State Capitalism

Cornell Studies in Political Economy

EDITED BY PETER J. KATZENSTEIN

State Capitalism –

PUBLIC ENTERPRISE IN CANADA

JEANNE KIRK LAUX AND
MAUREEN APPEL MOLOT

CORNELL UNIVERSITY PRESS

Ithaca and London

Copyright © 1988 by Cornell University

All rights reserved. Except for brief quotations in a review, this book,
or parts thereof, must not be reproduced in any form without
permission in writing from the publisher. For information, address
Cornell University Press, 124 Roberts Place, Ithaca, New York 14850.

First published 1988 by Cornell University Press.

International Standard Book Number (cloth) 0-8014-2079-2
International Standard Book Number (paper) 0-8014-9469-9
Library of Congress Catalog Number 87-47600

Printed in the United States of America

*Librarians: Library of Congress cataloging information
appears on the last page of the book.*

*The paper in this book is acid-free and meets the guidelines for
permanence and durability of the Committee on Production Guidelines
for Book Longevity of the Council on Library Resources.*

Contents

Preface

What role should the state play in the capitalist economy? In most industrial countries since 1945 the state has gone beyond regulation and redistribution to substitute itself for private-sector actors and directly assume the functions of investor, trader, and producer. No longer are state-owned enterprises limited to providing subsidized services or salvaging jobs. Certainly in Canada by the 1970s both federal and provincial governments owned commercial enterprises that produced goods and services for sale in national and international markets—from asbestos to aircraft to satellite communications.

The role of the state as investor and producer in competitive and profitable sectors of the economy—which we call *state capitalism*—clearly raises fundamental questions about modern capitalism and about the public enterprise as an instrument of policy. Why should the state in capitalist society, rather than merely ensure the conditions for private investment, itself seek to accumulate capital? If public enterprises are encouraged to compete in international markets and managers are given the autonomy they need to do so, can governments continue to exercise policy direction? Now that the conditions favoring state capitalism, an expanding world economy and acceptance of deficit spending, have radically altered with recession and fiscal restraint, what are the alternatives to public enterprises? To explore these questions we reconsider European experience, underscoring the shared features of state capitalism, and then focus on Canada, which has long accepted public enterprises and is highly vulnerable to changes in the world economy.

We argue that the reorientation of state enterprises and state investments toward competitive and profitable industries responded to an underlying shift in the conditions for economic growth—a shift often called the internationalization of capital—as production, financing, and competition increasingly took place on a global scale. Governments sought to capture the investment required by the national or regional economy to create the jobs and revenues that governments needed for political survival. Whether by targeting equity investments or by allowing public enterprises to diversify through subsidiaries, the state enterprise sector underwent a trend to commercialization in the 1970s as part of a broader industrial realignment. The norms governing public enterprises shifted accordingly, to emphasize "business logic," that is, to give primary attention to financial results.

In a series of case studies of Canadian commercial enterprises, we look at government efforts to achieve these neomercantilist ends. State ownership, we find, cannot be equated with state power (if we understand power as the ability to control outcomes). Both the relative autonomy required by managers of commercial enterprises and the impingement of market factors beyond the control of any one company or government temper the state's ability to use the public enterprise as an instrument of policy.

In the 1980s, chastened by the need for fiscal restraint, governments in Canada and in Western Europe, whether neoconservative or social democratic, have come to favor more flexible forms of state intervention—particularly mixed enterprises and joint ventures. New political coalitions not only challenge the assumptions of Keynesian political economy but promote the privatization of public enterprises. The rhetoric of privatization is now widespread, but we conclude that with the exception of Britain, we are witnessing not some wholesale dismantling of the public enterprise sector. Rather, we are seeing a streamlining of state capitalism. Governments sell off selected corporations and turn to the stock market to finance others. Yet they retain their discretionary use of investment, and they do so by making state intervention more acceptable, appealing to private-sector norms, invoking market discipline, and proclaiming their businesslike approach to the management of the state sector.

This book is the result of a long collaboration that commenced with a debate about whether Saskatchewan's decision to take over part of that province's potash industry could be explained by ideology or by practical politics and continued in joint investigation of other instances of direct state intervention in competitive industries. We have benefited greatly from discussions of all or parts of the manuscript with Duncan Cameron, who encouraged the project from the outset, Lynn Mytelka, Bruce Doern, Allan Tupper, Glen Williams, Stephen Brooks, David Bell, and Peter Hall. Peter Katzenstein and Roger Haydon of Cornell University

Press made many very useful suggestions that facilitated revisions; so did two anonymous reviewers.

Some of the material in this book has previously appeared in Jeanne Kirk Laux, "Public Enterprises and Canadian Foreign Economic Policy," *Publius: The Journal of Federalism* 14 (Fall 1984), pp. 61–80; Maureen Appel Molot, "Public Resource Corporations: Impetus and Evolution," in *Public Disposition of Natural Resources* (Calgary: Canadian Institute of Resource Law, 1984), pp. 285–305; and Laux and Molot, "The Potash Corporation of Saskatchewan," in Allan Tupper and G. Bruce Doern, eds., *Public Corporations and Public Policy in Canada* (Montreal: Institute for Research on Public Policy, 1981), pp. 189–220. Portions of the arguments in Chapter 1 were first developed in preliminary form in Laux, "Expanding the State: The International Relations of Canadian State Enterprises," *Polity*, Spring 1983, pp. 329–50.

Unless otherwise indicated, all figures are expressed in current Canadian dollars.

This project has been assisted by both our universities. The University of Ottawa, through its Humanities Research Fund, enabled Jeanne Laux to gather data in France, and the Faculty of Graduate Studies and Research at Carleton University underwrote some of Maureen Molot's Canadian research travel. The Research Secretariat at the University of Ottawa under the direction of Ginette Rozon performed yeoman service in typing the several versions of the manuscript.

Henry, Alex, and Edie Molot's patience and forbearance during the writing and revisions of this manuscript are enormously appreciated.

Finally, we salute each other and express mutual thanks for unswerving perseverance, good humor, and intellectual solidarity.

JEANNE KIRK LAUX
MAUREEN APPEL MOLOT

Ottawa, Canada

State Capitalism

Introduction

The shibboleth that has distinguished neoconservative parties in recent years is their cry that "government is not only too big, it also reaches too far into almost every corner of the economy."[1] Yet a quarter-century ago historian Maurice Dobb traced the growth of state intervention back to the fourteenth century in Western Europe. He concluded that "state intervention in the economy is a constant in capitalist systems. Only its degree and its forms are variable."[2] Has something changed? The twentieth century has seen three dramatic changes in the role of the state in the economy. First, there has been a trend toward increasing size, as measured by government expenditures, culminating in the full-blown welfare state. Second, with the "Keynesian revolution," state intervention shifted from being sporadic (in particular in wartime) to being accepted as intrinsic to economic growth. And finally, since World War II the state has extended its role in production, both indirectly through subsidies and planning and directly through the creation of public enterprises. This postwar shift toward state intervention in production, part of a conscious effort by government to manage the economy, led Andrew Shonfield to identify a new era of modern capitalism.[3]

Although national experiences vary, in most industrial economies state intervention clearly moved beyond redistribution and regulation as the state increasingly substituted itself for private-sector actors and directly assumed the roles of banker, trader, investor, and producer. As the *Economist* phrased it, whether parties of the right, left, or center are in power, "all governments, overtly or covertly, directly or at arms length, are in business."[4] No longer are state-owned enterprises limited to salvaging jobs or providing infrastructure for private industry. Now they engage in the production of goods and services that compete for sales in both national and international markets. Certainly they do so in Canada. The *Financial Post*'s listing of the top 500 industrial corporations in Canada in 1985 ranked by sales includes thirty-two companies wholly owned by government (sixteen federal, sixteen provincial) and another twenty-two that have substantial government investment. Worldwide, over the 1970s the increasing number of government-controlled firms on *Fortune* magazine's listing of large industrial corporations outside the United States provoked some American observers to see a threat to American business as state enterprises moved "from being protectors of domestic capitalism to competitors in world markets."[5] By the 1980s new political coalitions were calling for the rollback of the state. Spearheaded by the Thatcher government in Britain, they made the privatization of state-owned enterprises central to programs intended to tilt the balance of forces away from the public and toward the private sector.

Our study of public enterprise in Canada fits squarely within current debate over the role of the state in the capitalist economy. We examine the origins of commercial state enterprises, the limits to their use as instruments of policy, and the ongoing adaptation of the state sector to post-Keynesian requirements for economic growth and political survival. Part I considers the crucial matter of why the state in capitalist society should invest in profitable, competitive sectors of the economy. After all, liberal capitalist ideology makes ownership of the means of production, control over the production process, and the appropriation of economic surplus the responsibilities of private individuals. Decisions of societal import—what to produce, how to produce it, and for whom at what price—should thus be made by those competent to decide, that is, successful entrepreneurs and corporate managers in the private sector. The state should undertake only to assure conditions favorable for productive activity and then, in the interest of general social harmony, correct abuses by regulation and compensatory social welfare policies. In practice, however, we find that the state itself, through its commercial enterprises, frequently owns the means of production, engages wage labor, sells in the marketplace, and often reinvests the surplus generated. We are witnessing the accumulation of state capital and thereby the elaboration within the mixed economy of a sphere of production where the state no longer stands apart—in short, *state capitalism*.

To document and explain the emergence of state capitalism we begin by looking at the European experience. Comparative analysis across time and across countries reveals the relative importance of the state as investor or producer and permits us to underscore the new role played by state enterprises operating in competitive industries. To explain these developments, we turn to the major doctrines that purport to show why the state might assume ownership of the means of production in capitalist society—only to confront the poverty of explanations bounded by conventional Marxist or liberal ideology. Either doctrine seems to rule out state enterprises competing with private producers and pursuing profits over time. To understand the new commercial orientation of state enterprises we have to center attention on two developments underestimated by the traditional theories: the internationalization of production, and the fiscal crisis of the welfare state. These developments have altered the basis of capital accumulation and the capability of policy makers to affect outcomes. We argue that state capitalism is no longer exceptional, as liberal doctrine assumes, but has become inherent to capitalist development, now characterized by production, financing, and competition on a world scale. In the 1960s all governments, faced with a relative loss of control over their national economies in an increasingly transnational world economy, sought to reassert control through renewed intervention. We demonstrate that state enterprises in competitive sectors do not simply service private capital, as Marxist theory claims; they also express the dynamic of political struggles in liberal polities intensified by the fiscal crisis of the state. In the 1970s economic recession exacerbated the debate over the welfare state which centered on the costs of maintaining social programs and public-sector employment. Governments sought to demonstrate their ability to "manage" the public sector—and included initiatives to enhance the competitiveness of state enterprises.[6]

How does Canada fit into this pattern of emergent state capitalism? As Chapter 2 elaborates, historians and political economists emphasize the positive rather than the passive role that the state has played in Canada's economic development—a role often interpreted as a pragmatic response both to the obstacles of geography and to the provocation of expanding U.S. interests. Hershel Hardin goes beyond pragmatism. He argues that the centrifugal forces of regionalism and continentalism necessarily brought the state in Canada to promote nation building on the basis of a "public enterprise culture" distinct from American "free-enterprise liberalism."[7] And indeed, well before World War II, federal and provincial governments in Canada acquired control within such key industries as transportation, communications, and hydroelectricity by creating state-owned enterprises.

Only in the postwar period, however, and in particular since the 1960s, is it appropriate to regard direct state intervention in production as a common practice for both federal and provincial governments. One estimate suggests that some 76 percent of the several hundred provincially owned enterprises and 58 percent of the federal government's wholly owned enterprises were created after 1960.[8] By the 1970s Canadian state enterprises were active in manufacturing and resources, sectors where the state had not taken a direct entrepreneurial role before the war (Canadair; Eldorado Nuclear). Some engaged in direct competition with private enterprise (Petro-Canada), whereas others involved government in joint ventures with the private sector (Telesat Canada). Several extended their investments abroad to become multinational corporations (Polysar). Rather than simply providing subsidized services, as the leading business paper in Canada, the *Financial Post,* observed, "government is involved in a number of activities, from satellites to sheep, which are intended to return a profit, and, indeed, even in speculative activities that can return both an operating profit and an increase in the value of the investment."[9]

In turning to commercial state enterprises, Canada appears to fit into a European pattern of intervention whereby, Stuart Holland notes, "governments consciously sought participation in viable rather than failing concerns."[10] In a world economy characterized by the internationalization of production, policy makers in Canada as elsewhere sought to counteract their vulnerability to external change and assert greater control over domestic resources by extending the direct role of the state as investor and producer. Canadian historical experience, however, leads us to identify three limiting conditions to state intervention which distinguish Canada from other industrial countries. These are: (1) a world economy in which Canada is highly trade-dependent and has a relatively weak manufacturing sector; (2) a pattern of truncated industrialization that makes Canada very reliant on foreign (largely American) capital and technology; (3) a federal system with a combination of uneven regional development and high provincial government autonomy, which makes Canada appear a fragmented state.

Chapter 3 takes a close look at the universe of federal and provincial enterprises in contemporary Canada. General evocations of the hundreds of corporations owned by governments obfuscate more than they enlighten. Many, indeed most, such enterprises serve merely as convenient administrative substitutes for the government department or the subsidized nonprofit organization that carries out identical functions in other jurisdictions. The Canada Post Corporation and the National Arts Center are examples. Using a corporate legal form presents several advantages: bureaucrats can recruit personnel without the encumbrance of civil service procedures, and ministers can appear to reduce deficits by instructing a corporation to finance its operations through "off-budget borrowings." Nonetheless, Tom Kierans, president of Canada's influential investment brokerage firm McLeod Young Weir, ventures that "some 338,000 people are employed by 68 commercially oriented Crown corporations controlling almost $125 billion of assets." In his judgment, Crown corporations' growing share of national production indicates "a major expansion of their collective influence since 1975. It is probably much greater than most Canadians realize."[11]

We see something even more important than mere size. In the 1970s the state enterprise sector in Canada experienced fundamental reorientation, a trend to commercialization. In the first instance, commercialization involved an objective change in the market conditions faced by state-owned enterprises. Canadian state enterprises increasingly operate in competitive industries—whether in direct competition with private enterprises at home, or in indirect competition with producers of substitute goods (e.g., gas for oil), or by way of exports. The government itself has recognized this trend to commercialization; as the minister of privatization stated in 1986, "many of the larger corporations engage taxpayers' resources to compete directly with the private sector."[12] Rapidly evolving markets and technologies have even introduced competition to the proverbial natural monopoly, electricity. In the second place, commercialization involved a change in the basis of legitimation for state enterprises. Managers and politicians have turned away from an emphasis on social purposes to appeal to what we call "business logic," in other words a focus on financial results as selected Crown corporations are encouraged to pursue profit mandates.

The application of business logic to state enterprises in Canada fits within a broader response to the fiscal crisis of the state which we identified in Chapter 1. Across Europe, as the *Economist* appraised the situation, "government emerged from the calamities of the mid-1970s prattling of new public sector commercial discipline."[13] In Canada too the rising costs of social programs and the concomitant increase in budget deficits created a crisis of legitimacy and provoked a new political self-defense. The origin of this trend to commercialization may be identified in the Privy Council Office's 1977 report in which the federal government responded to the exposure of financial mismanagement on the part of two major state enterprises. The government proposed reforms that would henceforth assure management "on a sound commercial basis, to promote their efficiency and maximize the return on the investment of the Canadian taxpayer."[14]

The trend to commercialization has by no means gone unnoticed by the business elite. Paul Martin, Jr, president of a major private shipping company, objected that "it is often the drive for profit by the Crown in response to allegations of inefficiency that pushes it into unfair competition with the private sector." Martin is typical, if melodramatic, in warning of "public-sector imperialism" once ownership of competitive corporations is "concentrated in the hands of the government elite."[15] This notion that state ownership can be equated with state power, shared by the doctrinaire left, comes under scrutiny in Part II. It assumes, on one side of the equation, a political will to direct corporations to achieve outcomes other than those which would derive from purely commercial considerations. It assumes the intervening administrative capability to communicate, control, and verify performance criteria and the financial capability to act as shareholder by contributing capital for investment. Finally, it assumes a controlled environment wherein the state-owned enterprise is untroubled by externalities or by pressures to adapt its techniques, marketing strategy, or products to match the competition.

In fact, none of these assumptions can be taken for granted. In Part II, therefore, we undertake some case studies to appreciate whether governments in Canada have actually been able to use commercial state enterprises as instruments of policy. We investigate the genesis and performance of five state enterprises—the Canada Development Corporation, Canadian National Railways, Canadair, the Potash Corporation of Saskatchewan, and the National Asbestos Corporation—selected to represent different degrees of purposiveness on the part of government policy makers. Chapter 4 reconsiders the performance over time of corporations authorized to produce for profit without specific policy directives from goverment; Chapter 5 examines corporations created to serve regional development policy where governments had noncommercial objectives and intended to take a "hands on" approach to management. We speculate on the ways in which the trend to commercialization has exacerbated the classic tension in public enterprises between managerial autonomy and policy direction. The tractability of the commercial corporation as an instrument of policy in the mixed economy tends to diminish over time, we conclude, both because managers seek to enhance their discretionary powers and because governments' policy objectives are rarely synonymous with those derived from purely commercial considerations. If we understand power as the ability to control outcomes, then state ownership should not be equated with state power.

Part III asks what alternatives to state enterprises exist now that the conditions which favored both the growth of the public sector in general and the proliferation of public enterprises in particular have altered radically. These changes—from expansion to contraction in the world economy, and from acceptance of Keynesian spending to budgetary restraint in the national economy—have prompted most governments to emphasize forms of state entrepreneurship other than the large, wholly owned enterprise. Some governments propound the ultimate alternative to state capitalism—privatization. Other alternatives are investigated in Chapters 7 and 8, respectively the government-as-investor (buying into rather than buying out private concerns) and joint ventures that bring private and public enterprises together to undertake specific projects.

6

Although in other industrial countries the state uses equity as a discretionary instrument of policy, directed toward particular sectors or firms as part of a industrial strategy, in Canada the federal government proved unable to elaborate an investment policy, despite the creation of a new holding company, the Canada Development Investment Corporation, in 1982. With deepening recession, the government was caught up in a series of bailouts to resolve immediate problems in industries where failure would carry high political costs. Yet several provincial governments—notably Alberta and Quebec—demonstrate the possibility of more coherent investment policy as state investment agencies have oriented their portfolios to support regional industrial development. The controversies thereby generated, however, suggest that political limits exist for the state-as-investor.

Much less problematic is the joint venture, whereby public and private companies pool resources in a cooperation whose terms and conditions are normally set out in a negotiated contract. Falling investment has made the joint venture particularly attractive to provincial governments, dependent as they remain on the natural resource industries, as a vehicle to attract the capital, know-how, or long-term sales contracts needed to overcome the risks of exploration and development. Some Canadian governments established new state enterprises authorized to engage in joint ventures to promote "sunrise" or high-tech industries (here the government acts as venture capitalist and attempts to pick winners). Collaboration with private capital thus appears to be supplanting competition in the 1980s, although at the same time, by favoring one partner over another or by placing risk capital in projects outside provincial borders, governments-as-joint-venturers are altering established patterns of production and competition.

What general conclusions can we draw about the evolution of state capitalism? Across Europe in the 1980s political coalitions dubious about the merits of Keynesian political economy objected to an expanded role for the state as producer and investor in competitive industries. In the general search for new economic strategies the most extreme positions, which we examine closely as alternative models, have been Thatcherism, or the rollback of the state in Britain with a full-scale program to privatize state-owned enterprises; and Mitterrandism, or the directive role for the French state in industry with a program of full-scale nationalizations. In Canada the debate over the role of the state in the economy was revitalized by the advent of a Conservative government in 1984 dedicated to reducing the size and scope of government's economic activity and giving high priority to selling off Crown corporations. A flurry of conferences juxtaposed financial elites who glamorized "privatization in its broadest sense: 'the act of strengthening the market at the expense of

the state,'" and political elites who belittled the privatization crusade as
"in a sense, an attempt to settle our accounts with the past: past ideologies, old politics, nostalgic yearnings for the magic of the invisible
hand."[16]

In comparative perspective it seems evident that in Canada, as in all
European countries but Britain, privatization programs serve not to dismantle but to rationalize the public enterprise sector. Neither full-scale
nationalization nor wholesale privatization appears to be the wave of the
future, because formal ideologies have been chastened by the need to
adapt economic strategy to the exigencies of international competition
and fiscal restraint. Instead we find governments attempting to streamline their corporate holdings, waving the banner of profitability and
downplaying the large, stand-alone public enterprise in favor of investment through holding companies and mixed enterprises, which provide
greater flexibility. This streamlining ironically ensures the future for
state capitalism because it makes some direct state intervention in production ideologically acceptable to neoconservatives while it taps supplementary sources of capital for state enterprises valued by social democrats. Our conclusions therefore emphasize that state-owned enterprises
and state equity investments remain acceptable vehicles for policy regardless of political ideology. State capitalism—always variable in scope
and form—is inherent to the mixed economies of Europe and Canada.

PART I

COMPARATIVE PERSPECTIVES ON STATE CAPITALISM

CHAPTER ONE

State Capitalism in the
Industrial Countries

State-owned enterprises are at the center of international economic competition. By the end of the 1970s, over 50 of the 500 largest industrial corporations outside the United States were owned by governments rather than by private investors. Indeed, 36 countries were represented on the *Fortune* listing, and 27 included state-owned companies among their largest national firms. Putting aside Third World state petroleum companies, we find 21 industrial enterprises owned by European governments among the top 100 companies ranked by sales. These included, for example, France's car manufacturer, Renault (#9); Italy's petrochemical giant ENI (#10); Britain's steel producer BSL (#41); Holland's chemical company DSM (#60); and Germany's conglomerate Salzgitter (#88).[1] Across the 1960s and 1970s the average annual growth rate of these state-owned firms, in both sales and assets, exceeded that of the private companies on the same listing.[2]

Why in capitalist society should the state, rather than merely ensuring conditions favorable to private investment, itself seek to accumulate capital? This is the central question for Part I of our book. To situate Canada within the broader experience of industrial countries, we begin by describing the relative importance of public enterprises across countries and sectors in Europe.[3] Our attention focuses on the 1970s, both because this decade witnessed the creation of major commercial public enterprises in Canada and because, by the 1980s, new debates were raging over the role of public enterprises in Britain, France, and Canada which we will examine in detail in Part III. Here we review the principal theoretical explanations for public enterprise and offer an analysis of historical trends since 1945 to highlight and explain the emergence of *state capitalism*. By state capitalism we mean direct state intervention in production through commercial enterprises operating in profitable or competitive sectors of the economy.[4]

PUBLIC ENTERPRISE IN EUROPE

How important are state-owned enterprises within their national economies? Table 1 displays data for eight European countries over the 1970s, using three criteria to measure the size of their public enterprise sectors—share of total national employment, investment, and value added.[5] Clearly there are variations across countries and, to some extent, over time. The preeminent importance of the public enterprise sector in Italy and Austria is obvious. France follows, closely matched by Germany in terms of employment, by Britain in terms of investment, and by both these countries in terms of the value added by state-owned enterprises as a share of the gross domestic product. If we shift the basis of comparison to the European public sector as a whole, then the relative importance of each national public enterprise sector, based on an average weight for the three measurements used in Table 1, produces a ranking led by Germany (30.1 percent), France (24.4 percent), Britain (20.6 percent), and Italy (14.1 percent).[6] In Canada comparable statistics are not available, but the investment activity of public enterprises (both federal and provincial) ranged from 10 percent to 15 percent of total investment over the 1970s.[7]

The share of economic activity undertaken by public enterprises in Europe remained surprisingly consistent across the 1970s, despite the deepening economic recession. Some noticeable shifts did occur, however, particularly a dramatic increase in the overall importance of Italian public enterprises and the contrasting investment activity of public enterprises in France (upturn) and Germany (decline) at the end of the decade. These shifts, as in any ratio, are neutral as to a change in the activity of public enterprises, because a change in private activity can enhance or reduce the *relative* importance of the public sector. In Germany, in fact, the downturn is accounted for by an upswing in private investment at the same time as political controversy obliged the government to postpone start-ups of nuclear plants by state-controlled companies. In Italy and France, by contrast, recession dampened private investment, and both governments opted for a countercyclical strategy using new investment projects by state-owned enterprises.[8] But neither disparities across country nor over time should obscure the central fact revealed by Table 1: for most of Europe's industrialized capitalist economies at the end of the 1970s, public-sector *enterprises* (not including government services) were significant employers and investors.

Table 1. Economic Activity of Public Enterprises in Europe

	Employment[a]			Investment[b]			Value Added[c]		
	1973	1976	1979	1973	1976	1979	1973	1976	1979
Britain	7.6	7.9	8.1	23.6	26.3	20.0	10.0	11.8	11.1
Belgium	6.2	6.4	6.6	12.4	13.3	13.0	4.0	4.0	4.2
France	10.7	11.5	11.8	22.4	28.1	30.5	12.3	12.8	13.0
Germany (FRG)	10.3	10.8	10.5	16.9	17.1	12.7	11.5	12.4	12.0
Holland	5.4	5.6	5.8	9.8	12.1	10.8	—	—	—
Italy	14.1	24.6	25.4[d]	35.0	46.7	47.1[d]	14.7	23.8	24.7[d]
Austria	—	21.6	20.8	—	43.1	41.9	—	22.0	21.8
Spain	—	3.6	4.1	—	18.7	13.5	—	4.1	9.0

SOURCE: Statistics from the Centre européen de l'entreprise publique, correlated by Pierre Michel in his review of the Centre's 1981 study, *L'entreprise publique dans la communauté européenne*, in *Annals of Public and Co-operative Economy* 52 (September 1981), p. 398.
[a]Employees as a percentage of active population outside agriculture.
[b]Gross fixed capital formation as a percentage of GFCF for the economy as a whole.
[c]Gross value added as a percentage of GDP.
[d]Figures for 1978.

In several key areas of the economy the importance of state-owned enterprises appears overwhelming and leads to the observation that a core set of public enterprises was common to all European countries prior to British privatizations in the 1980s. The enterprises concerned were responsible for the post, telecommunications, electricity, and transportation (notably the railways but to a large extent airlines and buses as well). For example, the significance of public enterprises in transportation and telecommunications, measured in terms of employment, jumps in Holland to 43 percent in these sectors rather than merely 5.8 percent of total national employment; in Britain to 60 percent rather than 8.1 percent; in Belgium to 65 percent rather than 6.8 percent. In Italy, if we assess public enterprises in terms of their contribution to new investment, they account for 90.1 percent in the telecommunications sector and 96.3 percent in the energy sector, compared to 25.4 percent of new investment for the economy as a whole.[9]

Looking beyond these classic infrastructural sectors to industry, we find state-owned companies continued to dominate mining, particularly coal (Britain, France, Belgium), potash (France), and iron ore (Germany, Italy, Sweden)—legacies from war and depression usually inherited before 1945. In the manufacturing sector, however, the contribution of state-owned enterprise appears relatively insignificant when measured by the three criteria used in Table 1. The exceptions are Italy, where public enterprise generated 13.1 percent of employment and 15.3 percent of new investment in manufacturing, and France, where the corresponding figures are 6.2 percent and 9.9 percent.[10] Where national statistics permit, however, as in the case of France, more subtle comparisons become possible. Because industry in Western Europe is highly concentrated, for example, it is enlightening to compare public enterprises to the largest private companies rather to the entire manufacturing sector. On this basis, by the end of the 1970s their share of employment in manufacturing in France reached 15.8 percent, their share of sales 19.2 percent, and, perhaps most relevant to the government's industrial policy, these state-owned enterprises accounted for 35 percent of France's industrial exports even before the Mitterrand government's nationalizations.[11] In Spain the state holding company, Instituto Nacional de Industria (INI), accounted for 28 percent of Spain's gross industrial investment and 17 percent of its industrial exports. Within particular industries, INI's companies accounted for more than 30 percent of total national production of refined petroleum, steel, aluminum, ships, automobiles, and aircraft.[12]

To appreciate the role of the state as investor and producer in Europe we cannot, however, rely exclusively on official statistics, which tend to focus on those wholly owned state enterprises deemed to be carrying out a national purpose. Each government has its own definition of what constitutes a public enterprise. Britain's is perhaps most restrictive, Germany's most inclusive, but a few illustrations suggest how most of them underestimate the scope of the activity actually carried out by companies with state equity participation. British national statistics in the 1970s included none of the companies held by the state holding company, the National Enterprise Board. They thereby excluded major corporations such as British Leyland, Rolls Royce, and British Nuclear Fuels. In France, national statistics use 30 percent government equity participation as the cut-off for inclusion, and they exclude any company held by the subsidiary of a state-owned enterprise (regardless of the share of government control). In Germany, although the Financial Statistics Act restricts the term "public enterprise" to those firms with at least 50 percent state ownership, the Ministry of Finance's Annual Report takes into account all holdings over 25 percent regardless of whether they are directly or indirectly held. The broader picture of the German public enterprise sector thus is impressive—Salzgitter AG, for example, wholly owned by the federal government, has another 169 industrial holdings, in each of which the state holds at least a 25 percent ownership share.[13]

In Europe at the end of the 1970s, in short, the economic impact of state-owned enterprises was substantial. Such enterprises employed more than 8 million persons, 11.9 percent of the actively employed population outside agriculture; contributed 22.5 percent of gross fixed capital formation and 13.2 percent of value added. On a sectoral basis the importance of public enterprises across Europe was estimated at 70 percent in energy, transportation, and telecommunications; 30 percent in finance; and 7 percent in industry.[14]

EXPLAINING PUBLIC ENTERPRISES

Orthodox Theories

The importance of public-sector enterprises in Europe raises questions about the role of the state in the economy of advanced industrial countries. After all, liberal capitalist norms clearly make ownership of the means of production, control over the production process, and appropriation of economic surplus the responsibility of private individuals. The state is supposed to ensure conditions under which individuals may carry out productive activity and then should undertake to correct abuses in the interest of general social harmony through regulation, redistributive measures, and compensatory social welfare policies. Three broad explanations of public enterprises suggest why the state might assume ownership of the means of production in a capitalist society.

Marxist analysts, such as Claus Offe, explain the shift from one mode of state intervention, "allocation," to "production" by referring back to the broad function of the capitalist state, which "creates and maintains the conditions of accumulation."[15] New forms of intervention are state responses to market failure, which may stem from such causes as national or international competitive pressures. Direct state intervention in production, through the creation of state enterprises, appears aberrant, but orthodox Marxist theorists explain it as symptomatic of a new stage of capitalist development marked by extreme concentration and centralization of capital.[16] The very survival of the capitalist mode of production now obliges the state to become directly involved in the production process, absorbing costs in some sectors to allow for an increased rate of profit in others. Monopoly capitalism has been transformed, in Ernest Mandel's words, by its "capitalisation of super-profits and the comparative absence of fresh fields of investment for these capital surpluses." In this situation, "monopoly capitalism turns more and more to the state, in order to secure by state intervention in the economy what the formal working of the latter can no longer secure for it. The bourgeois state becomes the guarantor of monopoly profits."[17]

State enterprises in this orthodox Marxist interpretation are but one means (subsidies and government contracts are others) by which the state insures superprofits. In no sense do they constitute a separate or competitive sector, and the likelihood of their generating profits is negligible. The state may take over basic industries, "ensuring lower costs of production for the transformation industries"; salvage industries in crisis; or create industries in wartime, but it will then necessarily reprivatize them, "nationalising losses while restoring profits to private ownership."[18] Should state managers seek to carry out productive activity, perhaps to supplement inadequate tax revenues, they will ultimately fail. In James O'Connor's view, "monopoly capital employs many and varied methods . . . to prevent the state from acquiring and managing directly productive capital." Where, as in several European countries, the state appears to act as a profit maker, in fact "profits from state enterprise are either limited by statute, diverted to private consumption, or used to encourage the private sector at the expense of the state sector."[19] This first interpretation, in brief, assumes a basic compatibility between the persistence of a capitalist mode of production and the existence of state enterprises—it being understood that productive investment by the state is "out of the question."[20]

A second interpretation also reconciles the coexistence of public enterprise and private capital accumulation; it views state enterprises as an epiphenomenon rather than a systemic necessity. In this archetypal liberal view, individual cases demonstrate that the creation of a state-owned enterprise responds to specific circumstances that combine social needs with an inability on the part of private capital to fulfill them (because of uncertain returns).[21] In these circumstances, clearly, government must step in and, for example, open up new frontier areas by building railroads; promote national integration by creating a public broadcasting company; ensure national security by investing in the aircraft industry; avoid social disruption by salvaging a major employer. In general, commercial state enterprises are presumed likely to disappear, through outright or partial privatization, once circumstances change. Should such enterprises persist, they do so only to play the ancillary role of servicing the entire private sector. They may, for example, provide infrastructure (transportation), power (hydroelectric or fissile), or basic inputs (coal) without being seen as either encroaching upon private accumulation or favoring one group, monopolistic industries, over another.[22]

The third interpretation of the state's taking on a direct role in production in a capitalist economy is more a partisan position than an explanation of practice. Voiced by socialist and social democratic parties in Europe, Britain, and Canada, it regards state enterprises in key industrial sectors as decreasing the social power of private capital. It expects, therefore, that eventually state enterprises will ease the transition to a socialist mode of production by lessening areas of direct confrontation with the bourgeoisie and by enlarging the scope of resources—assets and expertise—immediately available to a governing socialist party attempting to launch a planned economy. In the meantime state enterprises offer an opportunity, especially when social democratic parties form the government, to temper the capital-labor relationship by creating a more humane workplace or by using profit for social purposes such as environmental impact research. Far from merely servicing private capital, state enterprises demonstrate the possibility of its elimination.[23]

The prevailing Marxist and liberal interpretations rule out the possibility of state enterprises competing with private producers and pursuing profits over time. Clearly they no longer correspond to reality. State enterprises now figure prominently among leading firms worldwide in both the traditional and the technologically innovative industries. Table 2 displays those companies on the *Fortune 500* list of the world's largest industrial corporations outside the United States which in the late 1970s either were wholly owned or had substantial equity positions held by governments in Western Europe and Britain. Examination of the largest corporations in each advanced capitalist country on the *Fortune* list reveals the relative importance of state enterprises among key players as well as the mixture of state, multinational, and national capital characteristic of industrial production in the contemporary world economy.

Table 2. Largest State-Owned Industrial Firms in Western Europe in 1979

Aerospace	Automobiles	Chemicals	Petroleum and Coal	Steel and Iron
Aérospatiale (France)	Alfa Romeo (Italy)	DMS (Holland)	BNOC (Britain)	British Steel (Britain)
British Aerospace (Britain)	British Leyland (Britain)	Entreprise minière et chimique (France)	BP* (Britain)	Cockerill* (Belgium)
Dassault* (France)	Renault (France)	Montedison* (Italy)	Butano (Spain)	Ensidesa (Spain)
MBB* (Germany)	Volkswagen* (Germany)	Norsk Hydro* (Norway)	Charbonnages de France (France)	Italsider (Italy)
Rolls-Royce (Britain)	SEAT (Spain)	VIAG* (Germany)	Compagnie française des pétroles* (France)	Salzgitter (Germany)
SNECMA (France)			Elf-Aquitaine* (France)	Statsföretag Group (Sweden)
			ENI (Italy)	Svenskt Stal* (Sweden)
			National Coal Board (Britain)	VOEST-Alpine (Austria)
			Neste (Finland)	
			OMV (Austria)	
			Saarbergwerke (Germany)	
			VEBA* (Germany)	

SOURCE: Adapted from A. Y. Lewin, "Public Enterprise, Purposes and Performance: A Survey of Western European Experience," in W. T. Stanbury and Fred Thompson, eds., Managing Public Enterprises (New York: Praeger, 1982), Table 2.2, pp. 68–69.
*State ownership share is less than 100 percent but more than 20 percent.

For example, Italy's ten largest industrial firms included three wholly owned state enterprises, one company with majority state ownership, two subsidiaries of U.S. multinationals, and four private enterprises. In West Germany, which had 63 firms among the Fortune 500, private enterprise dominated; just two mixed enterprises, Volkswagen and VIAG, appeared among the top ten, although the second decile included one wholly owned state enterprise and three U.S. multinationals. Britain's ten largest corporations, again as ranked by sales, included three wholly owned state enterprises, two companies in which the government held a controlling interest, and two U.S. multinationals (whereas the second decile was composed exclusively of private enterprises). Among France's top ten we find two wholly owned state enterprises, one mixed, and seven private (of which five were nationalized by the socialist government in the early 1980s). Austria had just four companies large enough to figure among the Fortune 500; three of these four were owned by the state.[24]

The Changing International Political Economy

The emergence of the state as investor and producer in competitive and often profitable sectors of the economy invites explanation. To appreciate the shifting role of state enterprises within the political economy of advanced capitalism, we briefly review the historical phases common to all countries since 1945, drawing upon Stuart Holland's distinction between the first-generation nationalizations of the 1940s and the second-generation state enterprises of the 1960s.[25] We then extend his analysis to the third generation of commercial state enterprises in the 1970s. The new commercial orientation of state enterprises, we believe, is best understood by focusing attention on changes in the international political economy and, in particular, the internationalization of production. These changes have altered the basis of capital accumulation and reduced the ability of national governments to control policy outcomes.

The public sector today in any Western European country is variegated, the particular national pattern resulting from the overlapping across time of enterprises created or acquired at specific historical moments. Typically, these range from tobacco, salt, or match monopolies acquired as part of royal prerogatives, to iron and potash mines inherited as the spoils of World War I, to strategic industries such as airplane construction which were subsidized and sometimes salvaged through nationalization during the interwar depression. With only a couple of exceptions—the main ones being takeovers by the Italian state under Mussolini and the nationalizations legislated by the 1936 Popular Front government in France[26]—the deliberate creation and/or consolidation of a public enterprise *sector* is a phenomenon of the postwar settlement in Europe. By 1950 the state in all European capitalist economies, as in Canada, had moved beyond regulation and redistribution to intervene directly in production. Wartime exigencies—the need to coordinate production to meet military priorities and to assure availability of strategic goods—had convinced governments to organize national planning boards, engage in state trading, and establish state enterprises. Rather than fully dismantle the wartime economy, as after 1918, the state continued its interventions into the postwar years.

Although precise circumstances varied dramatically by country, in general we can attribute the enlarged public enterprise sectors across Europe to a combination of passive and active policies. By passive policies, we mean that governments did not relinquish state control over industries they had inherited either from previous regimes or from the wartime economy. In some instances they were inspired by a concern to ensure basic services and key industrial inputs required for reconstruction; in others, by a desire to wield economic levers useful in the exercise of Keynesian economics, such as the national banks; and in still others, by a realpolitik calculation that the state would have to develop strategic technology (as in the nascent nuclear industry). By active policies, we refer to the wave of new nationalizations carried out by, or in response to pressure from, parties of the left. The electoral victories of socialist parties, radicalized by the experience of fascism and the resistance, were the catalyst for major state takeovers, particularly in France and Britain where entire sectors—electricity, gas, coal, steel—were brought under public control. In France the 1946 constitution went so far as to introduce the principle of nationalization for any industry providing a social service or having achieved a position of effective monopoly.[27]

The actual evolution of the public enterprise sector in Europe across the 1950s was, however, a far cry from any socialist project. This period doubtless served to reinforce orthodox liberal and Marxist views on the role of state-owned enterprises in the capitalist economy. As Stuart Holland accurately observes, "in the early 1960s, it appeared that a first postwar wave of nationalizations in Europe had come to an end. . . . Nationalization of the first-generation type had taken whole sectors into public ownership or had salvaged failing concerns in the private sector. . . . Many of the nationalized concerns had failed to show profits at all."[28] Acceptance of Keynesian demand management policies relegated state enterprises to a passive role. Located principally in those primary or secondary sectors reliant on demand from other sectors, state enterprise in effect serviced private enterprise at public expense.

By the late 1960s, however, as Holland argues, a second generation of state enterprises had emerged: "Most West European governments introduced new public enterprises in the late 1960s which were devoted either to the management or the financing of industry. In general these second-generation public enterprises contrasted with earlier nationalizations in that governments consciously sought participation in viable rather than failing concerns."[29] Why? Holland's explanation is twofold: contradictions in the pattern of national economic growth and changes in the international political economy revealed the limits to Keynesianism and demanded direct state intervention in production. In the 1950s and 1960s accumulation was certainly taking place, but the resultant pattern of growth was *politically* unacceptable. The distortions of capitalist development—"structural unemployment, regional unemployment, and sectoral underinvestment"—which a tendency toward concentration and uneven development generate, made it obvious to political elites, even in a period of rapid economic growth, that more than macroeconomic tinkering was necessary to avoid social dislocations and eventual economic slump. The state would have to play a directive rather than a responsive role. To stimulate industrial growth in less developed regions or to promote a new, highly capital-intensive industry such as electronics or nuclear energy, the state might have to become an entrepreneur.[30]

In principle these tasks might have been accomplished through other instruments of industrial policy, such as targeted grants or tax expenditures. But in addition to using these instruments, the state directly intervened in production again after years of allowing existing state enterprises to lapse into a passive, ancillary role. It did so primarily because of changes in the international political economy. In particular, Holland argues, the changes included "the new problems of economic management and government economic sovereignty posed by the opening of the EEC and the intensification of the multinational challenge."[31] New, state-owned holding companies were created or debated in most West European countries to provide equity financing not only to threatened industries but also to promising firms faced with external competition. In a leading sector such as electronics, the state used direct equity participation to promote the mergers or joint ventures required to place a national champion in international competition—Italy's Edison, France's Compagnie internationale pour l'informatique, Britain's International Computers Ltd.[32]

Certainly by the 1960s governments in all advanced capitalist countries, faced with a relative loss of control over domestic economic development in an increasingly transnational world economy, sought to reassert control through renewed intervention, including the use of state investment and state enterprises. The overlapping internationalization of trade, capital, and production made "interdependence" a cliché and rationalized the recourse to neomercantilist practices as each government sought to ensure the conditions for continued economic growth, and thus for social welfare, at home. Not only did exports and imports grow faster than output in the OECD, thereby enhancing the overall dependence of national income on trade, but trade among OECD countries became concentrated within the manufacturing sector and, indeed, increasingly within the same branch of an industry, for example, plastics or transport equipment. This specialization heightened national vulnerability to any shift in international production or trade patterns. Changes in communications and computer technology, along with the internationalization of banking operations, permitted rapid transfers of funds, which reached massive proportions in the 1960s and thereby reduced the efficacy of monetary policy, as Richard Cooper's *The Politics of Interdependence* so masterfully shows.[33] In addition, the creation of a transnational Eurodollar market allowed for transfers that central banks did not control. By far the most dramatic change in capital flows, however, was from portfolio to direct foreign investment—the internationalization of production as large national firms turned multinational. As early as 1969 the leading three hundred multinational firms accounted for some 15 percent of the world's gross product. Once the preserve of U.S. and British capital, internationalization had become a strategy for leading firms in all OECD states by the late 1960s, when the subsidiaries of foreign firms accounted on average for 17 percent of the total value of manufactured goods.[34] Both Marxist and liberal scholars could agree at the time that, in Robin Murray's words, "economic internationalization has opened economies and increased instability. At the same time the process has weakened the existing national State powers in their ability to control this instability."[35]

By the mid-1970s, however, important changes were taking place in the world economy. These changes called into question the assumptions of the 1960s regarding sustained growth for the advanced capitalist countries within a liberal international trade and investment regime. Instead, the industrialized countries were in crisis—a recession characterized by falling investment and profitability, rising unemployment and inflation. Many governments, losing faith in trade liberalization, resorted to neoprotectionist measures, erecting nontariff barriers such as voluntary export restraints or implementing nationally biased procurement policies. The "problems" that had confronted a government or an industry individually in the late 1960s now appeared as part of a structural crisis common to all advanced capitalist economies.[36]

The global recession can be attributed to the end of the Bretton Woods system of fixed exchange rates in 1971, the OAPEC embargo and subsequent oil price shocks after 1973, and the technological revolution in production as leading firms moved away from traditional manufactures to create knowledge-based industries.[37] The crisis can also be seen as the logical consequence of trends of the 1960s, specifically, increased trade dependence and internationalization of production. Both trade as a share of gross national product and manufactured exports as a share of gross output continued to rise steadily in the industrial countries across the 1970s.[38] For these countries, investment abroad constituted a rising share of total investment, while the average annual rate of increase in their capital stock held abroad accelerated most rapidly in 1971–75.[39] We can largely account for these increases with the enhanced role played by European, particularly German, and Japanese capital, because both U.S. and British shares of total manufacturing exports and of new foreign investments continued to decline.[40]

More fundamentally, these trade and investment trends formed part of a worldwide process of change in the structure and location of industrial production, a process effected by both multinational corporations and entrepreneurial states. An emergent "new international division of labor" altered the basis of competition and accumulation in ways that rendered archaic the notion of a national response to the multinational challenge. Not only did corporations based in the OECD countries relocate some labor-intensive production to the Third World, but they also evolved strategies of worldwide sourcing which made use of subcontracting, joint ventures, and licensing agreements rather than 100 percent control of a production unit abroad. An increasing share of world trade was in fact intrafirm trade, that is, exchanges between affiliated companies. At the same time firms from a select group of developing countries, the so-called newly industrializing countries (NICs), entered world markets directly as exporters of capital and consumer goods in such industries as shipbuilding, textiles, and clothing.[41]

In the view of the United Nations Industrial Development Organization, the 1970s witnessed an "international realignment of industrial capacity [which] spawned fears of 'de-industrialization' and led politicians to initiate programs designed to reindustrialize their economies. This concern has given impetus to the gradual but steady increase in the degree of government involvement in the manufacturing sector."[42] Clearly, once production is organized on a truly global scale, competition intensifies, not only among firms competing for sales but also among states competing for production sites. Governments in Western Europe, as in Canada, tried to ensure domestic levels of investment, employment, and technological capability necessary to generate private and public revenues that would guarantee social welfare—and political survival for the party in power.

These neomercantilist tasks were immensely complicated by a global

23

restructuring undertaken by international firms in such industries as steel, textiles, and petrochemicals which began in the late 1960s and accelerated with the oil crisis, the Japanese challenge, and the new competition from the NICs. This restructuring involved divestment and reinvestment across national boundaries; it gave political urgency to programs of reindustrialization and rationalized recourse to state capital. If Jean-Jacques Servan Schreiber's *The American Challenge* was the signpost for European thinking in the 1960s, Christian Stofffäes, in *La grande menace industrielle,* captured the priorities of the 1970s. Not protection but restructuring; not salvaging an industry but devising strategies for a whole sector; not grandiose development projects but selective support for the companies that might make it in global competition. In sum, the challenge of the 1980s would be not to resist the multinationals or adjust to external constraints but to participate in production, exchange, and accumulation on a world scale.[43]

Evolving State Capitalism

Within these shared exigencies we situate the emergence of a third generation of state enterprises in Europe and Canada in the 1970s, enterprises that move the state beyond the boundaries set by either orthodox Marxist or liberal theory. The evolution of particular sectors and particular enterprises demonstrates that European governments, in the new conditions of recession and industrial realignment, were willing to use state ownership to ensure national participation in internationally competitive industries, thereby expanding the sphere of production we call state capitalism. We draw examples first, from sectors where governments historically have intervened for security reasons—energy and defense—and second, from industries where state investment has been presumed to fulfill an ancillary function in support of private capital.

Douglas Lamont, in *Foreign State Enterprises,* documented the "expanding role of government-owned industrial firms as competitive corporations throughout the developed world" and identified eight companies wholly or majority-owned by European governments in the mid-1970s which had become multinational enterprises. Each of these state enterprises had at least 20 percent of its productive capacity, volume of sales, or employees located abroad.[44] It is not surprising to find three state-controlled petroleum companies among them. The oil crisis of 1973 provoked European governments to create or strengthen state-controlled oil companies to enhance security of supply and also to promote alternatives to hydrocarbons, especially natural gas and nuclear energy. In that year the British Gas Corporation replaced the Gas Council, which had simply purchased gas, and took on activities from research and exploration through production to retail sales. In Italy the state enterprise ENI expanded its control over domestic refining and distribution by buying out Shell; reduced its reliance on oil feedstocks by selling off refining or distribution subsidiaries in Africa; and diversified away from hydrocarbons by creating new subsidiaries to run pipelines to receive Soviet gas, buying into Norwegian and Egyptian gas companies, and taking an equity interest in another state-owned company developing nuclear energy. Although the primary motive in all instances was to achieve "energy security," government investment in the energy sector in fact brought the state into industries that were by their nature international, already highly competitive, and usually profitable.[45]

In a very different sector, aerospace, the creation of new state enterprises (Britain) or the restructuring of existing state enterprises (France) in the 1970s was not intended exclusively to preserve national autonomy in defense production. States also looked to ensure their national producers of a place in world markets for this high-technology sector. The aerospace industry has become both increasingly export-intensive and more oriented toward civilian aircraft (which rose from 12 percent in 1965 to 25 percent of total sales in 1980). European companies increased their market share in this U.S.-dominated industry—by the mid-1970s France and Britain contributed 11.3 percent and 9.4 percent respectively of world production, more than 1 percent of the gross domestic product in each country and a steady export surplus over the decade.[46]

In Britain the financial failure of the major airplane engine manufacturer, Rolls Royce, prompted a Conservative government to nationalize the company in 1971. When in 1977 the assets of four aircraft manufacturers were combined to create the state enterprise British Aerospace (BAe), however, the takeovers represented a strategic rather than a reactive salvage decision.[47] These companies were not in serious financial difficulty, but they did face intense international competition. What began as an ideological commitment by the Labour party's left turned quickly into an industrial restructuring policy, with BAe managers running a normal, commercial business. The consolidation and reorganization of production by BAe aimed to ensure the dynamism of the British aerospace sector—important for defense procurement, of course, but important also for international competitiveness, as over half of the company's production was exported.

In France the state, having nationalized several aircraft manufacturers in the 1930s and others after the war, progressively regrouped them into two state-controlled firms by 1970. SNECMA, 89.6 percent state-owned (with the minority shareholders including rival U.S. United Technologies), manufactures aircraft engines. Aérospatiale, 98 percent state-owned, divides its production almost equally among aircraft, helicopters, tactical weapons, and ballistic and space systems. Internationalization was seen as a key to success for France's aircraft industry. Between them, SNECMA and Aérospatiale in 1979 held equity interests in more than a hundred commercial enterprises from France to Singapore, not to mention their participation in such joint ventures as Airbus and Concorde. For Aérospatiale, although the French state remained its major client, exports' share of turnover rose from 39 percent to 48 percent during the years 1977–80. The profitable helicopter division, for example, depended heavily on exports (75 percent of turnover) with civil orders accounting for most of the sales. Internationalization of operations helped exports: Aérospatiale bought out an American helicopter company in 1974, and by the end of the decade this subsidiary was purchasing for resale over half the helicopters manufactured by the state-owned parent in France. In addition, Aérospatiale subscribed for 50 percent of the shares in a marketing and distribution company for Southeast Asia, Samaero, and 45 percent of a joint venture in Brazil, Helibras, to manufacture and sell helicopters in Latin America.[48] Thus governments in France, as in Britain, institutionalized their commitment to national defense production through state ownership, but they also went beyond military-security objectives to promote a profitable and internationally competitive aeronautics industry.

By no means has the expanded role of the state in competitive sectors been restricted to such strategic sectors as oil and aerospace. In the pages that follow we show how even those first-generation enterprises whose original purposes and activities appeared to conform to the orthodox Marxist analysis of state monopoly capitalism have, in fact, evolved to recast the state in the role of a producer in national and international markets competing with private enterprise. Increasingly, as Jean-Pierre Anastassopoulos argues, monopoly has become fictitious.[49] Every state-owned enterprise faces at least one of four possible forms of competition. In *direct* competition, other enterprises, either national or foreign, produce the same goods or services; in *indirect* competition, other enterprises, again either national or foreign, produce substitute goods or services (for example, telex rather than letters, trucking rather than rail freight). The internationalization of production has generated competition even for state enterprises that appear to be monopolies in their home territory, for example, the electricity supplier Electricité de France (EDF). A multinational firm will compare the rates per kilowatt hour offered by EDF to those available in another country when making a decision on plant location, as in the decision by the French aluminum giant Pechiney to build a smelter in Quebec.[50]

The commercialization of public enterprises did not, however, simply "happen" as industries evolved. Governments have acted to reorient their state sectors in five main ways. First, in the basic industries where state enterprises clearly serviced the private-sector companies up-stream—coal is a classic example—governments promoted the commercialization of their activities through restructuring and diversifications. Second, where the state intervened to protect jobs in a declining industry—automobiles or steel, for instance—governments encouraged the internationalization of these same enterprises to meet competition on *world* markets. At the same time, contrary to liberal assertions about the exceptional nature of state ownership, particularly in profit-oriented industries, direct state investment became an inherent part of industrial policy. Third, governments dramatically expanded the scope of state intervention in production by allowing established state enterprises to undertake further investments, a process French observers call *filialisation*. Fourth, and simultaneously, many governments institutionalized the use of equity as an instrument of policy by creating state holding companies. Finally, in contrast to either Marxist or liberal expectations, we find governments, faced with rising deficits under conditions of recession, instructing their commercial public enterprises to make a profit. These overlapping processes together have altered the complexion of the public sector in Europe since the 1960s and lead us to identify a state capitalist sphere of production within the mixed economy.

Diversification of Basic Industries

In France the state-owned coal industry underwent a major restructuring in the late 1960s, when some twenty-three of its subsidiaries were regrouped to create the Société chimique des charbonnages responsible for chemical activities. This new thrust was reinforced ten years later when the state holding company, Entreprise minière et chimique (EMC), ceded its ammonia and phosphoric acid-producing subsidiary to the chemicals group now known as CdF-Chimie, in return for a minority share holding. At the same time the creation of CdF-Chimie International, a holding company regrouping all interests outside Europe, institutionalized a focus on exports. Indeed, by the beginning of 1981, when CdF-Chimie was once again restructured to become a holding company—involved in equal measure in petrochemicals/plastics, fertilizers, and organic chemistry/paints/acrylics—the resultant industrial group derived 40 percent of its turnover from its international operations.

Meanwhile, back at the mines, the role of the parent state enterprise, Charbonnages de France, evolved away from its original functions, which were to guarantee regional employment in the north and provide cheap inputs to the steel industry. Employment in coal mining declined from 240,000 in 1958 to 87,000 in 1974, and even with a shift in policy to increase coal production after the first oil shock in 1973, immigrant labor from Morocco on short-term contracts made up the bulk of the new work force engaged. Although nuclear power has become central to France's energy security policy, coal is nonetheless considered a strategic resource. When faced with declining productivity and reserves in its coal mines, the state has sought to make Charbonnages commercially viable. A subsidiary, Charbonnages de France International, created in 1978, took minority equity positions in joint ventures in the United States (Hawley, a coal mining corporation), Australia (Wambo Mining Corp.), and Canada (Quintette Coal Co.). In addition to sourcing coal, motivations for the large capital infusion given to CdF International in 1980 were to acquire information on international markets and to sell engineering services.[51]

Examples of recommercialization of basic industries through diversification can be multiplied. The Norwegian government expanded its minority interest in Norsk Hydro to majority control and over the 1970s built the country's biggest industrial group by diversifying into oil and gas, metals and chemicals. In the Netherlands, Dutch State Mines no longer extracts a single lump of coal but instead has become one of the world's largest chemical companies.

Internationalization of Declining Industries

The crisis of overproduction in the automobile and steel industries in the 1970s reflected not only intensified competition among OECD suppliers in conditions of recession but also the appearance of new exporters from Eastern Europe and the Third World. Whether acting through established state enterprises (France, Italy) or creating new ones (Britain, Sweden, Belgium), the European state became an aggressive international competitor in these two industries in crisis.

In the world automobile industry both private and state manufacturers, faced with the problem of surplus capacity, undertook similar survival strategies: internationalization of production, including cross-investment with foreign competitors. Thus we find the French state-owned enterprise, Renault, responsible for some 44 percent of both national production and exports of vehicles in the mid-1970s, following a worldwide strategy facilitated by its Swiss-based investment subsidiaries Renault Holding and Renault Finance. In the early 1970s Renault set up manufacturing plants in Spain and Turkey, as well as distribution subsidiaries in Germany, Britain, Italy, and Belgium. Extending its activities to car rentals, Renault acquired Compagnie internationale Europcar, and the new state enterprise took third place in the European market, with more than half of its turnover from operations outside France. Cross-investments with competitors multiplied in the 1970s; examples include a joint venture with Alfa Romeo (state-controlled) and Fiat to produce diesel motors in Italy and investments intended to achieve production sharing, distribution rights, or access to technology with American Motors, Mac Truck, and Volvo respectively.[52]

In Italy a single state-owned enterprise, Finsider, has long produced most of the country's steel. It is clearly charged with a mandate to provide Italian industry with a secure national source of this intermediary input at a reasonable price. Many of the end-product manufacturers, however, are themselves state-owned, particularly in the automobile and shipbuilding industries, so that state capital serves state capital rather than subsidizing private profits. In fulfilling its mandate, Finsider engages in international competition in two ways. First, it exports surplus production through its subsidiary, Siderexport, which can charge higher prices than those applied in the home market. Second, because of Italy's shortage of natural resources, Finsider has undertaken direct investment in iron ore and coking coal facilities overseas. Through its subsidiary Finsider International, which controls another twelve companies, Finsider is well positioned to meet its objective to become "fully competitive at home and abroad."[53]

Filialisation

Diversification and internationalization have in large measure taken place through the creation of further subsidiaries (and joint ventures) by established state enterprises rather than by a formal extension of the public sector through legislation. In contrast to the liberal premise that over time state ownership will be limited to natural monopolies or enterprises performing a national service, behind the highly visible, "up front" state enterprises we find subsidiaries involved in a wide range of commercial activities. This expansion by filialisation responds both to market logic (that is, corporate managers pursue normal commercial interests related to their primary mandate) and to political logic (that is, governments use existing corporations whose further investments have low visibility and flexibility, thus reducing the political costs of state intervention).

In France as early as 1962 the Dolez Commission reported that if all subsidiaries or *filiales* were taken into account, then the holdings of state enterprises came close to nine hundred more than what Parliament officially monitored in its annual survey of public enterprises.[54] Filialisation has continued to be a characteristic investment choice for French state enterprise managers. The government's statistical institute concluded in 1975 that the importance of the public sector in industry was declining. A private study, however, brought the activities of subsidiaries into the picture to show that whereas the number of directly held state investments (in parent enterprises) did decline over the 1960s, the number of their holdings in subsidiaries rose by more than one-third.[55] The full scope of the activities of subsidiaries became clear only in the mid-1970s when the government began to request consolidated balance sheets. As a result, Renault reported on some two hundred companies, Elf-Aquitaine on one hundred forty, and even the national railways, SNCF, on eighty-five subsidiary companies.[56]

Often it is the subsidiaries of state enterprises which assume the major role as competitive producers. For example, the restructuring of France's state-owned petroleum and petroleum products enterprises in 1976 resulted in a complex organizational structure. A 100 percent state-owned parent corporation, ERAP, now has a purely formal existence and acts as a holding company for the key subsidiary, SNEA (Société national Elf-Aquitaine), in which it holds 70 percent of the shares, the rest being widely held by the public through the stock market. SNEA in turn has over three hundred subsidiaries, among them the 100 percent owned SNEA (Production) responsible for all exploration and production in France, as well as for petrochemicals, and the 60 percent owned Sanofi, which itself is France's second-largest firm in pharmaceuticals, first in veterinary products, and second in cosmetics—known to consumers through such trademarks as Yves Rocher.[57]

In West Germany, too, the characteristic pattern of new state investments, particularly in the 1970s, favored indirect holdings through subsidiaries, usually with minority equity participation by the government. Indeed, over the years 1977–79 all new equity investments by the federal government in industry (and these totaled some 13 billion Deutschmarks) were made indirectly through established parent companies. The six industrial companies with significant federal government participation accounted overall for some 375 further investments. Saarbergwerke AG, for example, 74 percent owned by the Bund (the rest by the Länder or state governments) and number 134 on the *Fortune* 500 list, is involved in coal, coke, mineral oils, fuels, machine tools, and rubber production through its fifty-eight subsidiaries.[58] In Germany the logic that generated expansion by indirect acquisition was as much political as commercial, as the example of the oil, mining, and chemical conglomerate VEBA illustrates.

VEBA, wholly state-owned until the 1960s, remained state-controlled after public share issues attracted some three million new investors but left the German government holding 43.8 percent of the shares at the end of the 1970s. Originally created as a holding company by the Prussian state within the Weimar Republic, VEBA became a state enterprise of the Federal Republic of Germany when the basic law of 1949 transferred the properties of the dissolved Prussian state to the new government. VEBA's holdings expanded substantially with the U.S. government's decision in the 1960s to release industrial assets seized by the Allies. Bonn was subsequently faced with the insolvency of the former proprietors; rather than save these beneficiaries of the Third Reich with a buyout, the government decided to transfer the assets to VEBA at the same time as VEBA's shares were being offered to the "people." Another turning point for VEBA came when the Schmidt government responded to the 1973 Arab oil boycott by buying into Gelsenberg, an oil exploration and refining company, to promote a regrouping of German petroleum interests. Within two years, however, the government transferred its majority interest to VEBA in a stock switchover deal, so that VEBA became, in large measure through these politically motivated acquisitions of companies, a vast conglomerate responsible directly or indirectly for the employment of some half a million persons.[59] So, in several European political economies, much of the expansion of the commercial public enterprise sector since the 1960s has taken place not by recourse to dramatic nationalizations but by way of existing state enterprises that extended their activities through subsidiaries.

Holding Companies

Faced with the need to restructure production in order to adapt to international competition, European governments of varying political complexions came to see equity participation as a useful instrument of industrial policy alongside traditional credits, grants, and fiscal incentives. In various countries, notably France, Britain, Belgium, Austria, and Sweden, by the end of the 1970s this acceptance of direct state investment in production as an inherent part of industrial policy had been institutionalized by the creation of government holding companies. All were in some sense inspired by the example of Italy's Instituto per la Ricostruzione Industriale (IRI) established in the 1930s. No mere pass-throughs for financing private enterprise, the new state holding companies fitted within industrial restructuring policies. It is the use of equity as a first, not last, resort and the intent to participate in strategic management decisions which distinguish these holding companies from the more passive development banks.[60]

France, for example, in 1970 set up the Industrial Development Institute aimed at small and medium-sized companies; in Britain, state investment in private industry was managed by the Industrial Reorganization Corporation (IRC). Created by the Labour government in 1966, IRC was mandated to assist in mergers and industry restructuring, even if new enterprises were needed to do so. By the time of its dissolution by the Conservatives in 1970 IRC was involved in management, naming directors to the boards of companies. The National Enterprise Board, established by the reelected Labour party in 1975 to replace the IRC, was well funded and organized as a holding company to extend state equity into "the competitive profitable sphere."[61] It managed dozens of government minority participations in commercial firms, as well as such newly nationalized companies as Rolls Royce and British Leyland.[62]

In Austria and Sweden, state holding companies differ somewhat from those elsewhere in that they focus on the existing state enterprise sector, but at the same time they have in common with others the underlying assumption that direct state intervention in production is a permanent feature of the mixed economy and may require a corporate management format to buy or sell when changing economic and commercial circumstances so require. Austria's OIAG oversees fifty-six wholly owned subsidiaries in industry (oil, iron and steel, chemicals) and holds several dozen majority and minority investments in private companies. Sweden reorganized its twenty-two state-owned commercial companies under a single holding company, Statsföretag AB, in 1970. Parliament specified that Statsföretag "should operate according to the same rules as apply to any other Swedish company." By the end of the decade the company was the country's second-largest enterprise in terms of assets, fourth-largest ranked by sales.[63] Belgium's Société nationale d'investissements (SNI), set up in 1962, operated in passive fashion for its first decade, but it has since been twice strengthened—first revamped as a holding company in 1976, then given a revised legislative mandate in 1978 which included the power to create new subsidiaries in response to government industrial policy directives and to carry out independent production and sales of goods and services.[64]

Notwithstanding their various powers and life spans, these state holding companies, together with exponential growth in the subsidiaries of established public enterprises, expanded the role of government as investor and producer in the capitalist economy; extended the scope of state activity beyond basic industries, and indeed beyond national boundaries, to competitive and profit-oriented companies; and in so doing signaled an assumption of continuous state intervention in production by means of equity participation in industry. The very flexibility afforded by indirect holdings—to invest or divest, to diversify or concentrate without needing new legislation—allowed for a "permanent" public enterprise sector, albeit with a changing composition.

Profit Mandates

Since the 1960s we also find an intriguing change in the legitimation of state enterprises. Governments began to ask managers to make a profit. The shift to a profit orientation for many public-sector enterprises expresses the dynamic of political struggle in liberal polities marked by the fiscal crisis of the state.[65] In the debate over expenditures in the public sector, governments applied "business logic" to the management of the public sector and of public enterprises in particular— that is, their rationalization of public enterprises appealed to a "non-ideological," managerial efficiency ethos. To protect programs already under their control and to validate the right to use equity as a policy instrument, bureaucrats sought to forestall cutbacks by demonstrating the ability to manage scarce resources (and to the extent that public enterprises proved self-financing, improved their bargaining over budget allocations).[66] Obeisance to the discipline of the market allowed politicians to defuse private-sector objections to interventionism. It also let them reject full responsibility for such unpleasantries as lay-offs by state enterprises—managers had to keep costs competitive, after all.[67]

The clarion call for a more "efficient and profitable" public sector came from the Nora Report, commissioned by President Charles De Gaulle in 1967. Observing that the state budget was expanding faster than gross national product and that some public enterprises were swallowing up a disproportionate share of tax revenues while others were crowding the financial markets, the Nora Report appealed to private-sector norms. It distinguished two groups of public enterprises—the industrial/commercial enterprises and mixed ventures that operated in highly competitive sectors, and the first generation of nationalized industries which retained market dominance while facing increasing competition. For the former, the Nora Report insisted that government should first set performance criteria aimed at ensuring an adequate return on capital invested and then allow top managers full autonomy to achieve improved productivity and profit rates in the face of international competition. For the latter, efficiency should be promoted by pulling back from political interference. The state should only define a broad sectoral policy—separating social obligations from commercial costs. In particular, administered prices should be freed so that these companies could begin to evaluate their performance on the basis of real returns.[68]

Reinforced by subsequent reports in 1975 and 1978, these recommendations were applied in part: performance contracts were negotiated with different enterprises, public-sector tariffs were permitted to rise faster than general retail prices. But at the level of political discourse, successive governments assimilated the Nora Report's standards. Thus the center/right government of Valery Giscard d'Estaing invoked both the need to adapt to international competition and the inability to accept current levels of public financing for state enterprises when it looked to justify applying criteria of efficiency and profitability to public-sector enterprises.[69]

Britain's postwar economic malaise has made concern over state enterprise financing long-standing, and the original statutes of most nationalized industries include a self-financing provision. A forceful White Paper on nationalized industries was published in 1967 and became the touchstone for subsequent government studies. It insisted, for example, that "investment projects must normally show a satisfactory return in commercial terms" and devised criteria for pricing and for financial targets "to ensure that public investment earned a return which was comparable with that of private industry."[70] The deepening economic crisis in the 1970s inspired a renewed attempt to reduce public sector-borrowing in Britain and to allow public enterprises to raise prices rather than use debt financing to cover operating losses. In 1978 another White Paper reaffirmed prior studies—it specified a 5 percent rate of return on new investment, required publication of performance indicators, and restricted borrowings by public enterprises.[71]

Elsewhere, too, increasingly defensive governing parties sought to reduce costs, attract private capital, and yet retain the social, political, or economic policy benefits derived from direct ownership of industrial enterprises. They proclaimed their respect for private-sector norms and vaunted their capability to manage public resources rationally. The Belgian state holding company, SNI, was enjoined in its revised legislative mandate in 1978 to apply "rules of good industrial financial and commercial management as well as to achieve normal profitability."[72] In Italy the Chiarelli Commission for the reorganization of state holdings insisted in 1976 that adaptation to national and international competition required a more rational use of resources. A succession of ministerial reports thereafter appealed for an end to bailouts, corruption, and excess bureaucracy in favor of directing state investments to key sectors and to competitive technologies. Where social or political considerations required underwriting investments, such noncommercial costs must be accounted for separately.[73] According to the chairman of Sweden's state holding company at the time of its creation in 1970, government policy specified that "our first priority was to take steps to improve the competitiveness, effectiveness and profitability of the companies within the group."[74]

Across Europe, therefore, we see that the context of fiscal restraint produced a preoccupation with demonstrating a businesslike approach to the public enterprise sector. But profit mandate and profit making must not 'be confused. Although many state-owned enterprises, and many more of their subsidiaries, do make money in the sense that they earn revenues sufficient to cover current operating costs, few earn enough to report a positive net income and fewer still have achieved a credible return on investment.[75] At first glance, indeed, the enunciation of a profit motive for state-owned enterprises appears to be an example of political mystification—governments wishing to give the appearance of being businesslike. The impression is true and is in itself revealing of how political discourse has espoused business logic. But as we have suggested, the articulation of private-sector norms to legitimize public enterprises has also had real policy consequences. It reflects underlying shifts in the political economy.

CONCLUSION

The role of the state in advanced capitalist countries is no longer circumscribed by the tenets of either orthodox Marxist or liberal doctrine. Comparative analysis across time and countries reveals the importance of the state as investor or producer, permitting us to underscore the new role played by state enterprises in competitive industries. The state does not stand apart from production; it has become a producer of goods and services for sale in both national and international markets. The public enterprise sector accounts for a substantial share of employment, capital formation, and value added in the major European industrial economies.

Yet it is also true that state ownership still concentrates in those sectors which serve the private sector as a whole (transportation, telecommunications, energy). Many of the largest state-owned industrial concerns were originally acquired under circumstances of market failure, and some still operate at a loss to protect jobs or supply inputs to private industry at low administered prices. Collaborative and competitive state capitalism coexist in the contemporary mixed economy. Naturally the state in capitalist society seeks to create conditions conducive to private investment. We can expect future governments to intervene in industry by providing equity financing to shore up national champions and salvage major employers.

State-owned enterprises, however, are no longer limited to subsidizing capital or salvaging jobs. Our historical survey highlights the appearance of a third generation of state enterprises in the 1970s, enterprises that operate in internationally competitive and even profitable industries. Moving beyond the reactive logic appropriate to the 1960s, the state as

35

investor and producer comes to play a direct part in the industrial realignment that the new conditions of production, financing, and competition on a world scale require. Accepting equity as an instrument of industrial policy at home, governments across Europe expanded the scope of state investment in industry, both through further investments by established public enterprises and through new holding companies.

These state investments, to be sure, are often collaborative in the sense that they are undertaken jointly with private investors. Minority positions may preclude control over the use of capital contributed by the state. And indeed, state capital need not always displace private capital. Once the public monies used to promote private enterprise take the form of equity rather than loans or one-shot grants, however, and once the managers of state portfolios are told to seek a return on investment that respects commercial norms, the governments no longer simply intervene. The state has itself become a participant in the process of capital accumulation.

In sum, we are witnessing the consolidation of state capitalism—a sphere of production within the capitalist mixed economy where the state does not stand apart from production but through its commercial enterprises owns the means of production, employs wage labor, and sells goods or services in competition with others.[76] We can best understand the commercial orientation of state enterprises by centering our attention on the internationalization of production and the fiscal crisis of the welfare state—developments that in the 1970s altered the basis of capital accumulation and the capability of policy makers in Europe and North America to affect outcomes. In emphasizing experience common to all industrial countries, however, we necessarily neglect the very specific ways in which these developments express themselves within each national political economy. In Chapter 2, therefore, we focus on those particularities of Canadian experience which are relevant to an understanding of the emergence of state capitalism.

CHAPTER TWO

The Political Economy of
State Intervention in Canada

Canada has long accepted a positive role for the state in economic development. Historians and political economists emphasize the active rather than the passive role that the state has played in facilitating economic development. Their explanations vary, but all agree that in large measure state intervention has been a response to the obstacles of geography and the challenges of a dynamic and more developed U.S. economy to the south. Though it can be argued that state intervention has been crucial to promoting economic development everywhere, the state in Canada went beyond merely assuring conditions favorable to private accumulation. Hugh Aitken, an important contributor to the debate on the role of the state in Canada, summarizes the "statist" approach thus:

> the standard interpretation of the entire history of the Canadian economy assigns to the state a major role in guiding and stimulating development: on any reading of the historical record, government policies and decisions stand out as the key factors. The creation of a national economy in Canada and, even more clearly, of a transcontinental economy was as much a political as an economic achievement.[1]

The character of state intervention has changed markedly in a century and a half, from the provision of infrastructure (canals, railways) to the current involvement of the state in the production of goods and services, often in competition with private capital. What is important for our purposes, however, are the continuity and acceptability of state intervention in Canada and the considerations that distinguish the Canadian experience from that of other advanced industrial economies. This chapter reviews arguments about the role of the state and then briefly

37

summarizes the history of state activity through the 1970s. We seek to identify the limiting conditions of Canadian development which have shaped the pattern of state intervention.

THE HISTORICAL ROLE OF THE CANADIAN STATE

The role of the state in the Canadian political economy is inextricably entwined with the nature of that political economy and its position within the world economy. Canada began as a British colony whose sole raison d'être was the provision of such staples as cod, furs, and later timber and wheat for metropolitan markets. The relevant state authorities—imperial Britain, the colonies, and since 1867 Canada—had to confront the need for transportation, without which staple commodities could neither be extracted nor moved over great distances for sale abroad. As a predominantly staples-producing economy, Canada depended for prosperity on foreign demand for primarily unprocessed commodities. The state assumed considerable responsibility not only for providing means to export these goods but also for the problems generated by troughs in demand and the resulting underused capacity in production and transportation. Changes in the accessibility and character of staples and competition from American routes for the staples trade necessitated ever more complex and expensive transportation links, first canals and then railways. State participation in the establishment of this infrastructure took different forms—from outright construction of the Rideau canal, to bailouts of bankrupt enterprises such as the Lachine and Welland canals and various railways, to generous land grants and loan guarantees for the privately owned Canadian Pacific Railway—but state involvement was constant. The intimate relationship between patterns of state intervention in the economy and political coalition building, common to all countries, was particularly blatant in a new nation. The most obvious illustration is state assistance for railway construction to link the eastern and western parts of the country to the center, part of the Confederation bargain that created Canada in 1867.[2]

The continuous state intervention to support and underwrite the costs of infrastructure is the theme of Harold Innis. His expansive scholarship has been instrumental to our understanding of Canada as a staples-producing economy whose economic well-being was a function of demand for its commodities in successive British and American metropoles. Innis views the Canadian state as almost a by-product of the requisites of staples extraction. In a political economy rich in resources but involving vast distances of difficult terrain, transportation was a key factor.[3] Developments in transport technology dramatically affected access to and exploitation of staples. As routes lengthened into the interior of North America and the commodities to be exported changed from fur alone to include lumber and wheat, the significance of water transportation heightened. And as recognition of the importance of canals grew, so did dependence on the state. Private capital started canal building to create the St. Lawrence system, but it was inadequate for the task, and the state intervened to purchase and finish the project.

The relationship between state activity and water transportation established a pattern that the railway era replicated. State involvement in the St. Lawrence canal system was followed by government construction of the Intercolonial Railway and generous state assistance to private enterprise that built the Grand Trunk and Canadian Pacific railways. At the turn of the century the Canadian state built the Northern Transcontinental and aided in the construction of the Canadian Northern and Grand Trunk Pacific. Overbuilt and debt-ridden, many of these lines (save for the Canadian Pacific) were merged by the state in 1919 into a publicly owned railway company, the Canadian National Railway (CN). The costs of these varied undertakings had important political ramifications. Both the Act of Union in 1841 and Confederation in 1867 were dictated in large measure by the need to create progressively larger political units able to underwrite the costs of the burgeoning transportation infrastructure. Moreover, state fiscal policy, of which the tariff was the central feature, reflected the demands of transportation improvements. Innis's conclusions are captured in these words: "Government ownership in Canada is fundamentally a phenomenon peculiar to a new country, and an effective weapon by which the government has been able to bring together the retarded development and the possession of vast natural resources, matured technique and a market favourable to the purchasing of raw materials. . . . Private enterprise was not adequate to the task."[4]

The uncertainties of staples production for export are a major but not a sufficient explanation for the role of the state in Canadian economic life. Comparing Canada with Britain, James Corry suggests that the demands of colonial life tempered the laissez-faire tradition and made Canadians much more prepared than the British to accept state assistance in the promotion of national development. Prior to Confederation the major problems in the colonies were those of organizing a concerted attack against nature. Following Confederation, as Canada moved more fully into the international division of labor, "the pendulum swung . . . toward more active intervention by the state in economic and social matters."[5] Corry's perspective is much like Alexander Gerschenkron's thesis on late industrialization in Russia and Germany.[6] Because private enterprise accumulated capital too slowly for many tasks, the state was the only agency that could command the finances necessary for costly economic ventures such as railways. However, where one industry predominated—frequently the case in a staples-producing economy such as Canada—the relative absence of competing economic interests allowed for easy agreement on the need for a considerable range of state action in the name of economic development. Corry's explanation for state intervention, comparatively late economic diversification, points to what has become an important theme in Canadian political economy, namely dependent industrialization.

Industrial development in Canada lagged two to three decades behind that in the United States, a function primarily of Canada's dependence on the exploitation of staples. The undiversified character of staples production retarded capital accumulation and, in the context of American aggressiveness, increased reliance on the state. A persuasive rationale for state activity in Canada centers on what Hugh G. J. Aitken has termed "defensive expansionism"—the political urgency of protecting the westward-moving Canadian frontier against the threat of American encroachment and the economic necessity of using state resources to promote investment. This pattern of state-sponsored expansion dictated by external constraints rather than by internal needs "meant that typically decisions had to be made and investment projects begun before the Canadian economy was 'ready' for them."[7] Successive Canadian governments defined and implemented strategies of economic survival which included among their most prominent features huge and continuing investments in infrastructure. Whether for the Intercolonial Railway in the nineteenth century or for the Trans-Canada gas pipeline in the twentieth, the Canadian state made its considerable financial contributions contingent on routes that contributed to national integration by linking Canadian centers rather than passing through or terminating in the United States. In sum, within the comparative context of North American economic development, Aitken portrays the critical role played by the Canadian state as a direct result of the omnipresent American challenge.

If state intervention in Canada was shaped by the demands of a new political economy that had to adjust to the rapid changes of industrialization and an advancing frontier within a continental environment, then, Alexander Brady argues, there was nothing unique about the Canadian state. Its role was similar to that of "other Dominions or indeed to that of other northern countries with moving frontiers of settlement."[8] Brady organizes his explanation for Canadian statism around the protection of Canadian interests and the Canadian community, going well beyond the federal state's involvement in infrastructure to include the cultural sphere. The Canadian Broadcasting Corporation, for example, established in 1936, served to develop and protect Canadian culture and thereby to promote a sense of national unity. For Brady, moreover, an analysis of "the state" in Canada has to emphasize the provincial experience with public enterprise, dating back to the early years of the century with Ontario's creation of a hydroelectric corporation in 1906 and its railway in 1907.

The justification for direct intervention by the provincial governments was similar to Ottawa's, that is, economic stimulus and territorial integration. In their decisions to take control of hydro-generating capacity or telephone service the provinces were also responding to the pressures of local interests—in Ontario, small manufacturers, merchants, and municipalities concerned about cheap, reliable sources of power for industry; in Manitoba and Saskatchewan, farmers who wanted telephones and rural electrification. In his discussion of government enterprise in the Canadian West, Brady combines a political culture explanation with economic necessity, suggesting a positive predisposition to collectivism as an explanatory factor for the western experience. Farmers' dependence on the féderal and provincial provision of infrastructure and the risks of staples production combined to make westerners more supportive than central Canadians of broad state intervention. Overall, like Corry, Brady argues that the increasing complexity of society and the responsibilities the state began to assume for the well-being and security of its citizens made inevitable the growth of state activity.

This conclusion might suggest a generic, not a nationally specific, interpretation of Canadian statism since the turn of the century. But Herschel Hardin argues that the defining characteristic of the Canadian experience is to be found in Canada's identity as a public enterprise nation. Against the centrifugal forces of regionalism and continentalism, Hardin asserts, state intervention in Canada permitted nation building on the basis of a "public enterprise culture" distinct from, and in contrast to, American free-enterprise liberalism. The political philosophies predominant in early Canadian and American history differed substantially: the impact of Lockean liberalism, critical in the United States, was severely tempered in Canada by the elitist, conservative ideas of English Canada and the feudal-clerical ideas of Quebec. The Canadian capitalist was thus very different in outlook from his American counterpart. Central to this difference was his readiness to press for, if not depend upon, government intervention and assistance in economic ventures.[9]

To Hardin's frustration and regret, Canadians have been unduly influenced by American ideology in their historical assessment of government intervention. As a result they denigrate their public enterprise tradition, believing it is "a somehow secondary or untrustworthy, even marginal phenomenon, although it exists on a substantial scale and in most sectors of the economy." To reveal this Canadian tradition of state enterprise, Hardin traces it from the canal and railway–building eras to the establishment of state corporations during World War II. His heroes are not the barons of private capital but rather such visionaries as Adam Beck, who pushed for the establishment of Ontario Hydro, and Henry Thornton, first president and chairman of CN.[10] Were Canadians less awed by the American style of entrepreneurship, they would recognize the creativity, dynamism, and significant technological contribution of their public enterprises.

This brief survey highlights the centrality of the state to interpretations of Canadian development—both economic growth and nation building. Several common themes emerge; although they may be explained differently, they combine to form an essentially *geopolitical* explanation for the preeminent role of the Canadian state. Important among these themes is the need to overcome the obstacles of geography in a new country of continental scale with a harsh climate and a sparse population. State intervention was deemed necessary to permit staples exploitation, to link distant settlements, and to insulate the nascent Canadian community against American interests. Whether we think of canals, railways, or pipelines, or even cultural institutions, the impetus for state financing or state ownership is the same—in Aitken's phrase, "defensive expansionism."

Fundamental to all interpretations of state intervention is Canada's relationship to the international political economy. First imperial Britain and eventually the American superpower assigned Canada a place within its own hegemonic organization of production, trade, and military security. As a staples exporter and a relatively small power on the periphery of empire, Canada and its successive governments encountered difficulties in assuring the basic conditions for either self-sustaining growth or political autonomy. These difficulties encouraged both the public and the policy makers to accept direct state intervention. Economic historians also emphasize the close if not symbiotic relationship between the state and private capital, all the while accepting that there are collective benefits to be derived from economic nationalism which overshadow the unequal gains to one class or region within Canada. Because of late industrialization, for a significant period the Canadian bourgeoisie appeared weak relative to the tasks at hand. It saw the state as the only agency capable of mobilizing the resources required for large-scale projects or of providing the political brokerage needed to secure access to foreign markets or protection from competition. And finally, the development of new staples generated regionally specific economies within a federal framework, so that state intervention in

twentieth-century Canada took place on two, often competing levels—
the federal and the provincial.

ECONOMIC DEVELOPMENT AND STATE INTERVENTION

This picture of the Canadian political economy requires considerable
nuance and expansion if it is to serve as a backdrop for explication of the
growth of state enterprises in Canada and their change in orientation
from infrastructure to commerce. To be sure, staples extraction was
crucial to early Canada, and staples dependence shaped the context for
much economic activity. The progression of staples, from fish and fur,
to timber, wheat, fuel and nonfuel metals and minerals, benefited different groups in Canadian society at different times, generated competition
among segments of Canadian capital, and forced adjustments in regions
whose staples were no longer in demand. Staples commodities remain a
significant component of Canadian exports in the 1980s, and heightened awareness of the value of these natural resources after the 1973 oil
crisis, together with concern about locales and rates of development, lie
behind recent state involvement in resource production (discussed below
in Chapter 5).

To concentrate exclusively on staples production and the infrastructure necessary to export these commodities, however, is to ignore the
particularities of industrialization in Canada and the state's role in that
process. A particular historical pattern of development distinguishes
Canada from other advanced capitalist countries. Its special features are
(1) a world economy in which Canada is highly trade-dependent and has
a relatively weak manufacturing sector; (2) a pattern of truncated industrialization which makes Canada very reliant on foreign capital and technology; and (3) a federal system in which uneven regional development
and high provincial autonomy make Canada appear a fragmented state.
Although the Canadian economy today shares many of the vulnerabilities of other open capitalist economies, Canada is notable for its
high levels of foreign ownership, its poor export performance in manufactured end-products, and its marked dependence on imports of
finished manufactures, including capital equipment.[11]

What was there in Canada's initial industrialization that might explain
the current structure of the Canadian economy? Economic diversification away from staples began in central Canada and parts of the Maritimes about the middle of the nineteenth century. Factories, spurred by
growing population and increased demand, sprang up to manufacture a
variety of consumer items and some limited producers goods. Some

43

three decades later Canadian industrialists were producing large quantities of relatively simple manufactured goods for local consumption. In certain sectors Canadian firms were supplying over 90 percent of domestic needs, and manufactured imports correspondingly declined. Railway construction was also important in industrialization, stimulating the emergence of a steel industry. As the century drew to a close, Canadian industrial production diversified further into commodities that required even larger capital investments and more complex manufacturing processes, such as rolling stock, appliances, and so forth.

What happened to this reasonably promising beginning was that the state adopted a policy of import substitution industrialization.[12] We do not suggest that decision makers were conscious of the long-run structural consequences of their policy decisions. Rather, we argue that with hindsight it is clear that some of the crucial decisions of the Macdonald government in the 1870s and of its successors thereafter—decisions frequently made in response to pressures from Canadian industrialists—meant that neither the state nor private economic actors took full advantage of the country's resources and opportunities.

As a strategy, import substitution industrialization has two defining characteristics: a tariff structure that permits domestic manufacturers to capture the home market and insulates them from foreign competition, particularly in consumer goods, and a reliance on imported production processes, machinery, and techniques developed by foreign entrepreneurs.[13] Canadian industrialization took place behind a tariff wall. Tariffs on manufactured imports were first imposed in 1859. With the National Policy of 1879, the policy of protecting Canadian industries to let them sell unchallenged in the domestic market was fixed as a tenet of the new Canadian state's economic policy. Indeed, manufacturers and politicians at the time expected Canadian industrialization to proceed satisfactorily by relying solely on domestic sales.[14] Massive exports of staples continued, but Canadian manufacturers either exhibited no interest in exporting their products, and thereby exposing themselves to the test of international competition, or were prohibited by licensing agreements from doing so. The National Policy tariffs were just one prong of a trio of policies—the others being the already established and heavily subsidized national railway system and the encouragement of immigration to settle the Canadian West—designed to consolidate a national economy in Canada.

Canadian industry developed in the shadow of the American economy. In the forty years after Confederation, when Canadian industry was expanding to serve growing local needs, American industry was already making the transition from small, localized firms to efficient, national companies using sophisticated technology. To Canadian entrepreneurs desirous'of producing goods as profitably and as quickly as possible for sale in Canada, the techniques and patterns of American production were extremely attractive. The Canadian Patent Act of 1872 made it easy for Canadian industrialists to gain access to American technology by permitting nonresidents to hold Canadian patents on the condition these be worked within two years of their registration.[15] Local manufacturers anxious to secure a foothold in the dynamic Canadian market were only too eager to license American production processes and technology. That these license agreements contained export restrictions and tied significant facets of Canadian industrial progress to innovation in the United States was of virtually no concern to either the Canadian state or Canadian entrepreneurs. In short, the combination of Patent Act regulations and National Policy tariffs ensured that the evolution of Canadian industry would largely depend on the fortunes of American capitalism. The staples sectors, on the other hand, remained tied to demand for primary commodities in Britain and the United States.

The strategy of import substitution industrialization seemed rational to Canadian state and economic elites preoccupied with the concerns of nation building in the contexts of North America and the British Empire. The wheat boom that began in 1896 continued and deepened Canada's historic role as a supplier of food to Britain. Between Confederation and World War I almost one-half of Canada's total exports went to Britain, and four-fifths of these were agricultural commodities. The commitments made at Confederation to link the Maritimes and British Columbia with the center and the subsequent opening of the Canadian West necessitated extensive foreign borrowing by the state and private capital, primarily for railway construction. In fact, investment in infrastructure and in farms consumed slightly more than 40 percent of all capital available for investment in the years from 1900 to 1915. As a result, capital available for investment in the machinery and equipment of production was sparse (approximately 7 percent) and was not much more than what was invested in agricultural implements.[16]

The American presence in the Canadian economy grew with the evolution of Canadian industry, in large measure as a function of import substitution industrialization. Even before U.S. direct investment was significant in Canada, the American presence was evident in the borrowing of technology. For many reasons, among them its protected domestic market and preferential trade status within the British Empire as well as its proximity and similarity of language, Canada became an attractive site for American entrepreneurs searching for new opportunities to invest their surplus capital. Although U.S. direct investment in Canadian industry began slowly, much of it was located in what, by the end of the nineteenth century, were fast becoming the most dynamic sectors of the economy—the chemical, electrical, and automobile industries. By 1914, through the establishment of branch plants, the takeover of existing Canadian companies, and licensing arrangements, U.S. firms had consolidated a prominent place for themselves in these crucial industries. There were more U.S.-controlled manufacturing companies in Canada than in any other foreign country, and Canada had become the major recipient of American capital outflows.[17] Some 40 percent of this American direct investment went to the production of the new industrial staples, minerals, newsprint, and fuel, which required complex technology for extraction and processing. Canadian capital, in contrast, retained its traditional dominance in the technologically less advanced and less capital-intensive sectors—such as footwear, textiles and clothing, furniture, and primary iron and steel—as well as in the production of the old commercial staples, though some Canadian-owned corporations had begun to invest heavily in newsprint capacity.

Canadian participation in World War I wrought changes in the political economy. Prior to the war the role of the state was limited to the provision of infrastructure and the creation of an environment conducive to the emergence of an industrial economy. With the onset of hostilities state activity changed dramatically: the state became more directly involved in the financing of economic activity, the distribution of goods and services, and, most significantly from our point of view, production. Moreover, the war accelerated changes in the structure of industrial capital which had begun before 1914.

The closure of the London money markets forced the state and Canadian entrepreneurs to find new capital sources to finance both wartime expenditures and expanded industrial capacity. Ottawa responded by consciously stimulating the domestic market for its bonds and securities and by war's end had raised more than two billion dollars from Canadians. In 1917 corporate and personal income taxes were introduced. During the war years the United States replaced Britain as Canada's major source of foreign capital, a position it retained thereafter. Whereas prior to 1914 Britain had provided three-quarters of Canada's foreign capital needs and the New York market only slightly more than 10 percent, by 1915 the relative importance of the two money markets had been virtually reversed as both state and corporate borrowers looked to the United States for capital beyond what they could raise domestically.[18] U.S. direct investment in Canadian manufacturing and resource extraction continued during the war, in part a function of the rapid economic growth that Canada's participation in the conflict generated.

State intervention in distribution expanded as the war dragged on: the establishment of the Board of Grain Supervisors brought the grain trade under federal control; Food and Fuel Controllers were appointed; and the allocation and rationing of a variety of commodities became the norm.[19] But perhaps the most significant instance of state intervention was the gradual nationalization of a major portion of the country's railways. Overbuilt and heavily debt-ridden, the railway system (other than the Canadian Pacific) was close to a collapse that would have threatened east-west transportation links and undermined the long-held state objective of national unity. Default on debt obligations, many of them guaranteed by the state, would redound negatively on Canada's credit rating. Lacking a practical alternative, the state acquired the assets of the three remaining privately owned lines between 1917 and 1923 and amalgamated them with railroads already under its control to form the Canadian National Railway.[20]

The state intervened directly in wartime production primarily through the Imperial Munitions Board (IMB), an agent of the Imperial Ministry of Munitions set up in 1915.[21] The IMB allocated contracts among Canadian munitions manufacturers and organized production to ensure adequate supplies of raw material and labor. The IMB also created separate departments to provide specialized technical information to firms that required it. Beyond organizing much of the Canadian economy for wartime activity, the IMB established seven factories under its control to manufacture essential commodities that the private sector could not provide. Many Canadian firms were reluctant to make the capital investments necessary to retool for munitions manufacture without purchase guarantees and most did not possess the requisite industrial technology.[22] To fill this vacuum state-controlled corporations assumed the initiative in war-related research and production. Enterprises to manufacture fuses, explosives, electrical steel, and aircraft were created under the authority of the IMB. The state made the rules guiding operation of these "national factories" quite explicit; the factories were to complement the private sector, according to Tom Naylor, not compete with it. Moreover, these wartime factories were "to be run on strictly commercial lines," with any operating surpluses used to defray the costs of establishment.[23] By war's end the national factories collectively had managed to retire their debt and return a small profit.

Finally, during the war years the Canadian economy became noticeably more concentrated and its different regions more highly specialized in what they produced. Large companies, those with annual sales in excess of one million dollars, became prominent in a number of manufacturing sectors. From 150 firms in 1911, producing 31 percent of the total value of manufacturing output, these firms grew in number to 410 by 1921, accounting for 51 percent of that output.[24] For reasons of transportation and proximity to capital and markets, moreover, manufacturing had become increasingly concentrated in central Canada, leaving the West, the Maritimes, northern Ontario, and large portions of Quebec to produce staple commodities, either for export or for Canadian consumption, and to consume the finished products of the center.

The transition to peacetime was difficult. With the end of hostilities those sectors of Canadian industry organized for war production had considerable excess capacity. Demobilization exacerbated the consequent unemployment, and there was significant labor unrest. The state was heavily in debt as a result both of the progressive takeover of bankrupt rail lines and of the costs of the war, which by 1920 included the expense of resettling soldiers and assisting the families of the wounded and the dead. The national factories, which might have been converted to civilian use, thereby providing a much needed fillip to Canadian industrial technology and possibly to Canadian exports of manufactured goods, were disbanded.[25] Canadian exports continued to rely heavily on staples, particularly wheat and the newer mineral resources. The markets for these staples reflected the new realities of Canada's economic ties—wheat exports continued to be sold across the Atlantic, but resource staples were sold in the United States. The poor export performance of the manufacturing sector did not improve in the interwar period. Canadian-owned industry was still concentrating on production for domestic consumption. Foreign-owned firms, increasingly dominant in the fast-growing consumer goods sectors, either were restricted by their parent companies from exporting or found imperial markets closed all too quickly as manufacturing capacity grew in the importing countries.[26]

State intervention in the interwar period returned to its traditional format—the establishment of nation-building institutions to protect Canada from the spillover of American interests. Two important Crown corporations were set up in the 1930s, a national broadcasting service, the Canadian Broadcasting Corporation, and a national airline, Trans-Canada Airlines (now Air Canada). Both were the creation of C. D. Howe, one of the most influential ministers in the cabinet of Liberal prime minister Mackenzie King.[27] Radio transmission in Canada had, in fact, been initiated by another state enterprise, Canadian National, in the early 1920s, and by Canada's fiftieth birthday in 1927 enough stations existed to allow broadcasting across the country. With the Depression and CN's precarious financial situation, these radio ventures came to an end. What few commercial stations did exist had become affiliates of the major American networks, and there was growing concern that NBC and CBS would expand into Canada.[28] In 1929 a royal commission, established by the King (Liberal) government and encouraged by the prime minister, who had been favorably impressed by the British

Broadcasting Corporation, recommended public ownership and control of broadcasting. This position, along with the idea that radio might be used to reinforce Canadian national identity in the face of American programs transmitted on commercial stations, had the support of both major political parties, as well as of the Canadian Radio League formed in 1930 to lobby for public broadcasting. The Conservative government of R. B. Bennett established the Canadian Radio Broadcasting Commission in 1932. The commission was superceded in 1936 when Parliament created the Canadian Broadcasting Corporation, empowering it to transmit radio signals coast to coast and to control all forms of broadcasting, public and private.[29]

By the mid-1930s air travel had become more than a curiosity. Canadian mail and freight were being flown by small regional carriers, and many Canadians were crossing the border to take advantage of air connections in the United States. Like railways many decades earlier, air routes offered another means to link the disparate parts of Canada, thereby countering the north-south pull that the growing economic importance of highways was then strengthening. The King government, returned to office in 1935, was concerned that American carriers might move into Canada to service growing demand; it moved quickly to develop an air policy. Recalling the expensive lessons of Canadian railway construction, the state determined to limit transcontinental air service to one major carrier flying between large Canadian centers. Rather than wholly private or wholly public, moreover, the ownership of the new airline company would be mixed, with capital coming from the Canadian Pacific and Canadian National Railway corporations. Each railway would nominate three directors to the board, and so would the state. Canadian Pacific declined to participate in the venture, feeling that the combined presence of CN- and state-appointed directors would ensure that policy decisions followed state preferences. Trans-Canada Airlines was then established as a subsidiary of CN, which was empowered to offer up to 49 percent of the airline's shares to other parties, providing the minister of transport, then C. D. Howe, approved of the purchasers. No shares were sold, and Trans-Canada joined CN as a state-owned transportation enterprise.[30]

Thus far we have focused on the particular pattern of Canadian economic development and the role of the national state in that process. But Canada's federal form of organization has both shaped development and limited Ottawa's ability to act unilaterally to ensure conditions favorable for capital accumulation. Before we continue the story into World War II and beyond, we must briefly recapitulate the role of the provinces in economic development up through the Depression. It is important to do so: the ebbs and flows of Canadian federalism before 1939 defined the parameters within which postwar tensions were played out between Ottawa and the provincial capitals. Although decentralized federalism has historically differentiated the Canadian experience from that of other advanced industrial countries, the constraints it imposes on federal intervention (and conversely, the opportunities it allows the provinces) would become more significant in the years following 1960. At the same time, some instances of direct provincial intervention were significant not only as examples of state-owned enterprises but also for the precedents they established of aggressive provincial governments determined to define their own priorities as against Ottawa's.

By the turn of the century provincial governments had already set up Crown corporations to integrate provincial economies and facilitate staples extraction. Ontario was the first to establish a provincially owned corporation when it took control of hydro production in 1906. Manitoba, Saskatchewan, and Alberta all brought telephones under public ownership before World War I. The rationale offered for the takeover of hydroelectric generation was that this power source was crucial to Ontario's economic development; it could not be left in private hands. On the prairies, private telephone systems were indicted for not servicing rural communities.

The creation of Ontario Hydro was just one of several policy initiatives taken by the Ontario government after 1890 to encourage economic growth. These initiatives challenged federal authority and undermined Prime Minister Sir John A. Macdonald's conception of Canada as a highly centralized federation. Within two decades of Confederation, in fact, there had emerged two distinct levels of power in Canada, the national *and* the provincial. It did not take long for provincial premiers, led by those of Ontario and Quebec, to test the limits of the federal bargain by establishing themselves as alternative sources of policy to Ottawa and in so doing to take full advantage of economic powers allocated to them under the British North America Act. Interpretations of legislative jurisdiction by the British Judicial Committee of the Privy Council, until 1949 the final arbiter of Canadian constitutional disputes, expanded provincial powers and constricted those of Ottawa. As a result, when Ottawa made modest attempts to alleviate the difficulties of Canadians during the Depression years by adopting policies reminiscent of those of the U.S. New Deal, such as pensions and unemployment insurance, the provinces successfully challenged the constitutionality of these measures, seeing them as encroachments on provincial jurisdiction.[31]

Reinforcing intergovernmental conflict and provincial autonomy were different economic groups that recognized the advantages federalism offered for pursuing their interests. Economic development in Canada unfolded in a decidedly uneven way over the interwar years, with manufacturing concentrated primarily in southern Ontario and the rest of the country dependent on agriculture and resource staples. As it did so, different groups within capital quickly learned which arm of the state they could rely upon for protection. As Garth Stevenson suggests, the provincial Liberal government of Ontario, in power from 1881 to 1905, became a rallying point for farmers and businessmen who opposed the federal Conservatives' tariff and railway policies.[32] For their part provincial governments were quite prepared to act as spokesmen for particular economic interests when it served their purposes of provincial aggrandizement.

With the outbreak of World War II and the imposition of the War Measures Act, the Canadian political economy again became highly regulated and centrally directed. C. D. Howe's Department of Munitions and Supply was responsible for organizing wartime production, and Howe was thus the minister most directly and continuously involved in economic decision making. As in the Great War, the private sector undertook the bulk of wartime production. Also as in World War I, moreover, the state created enterprises of its own for particularly sensitive activities. From Howe's perspective, winning the war was crucial, and the methods used to pursue victory were not at issue. He and his colleagues were prepared to establish state-owned enterprises where they deemed them necessary.

Over the course of the war some twenty-eight state enterprises, eleven directly involved in production, were created in different sectors of the economy where secrecy, continuity of production, the organization of complex projects, or risk taking unattractive to the private sector was of concern. Overall they employed some 12 percent of the manufacturing work force. Three of these public corporations were engaged in research and development on sensitive technology, including radar and jet engines, and one of the three, Eldorado Mining and Refining, which became publicly owned as a result of expropriation in 1944 (see Chapter 7 below), both extracted and refined uranium. A fourth company, Polymer Corporation, was established to develop and manufacture synthetic rubber for the war effort. In addition to these, the state owned and operated two munitions factories, two shipyards, an aircraft factory, a plant that serviced machinery used by government contractors, and another that constructed and operated communications equipment.[33] By 1945 the federal state thus had a productive capability in sectors that had become technologically significant during the war. Like governments in Western Europe, Ottawa retained under state ownership several strategic industries, Eldorado Mining and Polymer among them, which it saw as important to postwar security (nuclear) and research priorities (rubber). In the absence of political parties committed to public ownership, however, most of the wartime enterprises were returned to their original owners (shipyards) or sold to the private sector (aircraft, radar and optical instruments).[34]

THE POSTWAR POLITICAL ECONOMY

Canada emerged from World War II a highly centralized economy, the result of national mobilization for the war effort. Ottawa expected that this national economic direction would continue into the postwar era. Planning for postwar recovery began long before hostilities ceased, with C. D. Howe, the czar of wartime production, overseeing reconstruction. In setting postwar priorities the King government was heavily influenced by Keynesian prescriptions for economic stability, which assumed that national governments would, in Donald Smiley's words, "ensure appropriate levels of aggregate demand through generalized fiscal and monetary policies and through lowering barriers to international trade and investment". According to J. K. Galbraith, "Canada was perhaps the first country to commit itself unequivocally to a Keynesian economic policy."[35]

Among the attractions of Keynesianism was the preeminent role it envisioned for the national government in directing economic activity. In a federation in which battles over jurisdictional authority had hampered federal efforts to combat the Depression, policy makers were quick to seize upon anything that would buttress federal leadership in economic affairs. As the war drew to a close, Ottawa enunciated what Smiley terms "a new national policy," like its predecessor a trio of commitments designed to promote national prosperity. These were (1) national leadership in economic management to guarantee full employment and price stability; (2) national leadership in creating and maintaining a welfare state; and (3) cooperation with other states in international economic reconstruction through the removal of trade barriers and the establishment of a new monetary system.[36]

This new national policy began to unravel within a decade, however, for reasons to be found in the interrelationship between the structure of the Canadian economy and the postwar evolution of Canadian federalism. Economic production in Canada has always been regional in character: manufacturing industries are located primarily in the central Windsor-to-Montreal corridor, agricultural and resource staples come from the western provinces and the Maritimes. In all industries, and certainly in the staples-producing sectors, demand fluctuates, resulting in peaks and troughs in prices, investment, and employment. Ottawa's postwar economic strategies paid insufficient attention to the regional nature of the economy and to regional grievances founded on the historic economic disequilibrium among parts of the country.[37]

Unhappy with federal initiatives, the provinces began to challenge Ottawa's prescriptions for Canada's future. They had a new interest in international economic policy as well as in the changing balance of power within Canadian federalism, as owners of now much sought after fuel and nonfuel minerals and metals. Provincial government revenues rose as a result of royalty payments; provincial economic strategies focused on resource development. Exports of mostly unprocessed resource staples to the United States tied the health of many provincial economies as much to the growth rate in the United States as to that in Canada, perhaps more. Thus the balance of power within the federation, which had swung dramatically to the provinces by the end of the nineteenth century and lay overwhelmingly with the national state during World War II, began to move back toward the provinces in the late 1950s and 1960s. In the immediate postwar years, in sum, the federal state expected to be the major player in Canadian economic policy. But the unfolding of events in Canada and the international environment severely constrained its ability to achieve that role.[38]

Postwar trends in trade and investment further complicated problems of economic management for the federal government. European governments were voicing their concern about loss of sovereignty due to the accelerating internationalization of production; Canada, because of the extent of foreign ownership, appeared particularly vulnerable. The immediate postwar years had brought an enormous expansion in U.S. direct investment in Canada. If C. D. Howe had no ideological opposition to state enterprise when circumstances warranted direct government control, neither did he worry about the nationality of capital. Primarily concerned to prevent a postwar recession, Howe and the King government encouraged American capital to participate in the Canadian economy with a variety of taxation and investment incentives. U.S. investment continued to follow the interwar pattern, going both to manufacturing to serve the domestic Canadian market and to resource industries whose output was exported to the United States. A few statistics capture the magnitude of postwar U.S. investment in Canada. In 1939, 32 percent of Canadian manufacturing and 38 percent of mining and smelting were U.S.-controlled; by 1957 the figures had risen to 43 percent and 52 percent respectively.[39] A decade later, in 1967, overall foreign control reached 57 percent in manufacturing, 65 percent in mining and smelting, and 74 percent in petroleum and natural gas. In each sector residents of the United States accounted for over 80 percent of this foreign control of invested capital.[40]

The ramifications of this pattern of U.S. investment were considerable. In manufacturing, the most dynamic of the consumer goods sectors were heavily foreign-owned by the 1950s. Canadian branch plants, established to serve the domestic market, did just that and only that; many were prohibited by their parent companies from exporting. Where exports did make up a significant share of sales, as in transportation equipment, the majority of exports were intrafirm, that is, went to U.S. parent or affiliate companies and thus were little influenced either by market signals or by government policy incentives.[41] Of even greater significance for Canadian industry's vitality was the continuing dependence of these subsidiaries on their parents for machinery, processes, and patents. The organization of multinational corporations dictated that branch plants obtain much of their inputs from within the company, and so machinery, equipment, and parts for manufacturing flowed north across the border. A Canadian government study on foreign investment found that, during the 1960s, imports concentrated in sectors marked by foreign control, that foreign-owned firms imported an increasing share of their total purchases, and that 30–40 percent of these imports were procured from their own affiliates.[42] With most research and development undertaken at corporate sites in the United States, the R&D capabilities of subsidiaries were extremely limited. At best Canadian branch plants might modify products slightly to accommodate the tastes of Canadian consumers. In sum, in the postwar years the Canadian manufacturing sector came to exhibit all the characteristics of a branch plant economy, fragmented, inefficient, with limited technological capacity, and lacking "the size and sophistication needed to be competitive on world markets."[43]

In the resource sector, U.S. capital continued to invest in metals and fuel minerals important to the U.S. economy. Between 1946 and 1955, for example, approximately 70 percent of total U.S. direct capital investment went into the petroleum, mining, and pulp and paper industries.[44] The Paley Report, commissioned by the Eisenhower administration to examine future U.S. natural resource needs in the context of deteriorating East-West relations and the Korean War, identified Canada as a prime source of twelve out of twenty-nine key commodities. Most of the equipment for extracting these raw materials came from the United States, and the resources were sent south for processing. Like their counterparts in manufacturing, Canadian resource subsidiaries were part of vertically integrated multinational corporations. Over the 1960s, in both the mining and the oil and gas industries, more than 75 percent of all foreign-owned companies in Canada sent at least some of their exports to their parent or affiliate companies; for more than 20 percent the parent or affiliate was the exclusive customer.[45]

Policy decisions by the Canadian state facilitated this rush of American capital into Canadian resource staples. Postwar budgets contained lucrative tax incentives and generous depreciation provisions designed to attract investment in the resource sector. In early discussions under the auspices of the General Agreement on Tariffs and Trade, Canada pressed for lower tariffs on raw materials to ensure unfettered access for unprocessed Canadian resources in foreign, primarily American, markets. Resources were seen as the leading sector of the economy, and so, with the irony that sometimes characterizes history, one hundred years after industrialization had begun in Canada, staples were still the major component of Canadian exports. Differences did exist between the old and the newer staples, however, not only in the technologies required to produce them but also in the source of capital and demand (now concentrated in the United States) and in the nature of their trade, increasingly organized by multinational enterprises.

When we look at these postwar developments to compare Canada to the other industrial economies surveyed in Chapter 1, we find that, just as in Europe, Keynesian prescriptions proved inadequate to overcome structural problems or to compensate for uneven regional development. In Canada, however, the federal division of powers and the increasing autonomy of provincial governments—a function of new revenues and new interests generated by resource development—further exacerbated the inability of the central government to achieve its desired outcomes through macroeconomic policies. At the same time Canada, like other OECD states, became increasingly open to international trade and investment; however, this internationalization had a very uneven impact on national economies. In 1967, on average, 17 percent of the manufacturing output of OECD countries was produced by foreign subsidiaries; Canada was well above that average with 53 percent.[46] Unlike many other host countries, where foreign investment concentrated either in resource extraction or in manufacturing to serve domestic markets, in Canada foreign capital went to both the primary and the secondary sectors of the economy. The resultant intrafirm trade helped intensify north-south economic ties between Canada and the United States. As we now turn to examine how the Canadian state, like the state in Europe, expanded its direct intervention in production in the 1960s and 1970s, we need to remember the three conditioning variables that distinguish Canada from other advanced capitalist countries.

THE STATE AS PRODUCER AND INVESTOR

By the 1960s a recognition of the increasingly transnational nature of the capitalist world economy, and a preoccupation with Canada's relatively vulnerable place within it, prompted policy makers to look beyond traditional means of intervention.[47] In an era that saw economic growth as a political responsibility, both federal and provincial governments sought to assure the requisite economic conditions for social welfare and, by extension, survival of the party in power. Direct control over production through the state-owned enterprise looked like an attractive policy instrument. In turning to new commercial enterprises or in revamping the activities of established state-owned companies, Canadian governments responded in particular to the exacerbation of conditions that by the 1970s were endemic to Canadian development—trade dependency biased by concentration on the U.S. market, high levels of foreign ownership, and the competing statism of other governments within confederation.

International trade in the 1970s accounted for some 30 percent of Canadian GNP. More than two-thirds of imports and of exports involved the United States, and trade diversification seemed increasingly elusive.[48] If we omit a United States–Canada sectoral accord, the Auto Pact, then manufactures took just a 22 percent share in Canadian exports compared with a proportion of finished manufactures in exports of 50, 50, 60, and 61 percent in France, Britain, Italy, and West Germany respectively.[49] Official recognition of the cumulative impact of foreign investment and growing public concern about it came with the publication in 1972 of a government-commissioned report on foreign direct investment in Canada. This, the Gray Report, concluded that "the rise of the multinational enterprise creates a new situation that requires new powers in the hands of government."[50] Its recommendation that government review the terms of access for foreign investors was implemented with the creation of a Foreign Investment Review Agency.

The relationship between trade and investment patterns was confirmed by the rising share of Canadian trade accounted for by intrafirm exchanges. The Economic Council of Canada noted that, for some industries, intrafirm trade grew from 67 percent of Canada's imports in 1965 to 79 percent in 1979, with exports in these industries also rising from 63 percent to 80 percent in the same period.[51] Finally, the ability of any one government in Canada to formulate and carry out economic policies continued on occasion to encounter countervailing efforts by other levels of government. Export promotion, investment attraction, or resource development policies by provincial governments were often at odds with federal priorities. Recent cases in point include protracted negotiations over oil pricing with the province of Alberta in the 1970s, resort to the Supreme Court to settle ownership of offshore oil and gas rights in the 1980s, and introduction of legislation to restrict the activities of Quebec investment funds.[52]

State-owned enterprises thus fit within a broader Canadian effort to adapt to the new exigencies of production and competition on a global scale and to offset the nation's particular vulnerabilities. Some 72 percent of the several hundred provincially owned corporations and 58 percent of federal government enterprises have been created since 1960.[53] No longer can it be said that these corporations play a purely ancillary role like the earlier provincial development corporations, designed to provide debt or equity capital to private business. Nor are they restricted to the nonprofit delivery of government programs like the provincial and federal public housing corporations. Provincial governments moved directly into the highly profitable resource sectors through takeovers of profitable subsidiaries of multinational enterprise (Potash Corporation of Saskatchewan, National Asbestos Corporation in Quebec) and in joint ventures with private enterprise (Soquip, Saskatchewan Oil and Gas Corporation, Manitoba Oil and Gas Corporation). Even conservative governments, as in Alberta, did not shy away from statism to promote regional economic integration, as Alberta's 1974 takeover of Pacific Western Airlines demonstrated.[54] The federal government created corporations with an expansive investment mandate, such as the Canada Development Corporation (CDC) in 1971 to take equity positions in high-technology and resource industries, and Petro-Canada in 1975 to ensure secure energy supplies and reduce the level of foreign ownership in the oil and gas sector. Federal enterprises operated in the manufacturing sector where the state had not taken a direct entrepreneurial role before the war (e.g., Canadair). Some were engaged in direct competition with private enterprises, whereas others involved government in joint ventures with select private-sector partners (e.g., Telesat Canada). Long-established state enterprises extended their investments abroad to become multinational corporations (e.g., Canadian National Railways).

Particular state enterprises were used specifically to enhance benefits to Canada in an increasingly competitive world economy. The Export Development Corporation (EDC), for instance, created after the war, was reorganized and refinanced to promote capital goods and high-technology exports in the 1970s. Stressing exports in the power, aircraft, communications, and capital goods sectors, EDC financed a small number of firms—private enterprises regarded as winners in international competition, but also multinational subsidiaries and state-owned enterprises. By 1975 the Canadian state, through the EDC, was financing 40 percent of all of the nation's capital goods exports outside North

America. The EDC also added a Foreign Investments Guarantees Division to enable "Canadian companies to more confidently enter foreign markets" because they would be ensured "against the loss of their investment abroad by reason of political actions."[55] The Canadian Commercial Corporation (CCC), established in 1946 for military procurement purposes, was likewise reoriented in the 1970s to promote purchases of Canadian goods by foreign countries. In effect CCC is a state trader assisting foreign governments to purchase Canadian products and aiding Canadian suppliers in their sales to foreign governments and their agencies. Although U.S. customers, especially the Defense Department, account for the largest volume of orders—76 percent in fiscal 1982–83—the CCC acted on behalf of seventy-three foreign governments and international agencies in securing contracts for Canadian companies valued at close to $600 million.[56] In the 1970s, in short, the Canadian state acted as trader and as financier to assist Canadian-based capital to internationalize trade and production.

In attempting to explain the creation of competitive state enterprises, Jorge Niosi is one of the few contemporary political economists in Canada who has gone beyond a public administration approach to state enterprises. He argues that three interrelated factors account for state capitalism in Canada. First, the belated and dependent nature of Canadian industrial development provoked a weak bourgeoisie to look for state assistance to promote Canadian-controlled growth—for example, the creation of the CDC and the Société générale de financement. Second, uneven development across Canada stimulated provincial governments to make a defensive effort to control industrial development—for example, the takeovers of the steel companies Sidbec in Quebec and Sysco in Nova Scotia. Third, the class structure within Canada as a whole and within specific regions has generated political pressures that biased governments in favor of using a state enterprise to compensate particular groups within their electoral jurisdictions—for example, the creation of government marketing boards and credit corporations to respond to radical farmer movements after the war, and the nationalization of Hydro-Québec aimed at promoting Quebec businesses in the 1960s.[57]

Niosi, however, leaves the impression that the creation of competitive state enterprises is a uniquely Canadian phenomenon. As we have already seen, Canadian experience coincides with a broad shift in the orientation of the public enterprise sector throughout Western Europe during the 1960s and 1970s. In our view, state capitalism in Canada must first be understood as part of an accommodation to new conditions in the world economy. Provincial governments opted for state takeover of the regional steel mills Sidbec and Sysco, for example, after the divestment decision of a foreign multinational. Indeed, many of Canada's industrial state enterprises are bits and pieces dropped by American or British multinationals as these firms restructured to meet changing competitive conditions in the world economy—coal, steel, and aeronautics provide examples.

CONCLUSION

The state in Canada has moved beyond the circumscribed role that liberal ideology assigns to it. No longer is it limited to ensuring conditions favorable to private investment and involved in production only exceptionally, in instances of market failure. We now find the state itself owning the means of production, employing wage labor, selling on commercial terms, and reinvesting earnings. Contrary to orthodox Marxist assumptions, the state is clearly not excluded from the accumulation of capital. At times in collaboration with private-sector enterprises, at times in direct competition with them, governments are promoting a commercial role for selected corporations. In Canada's mixed economy the state no longer stands apart from production, attesting to the emergence of state capitalism in Canada.

The changing nature of the Canadian public enterprise sector stems from the changing nature of the world economy, in particular the concentration and internationalization of production that over the 1970s resulted in industrial realignment and exacerbated competition, not only among firms for sales but also among states for production sites. Many economists now believe that the state's role in most advanced industrial economies justifies comparison to its role in the mercantilist era. Rather than seeking precious metals to benefit a landed elite, however, governments now seek to assure "economic growth and high living standards based on technical superiority in new industries."[58] European governments, as we showed in Chapter 1, use state enterprises as part of a neomercantilist adaptation to the new conditions of capitalist development.

If we want to understand the role of state enterprises in Canada as part of an accommodation to new conditions of global capitalist development, we must consider not only what Canada shares with other OECD states but also what particular conditions shape the Canadian political economy. Our historical survey of Canadian development identifies three variables that express themselves differently at different moments but have always been present and that today distinguish Canada from other industrial countries. Those variables are worth repeating: (1) a world economy in which Canada is highly trade-dependent and has a relatively weak manufacturing sector; (2) a pattern of truncated industrialization which makes Canada very reliant on foreign, especially American, capital and technology; and (3) a federal system in which uneven regional development and high provincial autonomy make Canada appear a fragmented state. These limiting conditions act at one and the same time to incite direct state intervention in production and to inhibit the freedom with which state managers can use state enterprises to control the direction of economic development.

Chapter Three

Contemporary State Capitalism in Canada

We saw in Chapter 2 that the expanded postwar responsibilities of the Canadian state in the national economy and its vulnerability to changes in the international political economy led both federal and provincial governments to turn to direct intervention. State enterprises now produce goods and services for sale in national and international markets, and many are major economic players. Of Canada's top 500 industrial companies ranked by sales in 1985, 32 are wholly owned by governments (16 federal, 16 provincial), and another 22 have substantial government participation.[1] Table 3 displays the largest public enterprises.[2] The relatively weak industrial base and high level of foreign ownership in Canada—just forty-seven of the top hundred companies are wholly Canadian-owned—make these state holdings all the more significant.

To substantiate our thesis that the public sector in Canada, as in Europe, has evolved toward state capitalism, with state enterprises taking on commercial roles usually assumed by private enterprise, we need to look more closely at the universe of public enterprises. We also have to be more precise about how we define a "commercial" public enterprise—those corporations which we claim have moved beyond such traditional roles for state enterprises as salvaging jobs and providing services to the private sector. From among these commercial corporations we select the case studies of Part II to investigate the use of state enterprises as instruments of policy. The state's direct involvement in production, however, now extends beyond wholly owned public enterprises to "mixed enterprises" where governments hold equity conjointly with private-sector partners. In Part III we focus on this new direction in state capitalism.

The state's expanded role as investor and producer in competitive and

Table 3. Canada's Largest Crown Corporations, 1985

Company	Owning Government	Year Established	Revenue ($'ooo)
Petro-Canada	Federal	1975	$5,300,09?
Canadian National	Federal	1919	5,017,79C
Ontario Hydro	Ontario	1906	4,625,00C
Hydro-Québec	Quebec	1944	4,492,088
Canadian Wheat Board	Federal	1935	4,121,00C
Canada Post Corp.	Federal	1981	2,500,248
Air Canada	Federal	1937	2,273,57?
British Columbia Hydro and Power Authority	British Columbia	1945	1,953,00C
Alberta Government Telephones	Alberta	1908	1,048,931
Royal Canadian Mint	Federal	1969	965,57▪
Saskatchewan Power Corp.	Saskatchewan	1929	837,00C
New Brunswick Electric Power Commission	New Brunswick	1920	834,20?
Via Rail Canada	Federal	1978	724,99?
Canadian Commercial Corp.	Federal	1946	716,278
Société gen. de fin. du Québec	Quebec	1962	699,13?
Teleglobe Canada	Federal	1950	678,63C
Sidbec	Quebec	1964	507,748
Manitoba Hydro-Electric Board	Manitoba	1949	506,41?
Nova Scotia Power Corp.	Nova Scotia	1919	497,71?
Canadair	Federal	1976	438,01?
Saskatchewan Telecommunications	Saskatchewan	1908	423,678
Manitoba Telephone System	Manitoba	1908	342,89?
Newfoundland and Labrador Hydro	Newfoundland	1954	330,55?
Atomic Energy of Canada	Federal	1952	309,09?
De Havilland Aircraft of Canada	Federal	1974	299,61?
British Columbia Railway	British Columbia	1918	294,60C
Eldorado Nuclear	Federal	1944	219,79?
Canadian Broadcasting Corp.	Federal	1936	212,28?
Potash Corp. of Saskatchewan	Saskatchewan	1975	197,31?
CN Marine	Federal	1977	190,97?
Saskatchewan Oil and Gas Corp.	Saskatchewan	1973	161,12?
Cape Breton Development Corp.	Federal	1967	159,86?
Société nationale de l'amiante	Quebec	1978	115,71?
Ontario Northland Transportation Commission	Ontario	1902	106,16?
Canadian Arsenals	Federal	1945	103,75?

SOURCE: *Financial Post 500,* Summer 1986, and corporation annual reports.

profitable industries raises important questions for public policy. Students of political administration have long been fascinated by the contradiction inherent in the public enterprise—at one and the same time a corporation subject to the rules of the marketplace and a bureaucratic organization open to political direction. The present trend to commercialization exacerbates traditional tensions between autonomy and control. We are not speaking about a loss of control here, of "runaway" state enterprises, but about an adaptation to the requirements of capital accumulation. Once state enterprises are required to compete or to produce for profit, their managers tend to seek greater autonomy, it is true, and governments tend to give priority to financial performance, thereby neglecting the wider social and economic implications of corporate activities. Despite this new latitude, however, state enterprise cannot be equated with private enterprise. The exercise of direction and control over state corporations has long concerned governments in Europe and Canada, and a review of the ways governments administer their public enterprise sectors identifies the special challenges presented by the commercial corporation as an instrument of policy.

We speak of a *trend* to commercialization because we find in Canada, as in Europe, that the changing pattern of competition and the fiscal crisis of the state have altered the modus operandi of long-established state enterprises. We cannot merely count the corporations originally set up by government to carry out commercial tasks or compare the size of state-owned assets in manufacturing to those in communications, energy, or transportation which provide infrastructure for the private sector. Since 1970 many subsidized state enterprises have been refinanced and their management asked to seek a better return on investment, while some commercial state enterprises have extended their activities through subsidiaries. Even those state enterprises which traditionally were monopolies have had to reorient their operations to meet new competitive challenges or to overcome financial constraints. We end this chapter by demonstrating that even public utilities, which account for most of the corporate assets of governments in Canada, have evolved with changing market conditions to do much more than provide infrastructure or facilitate private investment.

Public Enterprises in Canada

In his 1982 policy statement introducing revisions to the legislation governing Crown corporations, Prime Minister Trudeau emphasized "the important role of these instruments of national purpose in furthering overall development strategies."[3] The activities undertaken by some forty state enterprises and their one hundred-thirty subsidiaries justified this claim: "Government corporations are vital participants in economic development through their actions across major industrial, financial and service sectors, deployment of some $40 billion in assets, receipt of annual revenues in excess of $7 billion and employment of more than 200,000 Canadians in all regions of the country."[4] At the same time, the corporate holdings of provincial governments in Canada greatly exceeded those of Ottawa, both in numbers and in total assets. A comprehensive survey carried out in the early 1980s identifies some 233 provincial state enterprises, several dozen of them having further subsidiaries.[5] Both the rapid growth in the numbers of provincial enterprises since 1960 and the expanded operations of the public utilities produced public enterprise sectors of significant size. So significant were they, in fact, that assets were over 20 percent of gross domestic product in eight of the ten provinces.[6]

How exactly can we identify a public enterprise or Crown corporation, and how should we then distinguish "commercial" corporations?[7] The federal government faced the same questions when it revised its Financial Administration Act in 1984 and determined that those corporations created by Parliament to perform "administrative, supervisory or regulatory functions of a governmental nature" would no longer be considered Crown corporations.[8] All other corporations, whether or not created by an act of Parliament, are deemed Crown corporations as long as they are wholly owned by the Crown (whether directly or indirectly, as subsidiaries of a parent Crown corporation). They must be listed on the schedules to the Act, thereby becoming subject to its administrative regulations unless explicitly exempted. What constitutes state ownership? For the federal government two criteria must be satisfied: all the shares issued and outstanding of the corporation in question must be held on behalf of (or in trust for) the Crown, and all directors (other than those who sit on the board ex officio) must be appointed by cabinet (or by a minister with cabinet approval). Provinces more typically define ownership by the government's holding a specified percentage of voting shares (more than 50 percent in British Columbia, at least 90 percent in Nova Scotia, 100 percent in Alberta). They then attribute control to government whenever cabinet appoints and removes a majority of the directors of the corporation.[9]

Public enterprises may come into being either through the takeover of existing companies (whether by expropriation or by purchase in the marketplace) or through a government decision to create a new company (either ex nihilo or by transferring activities from departments to a corporate vehicle). Also, some public enterprises are authorized to incorporate subsidiaries. However it is formed, the public enterprise, unlike other government agencies, takes corporate form and thus constitutes a legal person. In Canada the legal personality of the public enterprise may be expressed either by a special constituent act of a legislature or by incorporation under general companies legislation, whether the federal Canada Business Corporations Act or the provincial equivalent.[10]

From among the more than four hundred corporations that governments own in Canada, we use three criteria to identify enterprises that in effect extend the scope of state capitalism—function, market environment, and financing. We agree with André Gélinas that the true state *enterprise* is involved in commercial, industrial, and financial activities.[11] We focus, to adopt the language used by Statistics Canada, on those enterprises involved in "the production of economic goods and provision of services for sale . . . to the consumer" and thus exclude companies set up to supply government alone.[12] Among state enterprises so defined, we are particularly interested in those which are active in competitive markets and aim to be self-financing. The market environment we consider competitive where private enterprises also provide the same or substitutable goods and services (whether in Canada, or in export markets).[13] Thus we include some state enterprises considered to be monopolies, such as the large public utilities. Regarding the attempt to be self-financing, we take into account expectations as much as results: Is the corporation expected to be self-financing, that is, to cover its operating costs from its revenues? We thus exclude many financial intermediaries that serve primarily as conduits for government programs by offering special credit terms in such areas as housing and agriculture. These criteria identify approximately twenty of the federal government's Crown corporations and thirty of the provincial Crown corporations as commercial corporations. They sell goods or services to the public, confront competition, and are exhorted to cover their costs if not earn a profit.[14]

THE UNIVERSE OF MIXED ENTERPRISES

The state also plays out its role as capitalist in Canada in a collaborative manner as governments place equity in commercial enterprises together with private investors. The diversity of forms of mixed enterprises involving the federal government directly, or indirectly through its Crown corporations, reflects a multiplicity of "authorities" for equity participation and a general lack of coordination of investments. It is therefore not easy to determine the shifting contours of state capitalism, especially if we define state capitalism to include the full range of government-held equity in commercial corporations. Although legally required to disclose investments, moreover, the cabinet has a right to exempt corporations from this obligation, can exclude shares ostensibly held for security rather than control, and allows its ministers a high degree of discretion.[15] To present an approximate picture of state investments in Canada, we combine the official federal government listing prepared by its Treasury Board with the results of a recent independent study. Together those sources identify federal and provincial government holdings in mixed enterprises during the period 1980–83.

In reporting on the government's corporate holdings as of December 1982, the Treasury Board catalogued 106 investments beyond the wholly owned Crown corporations, from which we subtract those seventeen memberships in international organizations such as the World Bank which happen to take the form of a share subscription. Overwhelmingly the other 89 investments, whether majority (34) or minority holdings (55), were made by established Crown corporations, and all but a handful were undertaken by only four Crown corporations: Air Canada, Canadian National Railways, Petro-Canada, and the Cape Breton Development Corporation.[16] To complete the picture of federal government investment in the early 1980s we then must add some twenty equity positions held by the Federal Business Development Bank and the further investments of the mixed enterprise Canada Development Corporation. The CDC's *Annual Report* named 104 "consolidated subsidiary companies."[17]

Provincial governments, normally acting through established Crown corporations and agencies, are collectively as important investors as the federal government, in terms both of numbers of mixed enterprises and of the value of government equity. E. Craig Elford and W. T. Stanbury identify 167 provincial government investments and another 33 holdings of mixed enterprises.[18] Most provincial investments take the form of joint ventures (rather than continuous corporations) or minority portfolio placements. Quebec's Crown corporations and agencies play the dominant role, notably the Caisse de dépôt et placement and the Société générale de financement, both instruments of industrial policy that we analyze in Chapter 6. Outside Quebec, the resource and energy corporations (the focus of Chapter 7) created in Ontario and the western provinces to engage in joint ventures account for most instances of provincial government investment; one third of provincial mixed enterprises are in mining, metals, and mineral fuels.[19] The proliferation of government holdings in mixed enterprises is yet another way in which the state has enlarged its role as investor and producer in competitive industries. The vast majority of such investments have been made since 1980.[20]

With this summary sense of the contours of contemporary state capitalism in Canada, we now turn to the issues that surround the use of the corporation as an instrument of public policy. We focus on wholly owned state enterprises. It should be remembered, however, that questions of direction and control also attend investments in mixed enterprises, because in the majority of instances the state's share is held by a Crown corporation.

QUESTIONS OF AUTONOMY AND CONTROL

When the modern state decides, for whatever reasons, to take on activities of a financial, industrial, or commercial nature, it finds it desirable to vest decision-making powers in a unit outside government. In the view of Sir Herbert Morrison, whose thinking has influenced administrative practice not only in Britain but also in many Commonwealth countries, the public enterprise is extremely attractive because it promises "a combination of public ownership, public accountability, and business management for public ends."[21] The reasons for turning to a corporate vehicle are several. First, it is generally believed that the bureaucratic processes within government inhibit risk taking and thus are unsuited to a business environment where managers must reach decisions rapidly, often with regard to commercial confidentiality. Second, to attract top-caliber managers with appropriate business experience, government must be able to provide conditions comparable to those in the private sector, including competitive salaries and benefits, the right to hire and fire personnel, and the latitude to make and modify decisions. Third, because the short-run political interests of ministers may be at odds with the longer-term commercial objectives of the corporation, a separate board of directors provides the best protection from political meddling.[22] The Morrisonian ideal thus imagines an arms-length relationship between the government, which establishes broad policy and imposes ex post facto accountability, and the corporation. In Canada, certainly, this conceptualization has set the tone of debate over the role of public enterprises. Indicative is the opening to the federal government's major reform proposals in 1977: "How can increased responsiveness to public policy be reconciled with the arms-length relationship which the theory of public enterprise requires government, ministers and Parliament to maintain with Crown corporations?"[23]

The central dilemma—What is the proper balance between managerial discretion and political control?—has engendered considerable discussion. For the public administration specialist who starts from the premise that the departmental form of organization is a norm, the Crown corporation is one among many alternative instruments for delivering programs. The establishment of a public enterprise generates controversy mainly because it is part of a larger trend to transfer state activities to agents relatively autonomous from public control and notably insulated from scrutiny by elected representatives in the legislature.[24] In fact, however, few of the commercial public enterprises examined in this book were created ex nihilo or by extending functions previously assumed by a department to a corporation. More typically, these corporations substitute for the market, taking over activities previously carried out by the private sector. Rather than administering resources like bureaucrats, public enterprise managers generate new resources through investment and production. From the perspective of the economist, the question is not how far public enterprises should be allowed to deviate from the norm of departmental controls, but how far governments should be allowed to deviate from the norm of autonomy possessed by commercial corporations. Special privileges or special restrictions for the government-owned venture, it is believed, reduce incentives for managers to seek productivity gains or else inhibit market expansion and thus incur social costs through misallocation of capital.[25]

Even in countries that have never accepted the Morrisonian arms-length relationship as an ideal, such as France and Austria, debate over the administration of government-owned enterprises revolves around the same issue of control. The Nora Report on public-sector management in France sees the challenge as how to distinguish the two roles that every public enterprise plays simultaneously: the pursuit of efficiency and the advancement of socioeconomic goals set by government. Company interests and public policy interests frequently do not coincide. For example, optimal use of resources might lead a corporation to purchase foreign technology whereas government policy, concerned about strengthening national firms in international competition, requires local sourcing. How have governments resolved this basic dilemma of the dual allegiance of their state-owned enterprises?

Two decades of postwar experience taught most European governments the necessity of reforming their administrative regimes for public-sector enterprises. Senior bureaucrats recognized they had to know more about corporate finances simply to judge whether efficiency criteria were being met, and they also realized that boards of directors were often unaware of changing priorities in government policy. Ministers became receptive to bureaucrats' proposals for administrative reforms in response to three broad economic and political trends: first, inflation and tight credit had increased company costs and decreased political tolerance for subsidies; second, investment activity by public enterprises had increased the number of subsidiaries whose operations were less transparent; third, the moderation of socialist party doctrine in several European countries now permitted a more technocratic approach to running the public sector.[26]

What administrative reforms have characteristically been undertaken? Despite the expansion of state enterprises, few European governments instituted central administrative units to oversee their commercial enterprises; nor did many countries adopt comprehensive legislation to govern public-sector enterprises.[27] European governments typically sought to assert control over state enterprises and yet avoid undue interference in corporate decision making in three ways—financial controls, directive power, and appointments. All impose some financial controls, thus differentiating the state-owned from the private enterprise by the former's circumscribed independence. Limitations on borrowings, administered prices, or approvals for investments are normally prescribed, whether by company statutes, a general financial administration act, or regulations of treasury or finance ministries. To ensure compatibility between company and ministry objectives while respecting the claims of managers to clear lines of responsibility, some governments introduced formal directives (Britain) or "planning contract" agreements with the corporation (France).[28] Most governments reserve to themselves the right to appoint boards of directors and often senior management as well. They thus expect corporate activities to correspond to their evolving policy priorities (with dismissal the ultimate sanction).

CANADIAN ADMINISTRATIVE PRACTICES

In Canadian practice the general administration of Crown corporations is broadly similar across the country, despite special political traditions and economic conditions in different provinces. All administrative regimes conform to the basic tenets of the parliamentary system. A designated minister answers to the legislature for a corporation's activities, whereas cabinet, its committees, and a variety of central agencies—always including finance—exercise overall direction and control. Controls over Crown corporations are formalized to a widely varying degree, however, and usually reflect the general level of institutionalization of public administration in a jurisdiction. At one extreme is Nova Scotia, where face-to-face interactions still prevail among ministers and senior bureaucrats. Here the investment strategy adopted by a Crown corporation depends much more on knowing "what the minister wants" than on any formal guidelines. Ontario, on the other hand, has a classification scheme that tailors elaborate administrative and financial guidelines to different types of corporations.[29] Saskatchewan and Manitoba have made major innovations in administrative structures. Saskatchewan created a holding company to oversee large commercial Crown corporations; Manitoba became the first jurisdiction in Canada to create a Department of Crown Investments, in 1982. Only Saskatchewan and the federal government have general legislation to govern Crown corporations.

Different governments in Canada have dealt differently with the fundamental question of the corporation's broad orientation. All recognize that mandates set out in initial legislation tend to be both too vague and too time-bound (policies and technologies will both evolve). Four jurisdictions now request submission of a corporate plan. In Saskatchewan, for example, these plans are approved by the holding company that also operates as a committee of cabinet; in Quebec plans go before cabinet on the recommendation of the appropriate minister. Federal legislation requires every parent corporation to submit a corporate plan to Ottawa which must cover the activities of any wholly owned subsidiary, relate objectives to strategies, and assess annual performance in terms of past plans. Cabinet approves plans on the recommendation of the responsible minister.[30] In Ontario the chairmen of the boards of directors of commercial corporations and the responsible ministers negotiate memoranda of understanding; these serve as reference points for ministers in assessing corporate performance.[31]

The ways in which Canadian governments actually exercise authority over their corporations by way of financial controls, directive power, and appointments are extremely diverse. There are, for example, no uniform requirements for the submission of budgets by Crown corporations across the country, nor indeed within most jurisdictions. Normally corporations do submit capital budgets, whether as a formal requirement (Saskatchewan, Ottawa), as part of submission of a corporate plan (Quebec), or for information purposes on the request of the finance minister (British Columbia). These budgets must ultimately be approved by a committee of cabinet. Commercial corporations are not usually required to submit operating budgets; everywhere, however, there are controls over corporate borrowings. The degree of control ranges from provinces that borrow on behalf of their corporations (British Columbia, Saskatchewan) to those that encourage corporations to borrow on the market (Quebec). For Ottawa, controls are as varied as the corporations, because the individual corporation's statute grants or does not grant the power to borrow.

Virtually all governments in Canada issue directives to their corporations from time to time. These are typically communicated informally, either by the responsible minister or by public servant directors on the corporate boards. Directives have always been formulated by cabinet, whether in the form of a cabinet minute or as a condition attached to a capital contribution which requires it be used for a particular project. Only in Quebec and Ottawa have governments given themselves a legally binding directive power. Quebec has done so by revising the statute of each commercial corporation. Although certain federal government corporations have long been subject to binding directives under their constituent acts—for example, Air Canada, Teleglobe, and Petro-Canada—Ottawa legislated general directive power over all Crown corporations only in 1984. This legislation states that cabinet may, after consultation between the minister and the corporation's board of directors, issue a

directive if "it is in the public interest to do so." The board must implement the directive and is absolved from any liability incurred in carrying it
out. Each directive must be made public by being tabled in Parliament.[32]

Directive power is, in a sense, corrective power—binding directives
oblige boards to do what otherwise they might not have deemed to be in
the corporation's interest. Not surprisingly, directives are used only
sparingly. Under normal circumstances the board of directors is the
linchpin in the relationship between governments and Crown corporations. All corporations have boards, and virtually all board members are
appointed by cabinet. To use the boards of directors as policy conduits,
governments rely not on formal shareholder meetings but on informal
ministerial directives and often on the presence of public servants
and/or reliable political appointees on the boards. Government representation varies: in some provinces a minister always sits on the boards
(British Columbia, Saskatchewan), in others ministers may or may not be
directors (Alberta, Nova Scotia), and several provinces preclude ministers from serving as directors (Manitoba, Ontario). Wherever ministers
do not serve, however, it is standard practice to appoint one or two
public servant directors. Some fifteen federal government enterprises
have one or more senior bureaucrats on their boards of directors. The
deputy minister of energy, mines, and resources, for example, sits on the
boards of Atomic Energy of Canada, Eldorado Nuclear, and Petro-Canada. These divergent practices reflect an ongoing debate as to whether
government presence on boards represents a conflict of interests for the
public servant in question or a proper expression of the public's interest
in a public enterprise.[33]

With some understanding of how governments seek to resolve the
paradox of the public enterprise—at once a corporation subject to the
dictates of the market and a bureaucratic organization intended to serve
policy goals—we now can appreciate why the expanding number of
commercial state enterprises accentuates this classic paradox. The conclusion drawn from a large number of studies on European state enterprises is, in Harvey Feigenbaum's words, that a "goal of profitability and
the accordance of managerial autonomy to pursue this goal" reduces the
tractability of the corporation as an instrument of public policy.[34] This
generalization derives from bureaucratic, systemic, and ideological ax-
ioms, and it deserves explication before we see just how it applies to
Canadian experience. Its reasoning is *bureaucratic,* because it assumes
that the decision-making process within the bureaucracy is ill-suited to
the exigencies of the business world. In most advanced capitalist countries, therefore, the restrictiveness of control regimes varies with profit
mandate and market conditions—"normally, the less limited the profit-
making and the more competitive the context, the more should the

enterprise be independent."[35] Its reasoning is *systemic,* because it assumes that, in the capitalist mixed economy, survival of the firm under conditions of competition requires managers to respect market criteria. Governments are thus inhibited from introducing "noneconomic" performance goals. Finally, its reasoning is *ideological,* both because it presumes that market discipline can partially substitute for government direction (as private enterprises define what constitutes the right price or rate of return) and because many governments accept the notion that successful managers will be those recruited from the private sector. Overall, therefore, "the enterprises will tend to align their objectives and criteria more and more with those of their private-sector competitors; 'socially responsible' aspirations will be increasingly regarded as a luxury they cannot afford."[36]

THE TREND TO COMMERCIALIZATION

As in Europe, so in Canada we find the public enterprise sector undergoing a reorientation. Commercialization is part of political self-defense in a period both of fiscal constraint and of corporate adaptation to evolving market conditions. The Canadian trend to commercialization involves two distinct but interrelated developments that can be traced back to the 1970s. First, it involves a change in the legitimation of state enterprises; governments shifted emphasis from social purposes to invoke what we call business logic, that is, financial results ("the bottom line") became the principal criterion by which to evaluate performance. Second, the trend involves a change in the objective conditions governing performance as state enterprises increasingly confront competition.

The origin of the trend to commercialization may be identified with the Privy Council Office's 1977 report in which the federal government responded to criticism of financial mismanagement of major Crown corporations by proposing reforms that would assure administration "on a sound commercial basis, to promote their efficiency and maximize the return on the investment of the Canadian taxpayer."[37] This shift in performance criteria toward private-sector norms coincides with a crystallization of both political and economic pressures. The expanded activities of public-sector enterprises over the prior decade had given them greater political visibility. Numerous government corporations, and even more subsidiaries, had been set up without being scheduled in the Financial Administration Act, thereby diverting information expected by bureaucrats and Parliament. The press and parliamentary committees exposed several scandals, focusing attention on the political mismanagement of public enterprises. Some corporations had been allowed to engage in questionable commercial practices, at times contravening official policy.[38] The auditor general's 1976 report decried the "weak and inefficient" financial management of most Crown corporations, ineffective governmental direction, inadequate information provided in budgets, and thus the vital need for reform—beginning with the need to place all corporations on schedules that clearly delineated "purely commercial" enterprises.[39] In addition, the sheer size of several of the major public enterprises brought criticism of unfair competition from the business world and a reactive attempt by government to display a commitment to private-sector norms. According to a study commissioned to demonstrate the dangers of government in business, the "trend toward greater profit-orientation" by Canadian state enterprises can be attributed in part to "resentment among private-sector competitors."[40]

Economic constraints, especially the crisis in public finance, also incited government to find ways to rationalize its public-sector management. By the 1970s the recourse to deficit spending had become a new orthodoxy as government expenditures rose from 36 percent to 41 percent of the gross national product while revenues from taxation stayed constant.[41] Proposals to improve the management of Crown corporations were part of the broader debate on the costs of maintaining social programs and public-sector employment in the face of rising deficits. An increasingly defensive Liberal government claimed to be fiscally responsible, intent on improving the business climate, and able to "manage" the public sector. Ottawa introduced a series of experiments to enhance central agencies' control over resource allocation and set up a royal commission on financial management and accountability, the Lambert Commission.[42] In its final report, published in 1979, the Lambert Commission devoted special attention to Crown corporations. Noting that normally these corporations no longer operated under conditions of monopoly, the commissioners appealed to private-sector norms—boards of directors should be given a wider margin of autonomy, commercial objectives should be separated from social objectives.[43]

Although the government did not implement specific Lambert Commission proposals, the report's underlying business logic has been adopted both as norm and in practice. Revisions to the Financial Administration Act reconfirmed the principle that Crown corporations should be scheduled according to market conditions and financing. Some exemptions from budget controls were therefore permitted for the corporation that "operates in a competitive environment" and is "not ordinarily dependent on appropriations for operating purposes."[44] The rationale advanced for affording greater autonomy to commercial state enterprises replicates a logic familiar from the European literature:

"There is an essential need for a flexible relationship that allows corporations to operate effectively in a corporate form, manner and milieu and in accordance with sound business behaviour and practices."[45]

In practice the federal government sought new sources of financing for its public enterprises or at least ways to move some expenditures "off budget" to avoid the light of parliamentary scrutiny. It encouraged the commercial Crown corporations to finance projects on private money markets, thereby decreasing their demands on the public purse. The immediate advantages to the government of outside borrowing and the rationale provided by business logic are well expressed in the conclusion to the 1977 reform proposals, which explained that recourse to borrowing would "expose the commercial activities of Crown corporations more to market discipline and curtail the cash drain on the Consolidated Revenue Fund that results from Crown corporations borrowing from the government."[46] Several major Crown corporations, notably Air Canada and Canadian National Railways, were restructured. They were placed on a financial footing similar to that of their private-sector equivalents on the assumption that a comparable debt : equity ratio was a prerequisite to attracting private lenders. The revised legislation governing Air Canada now states that the company should have "due regard to sound business practices, and in particular the contemplation of profit."[47]

This shift in the legitimation of state enterprises to favor private-sector norms has not been limited to the federal government. At one extreme the neoconservative government in Saskatchewan, elected in 1982, accepted the recommendation of a government-appointed commission that its holding company "be given as its central objective the maximization of dividend payments to the province." In keeping with this new fiscal purpose, each Crown corporation was to be "clearly profit oriented."[48] In British Columbia the Social Credit government distinguished itself in the 1970s by undertaking a privatization program but subsequently promoted the commercialization of selected public enterprises. Thus the B.C. Rail Company was restructured and refinanced as part of a broader policy to facilitate private-sector development of coal reserves. As a result, "despite public ownership the railway operates in a commercial and competitive environment and it does so in expectation of profit."[49] In Ontario the traditional Conservative party (in power for over forty years until its defeat in 1985) created several new commercial companies in the late 1970s to promote particular policy objectives, such as technology innovation and energy security, and emphasized market criteria for assessing performance. Thus, for example, the government's memorandum of understanding with its Urban Transportation Development Corporation stated that "the Corporation shall operate in a totally commercial manner . . . and may compete in both the Canadian domestic and international marketplace."[50]

The trend to commercialization generally finds reinforcement among the Crown corporations. The companies present themselves, in annual reports and public relations, in ways highly imitative of the private sector. The chairman of the board and chief executive officer of Petro-Canada states that his company "has become a powerful competitor in the marketplace." Northern Transportation Company's annual report explains that "the Company is a profit-oriented commercial Crown corporation." The president of Atomic Energy of Canada, reporting on the corporation's "sixth profitable year in succession," underscores its capability to "diversify its product line" and "increase productivity" to survive in "a highly competitive market," while the chairman hopes for "greater business confidence" to spark renewed investment in the Canadian economy.[51]

The commercial reorientation of the public enterprise sector in Canada involves more than this normative shift, which, as we have seen, validates performance criteria derived from business logic. Changing market conditions have reintroduced competition in electricity, telecommunications, and other natural monopolies where government ownership is expected to ensure the low-cost provision of essential services to the public as a whole. This competitive challenge, combined with reduced domestic demand in the recession of the early 1980s, prompted the public utilities to undertake new activities that earned a return sufficient not only to cover costs but in some areas even to turn a profit. The commercialization of Canada's largest public enterprises underscores our theme that state capitalism is no longer exceptional—no longer is the state as producer of goods and services for sale in the market restricted to a small number of enterprises nor to enterprises with limited social impact.

Government-owned utilities in Canada have evolved in ways that recall the reorientation of basic industries in Europe over the 1970s (analyzed in Chapter 1). First, we witness indirect competition by way of substitution as alternative energy sources, in particular natural gas, erode quasi-monopoly positions. Second, we see competition for international markets (often between Crown corporations) as Canadian utilities export surplus power to the United States. Third, we find that competition for scarce capital leads governments to revise rate policies not only to cover rising interest rates but also to maintain a debt : equity ratio attractive to potential lenders and investors in bond markets. Finally, we see that in conditions of recession, corporate managers exercise their discretionary power to diversify activities and to compete in the new world market for engineering consultancy services.[52]

Quebec's state-owned hydroelectricity company, Hydro-Québec, is a giant by any standard, ranking in 1985 as Canada's second-largest industrial corporation in terms of assets and fourth in terms of capital expenditures.[53] Hydro-Québec's development plan, made public in 1983, set out a strategy that aimed to expand and diversify markets in response to adverse economic conditions—in particular inflation and the changing energy price structure, which favored gas over electricity. Because of its excess capacity, the corporation emphasized export sales, already the fastest-growing category in its sales. In spite of "tight competition," Hydro-Québec saw itself well placed to compete in export markets. It outlined a segmented market strategy whereby it would meet the needs of neighboring grids in Canada at a price high enough to permit it to sign long-term contracts with American utilities at a lower, competitive price.[54] The development plan also promoted diversification of product lines, in particular efforts to commercialize technology and develop markets for the corporation's know-how. Implementation has entailed $35 million in equity inventments—for example, Hydro-Québec's 33 percent interest in Electrolyser Inc. of Toronto, which is developing new processes for producing oxygen and hydrogen gases.[55] The main actor is Hydro-Québec International, a subsidiary set up to meet what company planners call "the lively competition in export markets for know-how related to the production, transportation and distribution of electric energy."[56] Hydro-Québec International has been involved in feasibility studies, joint consultancy projects with private firms, training of Third World engineers, negotiation of contracts for sales of turbines, and coordination of construction for electrical generating plants. When revenues declined in 1983–84, Hydro-Québec's president reinforced business logic, cutting costs by laying off 11,500 employees, pushing harder for sales, and looking for joint-venture partners to diversify more rapidly while spreading risks.[57]

British Columbia Hydro's corporate purpose, according to its annual report, "is to satisfy energy needs in British Columbia"; its corporate philosophy "is to operate as a business enterprise consistent with sound utility practices and financial principles."[58] In 1982 the provincial government took the exceptional step of issuing a directive to this government enterprise, which is already subject to a regulatory body, the Utilities Commission. It directed B.C. Hydro to "achieve a financial position enabling it to borrow funds on the most economic terms available."[59] Since the provincial minister of finance undertakes all borrowing on behalf of B.C. government corporations, one might have expected the government guarantee to be sufficient to attract investors. Private investors (largely American) are, however, presumed to take debt: equity ratios into account and, other things being equal, would place their money in another Crown corporation, Hydro-Québec, because of its favorable equity position. Explaining its difficulty in reaching the specified debt: equity ratio, B.C. Hydro noted, among other considerations, the drop in earnings from power exports to the United States due to "greater competition from other utilities for the available markets."[60] To position itself for future opportunities, B.C. Hydro applied for and was granted licenses to export electricity to the western United States from 1984 to 1988 and has since negotiated, for example, a $200 million sale to Los Angeles. Indeed, by 1985 export earnings enabled the corporation to report a profit despite rising debt service costs.[61] Like its Quebec counterpart, B.C. Hydro also moved into world markets to compete for contracts to supply technology and know-how. The two provincially owned utilities even formed a consortium with Canadian private enterprises to undertake feasibility studies for major hydroelectric projects in China.[62]

The other major public utility in Canada, telephones, government-owned in three provinces, is also moving into competition, both by ceasing to be monopoly supplier of phones and switchboards within a province and by diversifying product lines to sell in international markets. The evolution of Alberta Government Telephones (AGT) provides our final example of the trend to commercialization. Originally set up in 1906 as a department of government and transformed into a corporation in the 1950s, AGT now finances its operations from revenues or borrowings and does not receive any budgetary appropriations. In 1982 AGT incorporated two wholly owned subsidiaries, Alta-Can Telecom Inc. and Alberta Telecommunications International (ATI), and entered into a joint venture with Canada's eighteenth-largest industrial company, NOVA, to be known as Novatel.

In different ways each of these new ventures expressed a newly commercial orientation for a former monopoly that was intended to supply a service to the Albertan public. Alta-Can was mandated "to be a profitable business enterprise"; its objective was to undertake joint ventures with local industry, thereby internalizing "ideas and skills" the better to compete with other equipment suppliers following the liberalization of its monopoly position. ATI responded to the challenge posed by recession—AGT's president had already noted the "severity of the economic downturn [which] . . . had a devastating effect on AGT's revenue base."[63] ATI was set up to bid on international contracts so as to market AGT's technical skills and thereby "generate additional revenue" and "provide more challenging job opportunities" for the many engineers and technicians then underemployed. Finally, the joint venture with NOVA was sought to commercialize new technology, in this instance a cellular mobile radio telephone system, which AGT's R&D subsidiary, Westech Systems, had developed. Novatel would then market the system "on a global scale."[64] In trying to penetrate the Asian market, Novatel directly confronts competition from the world's leading telecommunications companies, for example Sweden's Ericsson. Overall AGT's evolution shows that "there is a clearly established trend to increased competition. In 1952 only 2% of AGT's total revenues were subject to competition; by 1972, 12%; and . . . in 1982, 28%."[65] No longer are the large public utilities that dominate Canada's state enterprise sector merely providers of infractructure to the private sector.

CONCLUSION

By the 1980s the public sector in Canada had come to resemble that in Europe. At both federal and provincial levels, governments have assumed a direct role in production, increasingly in competition with private capital, whether domestic or foreign. Even public utilities, the archetypal infrastructural corporations, have moved into competitive commercial activities as they vie for export markets, capital, and offshore contracts. But state capitalism extends beyond wholly owned state enterprises to include large numbers of mixed enterprises wherein the state and private capital combine in commercial ventures that then confront other competitors. The emergence of state capitalism belies the assumption that while the market is productive, the state is unproductive—increasingly the state is producing for the market.

Concomitant with the expansion of state capitalism has been a shift in the basis of legitimation of state enterprise toward the application of business logic. Governments have tended to substitute so-called market discipline for political direction in an effort to meet two imperatives. First, they attempt to reduce subsidies and to demonstrate their ability to manage the public sector in a time of restraint. Second, they seek to respond to the need of corporate managers for sufficient latitude to maneuver in industries marked by competition and buffeted by rapid technological change. Market discipline exacerbates tensions, however, between the autonomy required by and afforded commercial state enterprises and the ability of governments to ensure that corporate activities address evolving political priorities.

This trend to commercialization undermines the assumption that we can equate state ownership with state power understood as the ability to control outcomes. We have reviewed the ways in which various governments seek to administer their public enterprises in order to avoid the oversimplified conclusion that state enterprises are "out of control." Once governments become convinced that market conditions require "letting the managers manage," however, the prevailing ideology inhibits the reintroduction of noncommercial policy objectives. In order to appreciate more fully the implications of the trend to commercialization for public policy making, we turn now to detailed case studies.

Part II

THE LIMITS OF
STATE CAPITALISM

CHAPTER FOUR

Business as Usual:
Public Enterprises and Public Policy

The president of Canada's oldest and largest federal Crown corporation, Canadian National Railways (CN), has argued "that running a business at a reasonable profit and high efficiency is the best way for the
corporation to discharge its fiscal and social responsibility."[1] Yet in the
view of the auditor general, whose much publicized 1982 annual report
focused on the lack of control over government corporations, "the fact is
that the broad public purposes for which these corporations were established are frequently not spelled out either in legislation or anywhere
else in a public document. It is hardly surprising, then, that accountability for public policy objectives by these corporations is an elusive target."[2] The auditor general thus raises the question of the extent to which
governments can use commercial state enterprises as instruments of
policy.

To explore this question, we analyze the activities of five commercial
state enterprises in Canada, all of which operate in competitive industries. In this chapter we look at corporations that were asked to produce
for profit and given a wide margin of managerial discretion to do so:
Canadian National Railways; Canadair; and the Canada Development
Corporation (CDC). Not that these state enterprises lacked purpose beyond profits—each was intended by government to favor broad socioeconomic goals: to promote national integration (CN), secure a high-
technology industry (Canadair), or enhance Canadian ownership (CDC).
But in the 1970s management and government shared the assumption
that commercial success was synonymous with the advancement of these
objectives. The companies were not subjected to policy directives by
government but were expected to run railroads, sell airplanes, and invest Canadian capital in growth industries.

These three state enterprises differ markedly in terms both of their origins and of their formal relationship to government. CN, established in 1919, provided transportation at a high cost in public subsidies until its reorganization in the 1970s. It is a Crown corporation governed by special statute and subject to regulation by the Canadian Transport Commission. Canadair, nationalized when government bought assets divested by a multinational corporation in 1976, was expected to return a profit while restoring Canada's place in the world aircraft industry. Incorporated under general companies legislation, Canadair had no formal reporting requirements until the mid-1980s. The CDC was established by special legislation in 1971 to act as a vehicle of clearly stated investment policy. Given the right to issue shares to the public, the CDC was not a Crown agency and thus was exempted from any accountability to government other than by way of its government-appointed directors.

Despite their differences, all three cases show that the tractability of the corporation as a policy instrument tends to diminish over time. The latitude afforded to management of the commercial state enterprise will progressively distance corporate decision makers from government policy makers. In the experience of Maurice Strong, former chairman of the board of both Petro-Canada and Canada's state holding company, CDIC,

> the tendency is for a determined and independent-minded management to prevail in maintaining a high degree of independence once it has achieved this. . . . This tendency will inevitably be reinforced when most of its new initiatives can be financed from internally-generated resources and more and more of its senior management consists of people with little experience of government.[3]

In addition, Robert Sexty notes, once commercial state enterprises are encouraged to seek outside financing, a move rationalized in part by reference to market discipline, "the management of the Crown corporation has yet another constituency to please," that is, the outside lender.[4] The government's ability to assert direction is further constrained because management claims that creditworthiness depends on the company's commercial performance, which the imposition of "noneconomic" performance criteria could undermine.

Yet even where government is content to respect managerial autonomy, the corporation in question is still state-owned, and so business-as-usual will likely become business-as-politics. When the activities of a state enterprise, however inadvertently, jeopardize public monies or public policies, the government-as-shareholder finds itself obliged to absorb political costs. In concluding this chapter, we attempt to reach some generalizations about the use of commercial corporations as vehicles for policy by drawing together factors that delimit corporate autonomy.

BUSINESS AS USUAL: CANADIAN NATIONAL RAILWAYS

Although transcontinental railways take on near-mythical qualities in Canadian historiography as the basis for national economic unity, the formation of Canadian National Railways (CN) after World War I was not strictly an act of purposive state building. Rather, as a leading economic history textbook says,

> nationalization was undertaken not on grounds of principle but as a pragmatic necessity, to prevent the bankruptcy of enterprises in which many individuals had invested their savings ... and the possibility of serious damage to Canada's credit in foreign capital markets. The major argument in its favour was not its intrinsic desirability but the impracticability of all possible alternatives.[5]

Despite CN's original mandate to operate railways "on a commercial basis under its own politically undisturbed management," for fifty years the corporation typically suffered financial losses, requiring government subsidies and refinancing to overcome its three handicaps—heavy indebtedness inherited from predecessor companies, the obligation to service unprofitable routes, and competition from a successful private company, Canadian Pacific Railways.[6]

Clearly Canada's oldest and largest federal Crown corporation represented what Stuart Holland calls a first-generation public enterprise, one created when governments "salvaged failing concerns in the private sector," using them to provide infrastructure for the development of private enterprise at public expense.[7] CN was a Crown corporation required by its legislation to get cabinet approval of both its capital and its operating budgets. Its reliance on government funding exposed the corporation to parliamentary scrutiny, while its obligation to provide noncommercial services, such as intercity passenger service, made it highly visible to officials in the Department of Transport, not to mention the public and politicians. In the 1970s, however, as Garth Stevenson observes, a rather extraordinary turnaround took place when the reorganization and refinancing of CN "reinforced its ability and inclination to act as a profit-seeking enterprise virtually independent of the state."[8]

CN's new status—as a profit-seeking, diversified, international corporation—was made possible by permissive changes in regulations for the transport sector as a whole; hard bargaining by aggressive management; and concessions by a government determined to place Crown corporations on a better financial footing. The 1967 National Transportation Act gave all companies greater leeway in setting rates and established the principle that government would pay companies compensation for providing nonprofitable services deemed in the national interest.[9] Yet only after forceful management—largely in the person of Robert Bandeen, CN president from 1974 to 1982—introduced organizational changes was the basis set for restructuring the corporate-government relationship. In particular, CN managers revised their control system to define profit centers in such a manner as to isolate commercially nonviable operations. In 1977, for example, they made CN Marine (coastal ferry services) a subsidiary with separate accounts and incorporated VIA Rail (passenger rail services) under companies law.[10]

The federal government facilitated these changes by taking over VIA Rail's stock and proclaiming it a new Crown corporation. It then assuaged private-sector opposition by having VIA assume passenger rail service for Canadian Pacific as well, under contractual arrangements, and minimized parliamentary objections by slipping this important innovation through as an item in a Supplementary Estimates rather than tabling legislation for debate.[11] The final precondition for CN to become relatively autonomous, self-financing, came with passage of the Capital Revision Act in 1978. The act gave CN the right to borrow on its own credit in the money markets to cover deficits and the right to retain any earnings after paying a 20 percent dividend to the government.[12] These legal changes, along with the government's decisions to convert its preferred shares to common stock and to capitalize outstanding CN debt, thereby rendering the state enterprise's debt: equity ratio equivalent to its private-sector competitors', enabled CN to attract outside funding and thus freed management to make choices on a primarily commercial basis.[13] Results from the perspective of corporate performance, measured by market criteria, have been impressive, but contradictory from the perspective of public policy making. We examine success and contradiction in turn.

In the 1980s CN has become a major corporate player in transportation, telecommunications, real estate, shipping, and trucking. With some fifty-four wholly owned subsidiaries and investments in another thirty companies, CN ranks as Canada's thirteenth-largest corporation in terms of sales and fifty-third for net income. According to the business press, "management has pursued an aggressive policy of expansion and diversification, using new companies and takeovers to enter new fields and to rationalize existing operations."[14] In so doing, CN extended its international operations, particularly in the United States. The corporation's consolidated earnings record has enabled it to pay multimillion-dollar dividends to the government in most years since 1978.[15]

One CN investment, however, in the Cast shipping group, demonstrates how, in the absence of clear a priori policy guidelines, CN's very success in expanding and diversifying has created contradictions for government in two vital areas of policy: ocean shipping and regional economic development. Once the implications of the investment were recognized, normal government financial controls were apparently inadequate to correct corporate activity a posteriori. Faced with a highly visible controversy, under new conditions of economic recession, government officials felt obliged to salvage the situation by accepting business logic. They protected the investment rather than reconsider the surrounding public policy issues.

Canada's shipping "policy" since World War II has been strictly laissez-faire. Despite the importance of international trade, no Canadian legislation relates to deep sea shipping, nor do government incentives encourage shipping by Canadian flag ships. According to the Department of Transport in 1974, at the time of the CN investment in Cast,

> In Canada shipping policy is fragmented between different departments and agencies. . . . There exists neither a definition of objectives, a unified administration, an authorization of power for dealing with the subject matter nor any community of purpose or effort. Interventions, where possible at all . . . are necessarily limited to the vague generalities that are all that can safely be deduced from the equally vague guidelines.[16]

Yet the world shipping industry, particularly after the shift in the 1960s to more capital-intensive containerization, has become increasingly concentrated as national firms have formed consortia backed by preferential state financing and shipping policies. As government recognizes, "Canada, with its hands-off policy, is close to becoming a unique case among the world's main trading nations."[17] Over the 1970s, as world trade shrank, the industry also become susceptible to problems of surplus capacity and increasingly characterized by cartelization—a trend accelerated by the 1974 UNCTAD Convention on a Code of Conduct for Liner Conferences. The code, which had fifty-eight signatories when it came into force in 1983, permits countries to earmark as much as 40 percent of their imports and exports for national ships. These new realities "render a passive reliance on international competition inadequate to protect national interests."[18]

In 1975, without resort to government for approval, CN chose to invest U.S. $12 million in the Cast Group to confront the competition for freight forwarding in a new growth area—container ships offloading at the port of Montreal with goods destined for western Canada and the U.S. Midwest. Although CN already had direct investments in port facilities at Halifax, Nova Scotia, management considered that decisions by both Canadian Pacific Ships and Dart Containers to move to Montreal obliged CN to enter this market as well. Eurocanadian Shipholdings, a Bermuda-based holding company, held controlling interest in the Cast Shipping Line and was itself controlled by a Swiss-based holding company, Intercast SA. Cast's leased carriers offered both bulk and container service across the Atlantic between Antwerp and Montreal (where Cast owned a container terminal).[19] By its investment CN became one of three owners of the Cast Group with an 18 percent share of the voting stock of each holding company. Despite this minority position, the shareholder's agreement made a CN nominee one of the three members of each holding company's Executive Committee, where "general policy matters and pending major decisions relating to the administration, management and operation of the Cast Group" were to be discussed. In addition, it was agreed that "each shareholder shall use his best efforts to ensure that all traffic . . . be routed by rail and/or highway within the continent over lines or routes of CN."[20] In the eyes of corporate management the investment clearly made good commercial sense.

The state enterprise was not entirely free to undertake its investment decision, however, because the National Transportation Act required CN to notify a regulatory agency—the Canadian Transport Commission (CTC)—of its intent to buy into Cast. During subsequent hearings various interested parties raised objections. Canadian Pacific Railways protested that CN's real aim was not investment but control of Cast's rail business, while both the Canadian Shipowners Association and the Seafarers International Union of Canada objected to a state-owned enterprise transferring $12 million to a foreign-based concern. The CTC, however, approved the transaction, apparently accepting CN's position that its "sound investment" would neither restrict competition nor otherwise prejudice the public interest, and thus the hearings over a minority shareholding constituted "a tempest in a teapot."[21]

The political implications of CN's involvement in Cast became clear only in 1980–81, when the corporation decided to increase its financial commitment to Cast by purchasing preferred shares for an additional U.S. $42 million, thereby gaining the option (through a conversion clause expiring on December 31, 1981) to increase its ownership share to 26 percent. Cast wanted the new capital infusions to place orders for six new ships, which would make it Canada's largest shipowning company, just surpassing Canadian Pacific in tonnage. Indeed, commenting on the increased investment in Cast, CN's president heralded CN's new "world shipping role."[22] In effect, CN's investment in Cast now called into question established patterns of competition in deep sea shipping and, the Nova Scotia government claimed, undermined regional development policy by reducing traffic to the Maritime port of Halifax. Yet the state enterprise had acted without policy guidelines from the federal government.

In the absence of a coherent policy on ocean shipping, government could only react to CN initiatives. Its established bureaucratic procedures for financial control, however, were clearly unsuitable for altering corporate preferences. Even though CN must submit capital budgets through its responsible minister for approval by the minister of finance, the president of the Treasury Board, and ultimately the cabinet, the process often appears merely pro forma. Budgetary analysis may not be completed until well into the actual budget year, and de jure penalties for deviating from budget are nonexistent. Although formally CN needs cabinet approval for its investments, the corporation disposes of its own funds, and management need give only perfunctory notification of their intentions.[23]

Typically, major Crown corporations such as Air Canada and CN negotiate deals with the legal proviso "subject to Governor-in-Council [cabinet] approval" and, as in the case of Cast, inform the Treasury Board just a few days prior to the closure date. Elaborate memoranda to cabinet may set out the costs and benefits of various scenarios, but usually the company has precluded most of the options. Government is placed in a reactive posture: veto is always possible, but not true policy making. It was the chorus of objections from affected parties (the government of Nova Scotia, other shippers, and unions) which brought about a second inquiry by the Canadian Transport Commission, an inquiry under the Anti-Combines Act, a Supreme Court case, and a swirling controversy in the press during 1981–83.

The objections raised before regulatory commissions and the Supreme Court indicate the range of policy arenas affected by activities that CN undertook "in the normal course of business." Among them were use of foreign ships and crews by the Cast Group; location of the tax base outside Canada; payment of rebates by CN to a Cast subsidiary to secure contracts for forwarding freight westward from Montreal by rail; unfair competition from a government enterprise; and the conflict of interest in CN's investment in a Montreal-based container terminal when CN was responsible for the sole rail connection between Halifax and central Canada (the destination for 85 percent of goods offloaded at Halifax).[24]

Changing economic circumstances rather than political pressures convinced CN's Board of Directors in early 1982 not to raise their ownership share in Cast after all. Cast had hit hard times. Declining world trade, high interest rates, and a management mutiny in which some staff broke off to form a competing company rocked Cast to the point where it had to pledge three ships to its creditor, the Royal Bank of Canada. Although the state enterprise could, and eventually did, write down the $62 million at risk, government remained susceptible both to the political costs of Cast's failure and to the more immediate pressure of a fait accompli when the major Canadian banks involved put together a new financing package to protect their investments. Government clearly had no leisure to reconsider broad policy objectives, but it did agree to play its part in an urgent $200 million refinancing by approving a $10 million payment from CN to Cast, in return for which CN would acquire a container terminal in Montreal (thereby refueling Nova Scotia's fears of conflicting interests). CN also acquired the right to convert its shares in Cast to achieve a 75 percent controlling interest, thereby reasserting the railways' role in ocean shipping.[25]

The government, too, sought to cut its losses. One year after the refinancing, when CN sought cabinet approval to buy out Cast's rival spinoff, ministers refused to issue the necessary order-in-council; they reportedly accepted the arguments of CN's competitors that this expansion would constitute unfair competition by the state. Yet shortly thereafter, when bankruptcy again threatened Cast, CN succeeded in convincing cabinet that it could exercise its takeover option. This infusion of new capital would salvage the shipping company and reassure its creditors, including Canada's Royal Bank. CN's commercial interests, not government policy considerations, dictated the surprise outcome. When other shareholders objected to the terms proposed by the Crown corporation, CN pulled out altogether in the summer of 1983. Cast's holding company, Eurocanadian Shipping, declared voluntary liquidation, and the Royal Bank took possession of the ships and eventually control of the restructured company.[26]

The CN-Cast case shows the government obliged to react to the consequences of decisions by commercial state enterprise over which it had exercised little prior policy direction. In the absence of established policy priorities for the transportation sector in general, and the shipping industry in particular, the normal business activities of a state enterprise could and did generate contradictions between the indirect role of government as investor through its Crown corporation and government's direct responsibility to make policy.

LETTING MANAGERS MANAGE: CANADAIR

When the federal government purchased Canadair from U.S. General Dynamics Corporation in 1976, it was enacting one more scene in the continuing drama that surrounds the aircraft industry in Canada. The Canadian government and large British and American corporations have been the major actors, although the script has sometimes been revised by the U.S. government whose defense and procurement policies since World War II have helped define the market for Canadian-based production. Once the Canadian government stopped providing subsidies for aircraft development in favor of buying off-the-shelf technology in the late 1950s, it eliminated a domestic market assured by Canadian defense procurement. Eventually, in the early 1970s, as part of a restructuring of the world industry, two leading aircraft producers, U.S. General Dynamics and the British Hawker Siddeley Group, opted to divest their Canadian holdings. Reluctantly, Ottawa purchased the two subsidiaries to preserve the technology, skilled jobs, and export earnings they represented. So the government, through state-owned Canadair and De Havilland, found itself a producer in the high-risk, high-technology aircraft industry, competing with established international companies for sales on the world market.

Aircraft production in Canada had begun after World War I when Canadian Vickers, a subsidiary of the British multinational, set up an aircraft division near Montreal to design and manufacture amphibious planes. Meanwhile British De Havilland incorporated De Havilland Canada near Toronto to assemble and later to manufacture small planes under license, mainly for the air force. During World War II, as noted in Chapter 2, the coordination of production under the powerful minister of munitions and supply, C. D. Howe, involved both nationalization and creation of new state-owned enterprises—including the engine manufacturing plant Turbo Research, the airplane manufacturer Victory Aircraft, and a new aircraft plant built in Montreal and operated by Canadian Vickers. Following the advice of the Committee on the Post-War Manufacture of Aircraft, a private-public consulting body set up in 1943 which had recommended a Canadian-based industry to be supported by government contracts, both Turbo and Victory were sold to the British company Hawker Siddeley in 1945.[27] Foreseeing a fall-off in orders after the war, British Vickers determined to move out of aircraft production altogether. Rather than close down the plant it was leasing to Vickers, Ottawa established a Crown corporation in 1944, Canadair, and gave it the order for a new plane, the North Star, intended for both civilian use by government-owned Trans-Canada Airlines and military use as a transport plane by the Royal Canadian Air Force. As soon as an interested private investor was found, however, Ottawa sold the company in 1947 through a lease-purchase agreement. The American parent company, reorganized shortly thereafter as General Dynamics, not only was assured of substantial orders for the North Star but also received a Canadian government contract to develop a new fighter aircraft.[28]

The government's decision to abort the Avro Arrow fighter being developed by Hawker's affiliate, A. V. Roe, in 1959 marked the end of private research and development insured by firm defense contracts.[29] Henceforth the maintenance of a viable aircraft industry in Canada would require the government to act as supplicant—seeking to convince the American defense establishment to place orders and/or share subcontracting work, all the while offering incentives to the multinationals to retain Canadian-based production sites. Despite these incentives, however, two major changes in the aerospace industry over the 1960s convinced the multinational parents of both De Havilland and Canadair to relocate production away from Canada. The first was the U.S. Defense Department's policy of sourcing aircraft within the United States; the second, the Vietnam war notwithstanding, was a worldwide trend in the aerospace industry away from military to civilian and space program end-users. Both General Dynamics and Hawker Siddeley, which had absorbed De Havilland, chose to retrench by giving orders to their domestic plants, and dramatic lay-offs and repatriation of skilled workers from Canada prepared the way for divestment in the early 1970s.[30]

Looking back in 1983, the minister responsible for Canadair reconstructed the reasoning behind the government's takeover decision. Mindful of "the fateful decision" to cancel the Arrow and its negative impact on Canadair engineering and technology, the government by the mid-1970s believed that "Canada lacked the critical mass to remain its own supplier for these larger and more sophisticated aircraft." Despite declining U.S. military orders for small planes and thus a shrinking work force, "Canadair represented a high level of production skills. It was an important vehicle through which to obtain military and commercial aviation manufacturing offsets for Canada." Even if one adopted the more modest perspective of a continental subcontracting role, only continued production in Canada could foster the requisite engineering and design skills. In this official view of past and future, nationalization of Canadair—presented as a transitional strategy until private-sector interest revived—took on great symbolic importance: "Canadair was, after all, one of the only two aircraft manufacturers in Canada. To reduce Canada's ability to produce aircraft would increase Canada's trade deficit in manufactured goods. It would also signal a Canadian reluctance to face the risks of high technology."[31]

Canadair is thus a third-generation public enterprise, one that brings the state into competitive and profitable industries as part of a response not to market failure but to the effects of global restructuring by successful international firms. To ensure a national presence in leading industries, the state becomes an entrepreneur. In doing so its objective is not exclusively to serve social goals regardless of commercial viability but to protect productive assets in the short term and to promote the adaptation required to make nationally based production sites internationally competitive. In principle, state ownership is a means and not an end, yet the goal of eventual reprivatization obliges the state to take part directly in global competition so as to demonstrate to prospective buyers the company's ability to produce for profit.

As a commercial corporation purchased to enable Canada's aircraft industry to adapt to changing conditions in the world industry, Canadair was not treated like other Crown corporations in terms of direction, control, and accountability. Management was given wide discretionary power. No special legislation established the company's mandate or its reporting responsibilities. Instead, supplementary letters patent signaled the change of ownership in 1976. Incorporated under the general companies law, and not listed on the schedules to the federal Financial Administration Act, Canadair had no formal obligation to submit capital or operating budgets. As members of the board of a company financed by commercial bank loans, its directors had only to approach the responsible minister—and the minister to seek approval of a cabinet committee, the Treasury Board, thereafter—if and when they required a guarantee for loans. Only if such guarantees surpassed the ceiling initially set and approved by Parliament would there be reason for Parliament, the auditor general, and the public to become cognizant of company financing, activities, or results. Indeed, during its first seven years of operation as a state enterprise Canadair published no annual report.

Although the federal government, as sole shareholder, now appointed all members of the board and included among the fourteen directors the assistant deputy minister of industry, trade and commerce, Canadair's board played only a passive role. Concerned about the company's commercial viability, government had retained private-sector managers, notably the chief executive officer, Frederick Kearns, who had joined Canadair in 1949 and been its president since 1965. Even public servant directors saw their responsibility as explaining the company's needs to government, relying on senior management for expertise in this high-tech and high-risk enterprise.[32]

At first Canadair appeared to be a success under public ownership. The aircraft, or more precisely airframe, industry was maintained in Canada.[33] Canadair developed a new plane for the civilian market, the Challenger executive jet, incorporating innovative design features. Within three years the company had climbed back to 6,000 employees (from 1,500 at the time of takeover) and to profitability. By the 1980s, however, with the failure to reach sales targets for the Challenger, Canadair could not meet mounting interest payments. It became evident that independent management had led Canadair into a financial débâcle.

Tardy government efforts to rectify the situation only escalated it into public scandal.

After reporting profits for some years, Canadair published financial statements in spring 1983 revealing enormous losses. Press, Parliament, and public were stunned. Canada's national newspaper headlined the story "Canadair's $1.4 Billion Loss Biggest in Country's History."[34] Public attention had already been drawn to Canadair when a popular television program had devoted an hour of prime time to expose the company's problems and concluded that its product was no longer competitive; that the costs incurred in developing the Challenger could not be recouped; and that the taxpayer was at risk through the government's policy of guaranteeing Canadair's bank loans.[35] The business press recounted how the "Challenger dream" had turned into a "colossal nightmare of mishaps, miscalculations, bad luck, and bad judgment." Parliamentarians blamed the company for having misrepresented its financial situation; the *Financial Post* saw government as culpable and concluded that "the time is over for vague, flag-waving generalizations about aviation, technology and national interests."[36]

How should we account for Canadair's spectacular losses? Certainly any entrepreneur, private or state, seeking to develop a new product for world markets in a highly competitive sector is susceptible to failure. This is particularly true in the absence of government contracts to assure the sales required to break even, what is normally the case for European and U.S. aerospace companies.[37] In addition, Canadair's management made several miscalculations, notably an overcommitment of resources to one program, the Challenger executive jet, and a modification of its design without due regard to the consequences for performance.[38] But beyond these general business risks, we argue, the Canadair fiasco demonstrates limits to the use of commercial public enterprises as instruments for economic policy without the actual exercise of policy direction. Asked simply to produce airplanes for profit, company managers saw themselves not as subject to the "discipline of the marketplace" but rather as insured against financial risk by the safety net of government loan guarantees. At the same time government, having accepted business logic in "letting the managers manage," did not see itself as responsible for policy direction. Indeed, government assumed it was insured against political risk by the fact that no budgetary appropriation (and thus no parliamentary scrutiny) was involved. This combination of two irresponsibilities permitted first the build-up of the company's financial exposure and then government's complicity to avoid political exposure. Ultimate disclosure was inevitable, and the scale of losses helped discredit the government's interventionist approach to industrial adjustment.

The extent to which Canadair's senior officers had taken advantage of their relative autonomy and the presumption of government financial backing became painfully clear over 1981–82. The company received approval for development of the Challenger based on forecasts of a peak financial requirement of $128 million and sales of 236 planes by 1983, but its real needs turned out to be $1.9 billion and its real sales well under a hundred planes. Increasing cash requirements resulted from "the costs of redesign and modifications, delays in engine deliveries and certification, failure to achieve sales forecasts . . . over-ordering of parts . . . foreign exchange losses and . . . rising interest burden on borrowed money."[39] Over 1981 the company repeatedly appealed to the minister and the minister to the Treasury Board to guarantee the multi-million-dollar loans that it needed to survive another few months but that the banks would not finalize unless government agreed to specific conditions.

Reluctant to go to Parliament to raise the authorized level for loan guarantees without a better understanding of the company's prospects, the government set up an interdepartmental task force in May 1981 to examine the situation at Canadair. Meanwhile, however, the company's financial emergency pushed ministers into signing "interim letters of comfort" (pending parliamentary approval) involving such commitments to the banks as the maintenance of government ownership, the funding of future Challenger cost overruns, and payment to creditors in the event of default. When cost overruns on a new engine obliged Canadair to raise the ante in early 1982, ministers must have been outraged at the evidence of company management's lack of full disclosure to the task force just a few months earlier. Yet they were trapped by business logic—if they fired managers or removed directors, they would only undermine the marketing of the Challenger, which was required to recoup development costs. So the directors were retained and further interim letters of comfort issued, and Parliament was asked to raise the loan guarantee ceiling from $150 million to $1.35 billion.[40]

Such was the scale of government liabilities and of Canadair's commitment to the Challenger program that financial restructuring clearly was required to permit equity infusions. The financial disclosure that would make such restructuring plausible to Parliament necessitated greater government control. As the government saw it, "management frequently failed to communicate to the board the information required to permit a proper assessment of the company's problems," while "government, in turn, believed that the private sector directors are ensuring commercial standards."[41] Thus Canadair, along with several other government-owned commercial corporations, was made a subsidiary of a new state holding company (the CDIC) as of November 1982. As it turned out, this effort to reestablish control came too late to avert the political fallout from past mismanagement. In auditing Canadair's 1982 accounts, CDIC found that the company had been using what it delicately called "over-aggressive" accounting since the onset of the Challenger program—in effect misrepresenting its financial situation to its board and to lenders. While most aviation companies at that time were following the "program method" of accounting, which capitalizes the costs of developing new planes (based on their expected sales) to even out earnings, Canadair had not merely overestimated future sales but applied somewhat unorthodox costs such as interest, marketing, and administration overhead to the Challenger program. The company thereby inflated its apparent assets and could report "profits."[42]

Disclosure of Canadair's true financial picture revealed the high political costs of having let the company run itself. These revelations undermined the Liberal government's intended aerospace policy. Goverment's requests for equity infusions over 1983–84 met a barrage of press criticism and prompted a parliamentary inquiry, inspiring the newly elected Conservative government to reap political gains in 1984 by announcing the sale of Canadair to the highest bidder.[43]

EXERCISING SHAREHOLDERS' RIGHTS:
CANADA DEVELOPMENT CORPORATION

The origins of the Canada Development Corporation, a state holding company directed to invest so as to "develop and maintain strong Canadian controlled and managed corporations," are inseparable from a decade of debate over the consequences of high levels of foreign investment in Canada, and especially over the role of American branch plants. The Trudeau government designed legislation in 1971 that would effect a compromise between an industrial policy favoring Canadian ownership and a concern to promote private investment rather than substitute for it. The prime minister's parliamentary secretary explained this compromise during the debates on the CDC:

> I believe it [CDC] to be the first substantial step to help us "tip toe" through the intricacies of maintaining a substantial inflow of investment capital, still essential in the view of my party to the dynamic growth of our economy, and the imperative of assuming an increasing degree of control over the business and economic decisions which very much affect our sovereignty and our development.[44]

Government, by providing capital to a state enterprise that imitated private enterprise in having the right to issue shares to the public and in being asked to carry out its activities "in anticipation of profit," sought to minimize the intrusion of the state into the marketplace. To emphasize the relative autonomy of the CDC, the enabling legislation specifically stated that the corporation was "not an agent of Her Majesty or a Crown corporation within the meaning of the Financial Administration Act."[45]

Although government eschewed the control and accountability regimes standard for Crown corporations, it nonetheless made it perfectly obvious that the CDC was to be an instrument of policy. Formal government control was guaranteed by the requirement that the government retain at least 10 percent of the voting stock outstanding; other shareholders were restricted to 3 percent. During its first three years of operations, in fact, the CDC was wholly state-owned.[46] The nationalist impetus was made explicit in the act, which specified that directors of the board must be Canadian citizens and, in majority, resident in Canada, and shareholders must be either residents or citizens. Investments should aim at "substantial holding of shares carrying voting rights" to ensure Canadian control.

After its first decade of operations the CDC could be judged a commercial success. It had multiplied assets to $6.5 billion; built up Canadian high-technology producers (AES Data for word processors); bought into foreign firms (Savin Corporation in the United States for photocopiers); and bought out the Canadian holdings of international corporations (Elf-Aquitaine of France for oil, gas, and sulphur). Through CDC's many subsidiaries the state became involved in companies that competed with private enterprises in such leading industries as electronics, biotechnology, and petrochemicals.[47] The CDC's success in building a diversified corporation created the basis for subsequent autonomous action by management. Two episodes—the controversy over the commercial practices of Polysar, and the attempt by government to enlist CDC's participation in a bailout of Massey Ferguson—illustrate the divergence between commerical interests as defined by a relatively autonomous corporation and the public interest as defined by the government of the day.

In pursuing its corporate strategy "to develop companies that can become world-scale and develop sales in foreign markets to gain the size needed for full operating economies and efficiencies,"[48] the CDC created a multinational empire of subsidiaries and affiliates whose commercial activities were subject to no political direction or government approval. In the process, as the Standing Committee on Public Accounts reported to the House of Commons in 1977, Polysar International SA, an indirectly held Swiss subsidiary of the CDC, had engaged in questionable commercial practices, specifically kickbacks. The company desisted only after press leaks led management in the parent firm, Polysar Canada, to undertake an inquiry. In the course of testimony before the parliamentary committee it became clear that corporate officials considered such practices acceptable because they "are fairly prevalent today in the operations of multinational corporations." Indeed Canada's auditor general, having learned of the kickbacks, informed the prime minister that he had not publicly revealed them because "to have done so would in my view have been contrary to the best interests of Polymer [Polysar] as a multinational corporation trading in world markets in a highly competitive field." Clearly, company directors saw their mandate "to be no different from that of a company in the private sector," particularly as the government had not made a formal policy statement on commercial practices for state enterprises before 1976. Moreover, the Polysar group of companies engaged in intercompany pricing policies apparently "designed to reduce Canadian corporation taxes," and officers were unwilling to provide the committee with information "because the laws of a foreign country restrict public disclosure of the business transactions of that subsidiary." Not surprisingly, the parliamentary committee concluded that conflicts existed between the autonomy afforded to commercial state enterprises, whose officers then followed "normal business practices," and the interests of public policy makers.[49]

A more direct challenge to government authority came in 1981 with the conflict between the CDC and the federal government regarding investment policy. This confrontation stemmed from the corporation's particular mode of financing. The effect of issuing shares to the public was to revise radically the original government-corporate relationship, both formally, as government had intended in devising the CDC's legislation, and informally, which it had not expected. Formally, public share issues reduced the government's holding in the CDC from 100 percent in 1974 to 68 percent in 1978 to 48.6 percent in 1981. In fact the government owned 87.7 percent of the more than 35 million common shares issued by year-end 1981, but votes were attributed on the basis of fully diluted shares. To attract private capital, the government sought to reassure potential shareholders that the CDC was "a sound business investment" by writing a letter of understanding to the Board of Directors and by refraining from exercising its right to vote in favor of the option to nominate 4 members to the 18-to-21-member board. Informally, once the CDC had changed its status from a corporation wholly owned by government to a publicly traded company with government as the largest shareholder, CDC managers—encouraged by the financial press—used their responsibility for protecting "the return on investment" as a means to deter any "government intervention," which, they asserted, would frighten the market and dilute the value of CDC shares.

The CDC president expressed this inhibitory business logic well in a speech reviewing the company's problems:

"A third weakness is the uncertainty in investors' minds surrounding Government intentions toward CDC. . . . Until the Government makes a clear public statement of its intentions, the stock is going to be unusually depressed. It will accordingly be more difficult to finance on reasonable terms than it should be."[50]

It became clear during the 1981 standoff over investment policy that the logic of corporate financing and the ideology of private-sector management were combining to deprive the government of directive power over the CDC. With the reelection of the Liberal party in 1980 after a brief Conservative interregnum, new priorities for industrial adjustment in a major recession seemed urgent. The prime minister announced that the CDC would be "revitalized and play in the manufacturing sector the more positive role that Petro-Canada has played in resources."[51] Overcoming its passive shareholder role, the government, in the person of the minister of industry, trade and commerce, invited the CDC to participate in an equity infusion to refinance one of Canada's leading multinational corporations, Massey Ferguson. When CDC refused, the government lobbied board members before the 1981 annual meeting, asking them to elect Maurice Strong, long-standing Liberal party supporter and former chairman of Petro-Canada, to chair the CDC board. Once again the board refused to accede to government's wishes, and the business press exploded with such headlines as "CDC Must Keep Its Independence" and "Plan Subverting CDC Would Be a Betrayal." A major policy reconsideration took place.[52]

Inability to reassert government control over the CDC led to a decision to divest. At its June 1982 annual meeting the CDC board of directors accepted Ottawa's proposal to sell all government shares when market conditions became favorable and to seek parliamentary authority to allow other shareholders to augment their holdings. At the same time a new company, the Canada Development Investment Corporation, was incorporated under companies legislation to hold the government's equity. In explaining this decision, the minister responsible denied that government had ever interfered in the company's business decisions, though he acknowledged that "there have been important differences of views on CDC's relationships to the Goverment." All in all, however, everyone should agree "that the public policy considerations leading to the creation of the CDC by Parliament have matured. It is a successful commercial vehicle and has contributed significantly to Canadian ownership in the economy." Cabinet, however, sought a more tractable instrument of policy. The minister concluded that the CDIC "will not only provide a vehicle through which the Government's ongoing investment can be held, but will also be available for other public policy initiatives."[53]

CONCLUSION

Our analyses of CN, Canadair, and the CDC suggest that the relative autonomy of state-owned enterprises, most pronounced in commercial enterprises with a profit mandate operating in competitive markets, inhibits the ability of government to use such corporations as vehicles for policy. We derive this conclusion from a small selection of cases, of course, and other, comparative studies can both confirm it and provide nuance. Philippe Faucher cogently argues, on the basis of Canadian, French, and Brazilian experience, that state enterprises are not passive subjects of government influence but political agents actively seeking greater autonomy. The degree of autonomy they achieve will differ in different decision-making spheres—strategic planning, operations management, financing, investment—but overall, state enterprise managers attempt to distance themselves from government controls and align their company's behavior with private-sector norms.[54] Taieb Hafsi derives his model of state enterprise decision making from in-depth interviews in Canadian, European, and Algerian firms. He argues that an evolution in corporate-government relations from cooperation through confrontation to autonomy constitutes a predictable life cycle for state-owned enterprises.[55]

If we are interested in the tractability of the corporation as a policy instrument, therefore, we ought to examine those factors which appear to enlarge or diminish the area of relative autonomy for managers of commercial state enterprises. Extrapolating from the cases considered in this chapter, we focus upon legal regime, corporate financing, political salience, and type of commercial operations. Once again analogues in comparative research from Europe are striking, as these factors closely parallel the variables affecting managerial discretion identified by Yair Aharoni.[56]

To start with, it is clear that the relative autonomy of a commercial state-owned enterprise in Canada varies according to its enabling legislation and the consequent administrative regime for control and accountability. Autonomy is greater for a state enterprise incorporated under general companies legislation, such as Canadair, than for an enterprise established by special statute of the legislature. Among "special act" corporations, autonomy is greater for corporations not scheduled in the Financial Administration Act, which may be exempted from budgetary approvals or financial reporting requirements. The CDC's enabling legislation denied the corporation Crown agency status, foreseeing eventual mixed ownership, but CN had to respect a series of reporting obligations.

More important over time than the legal regime, the cases suggest, is the state enterprise's mode of financing. For both political and economic reasons the mode of financing directly affects how control and accountability regimes are applied. In the first instance, either a state enterprise is intended to be self-financing or it is not. Self-financing refers to the absence of direct government funding after initial capitalization (or refinancing, as in the case of CN). If a state enterprise requires budgetary appropriations or even nonbudgetary loans or advances from the government, these must be voted by Parliament. Bureaucratic procedures are required, and greater political visibility follows. If an enterprise is self-financing, the converse is true. In the second instance, we must distinguish among self-financing corporations in terms of their likely autonomy from governmental directives or bureaucratic controls. At one extreme, equity financing through public share issues greatly distances the corporation from government, both because of the logic of investment financing observed in the CDC case and because of the need to respect the legal rights of other shareholders. Debt financing from commercial lenders rather than from government inhibits government from introducing other than commercial criteria, a point that the cases of CN-Cast and Canadair bring out. Where the corporation is obliged to return to government for loan guarantees, however, government gets a renewed opportunity to exert control.

The likelihood that government will impose direction, whether through explicit directives or revitalized bureaucratic controls, seems to vary over the life of the corporation and to depend upon the political salience of its activity. The less "visible" the corporation, the more likely it is that management will benefit, acquiring the relative autonomy to follow business logic in decision making. Visibility may be generative, coincidental, or derivative. At their origin, that is, some state enterprises were set up for the precise purpose of giving political visibility to a top government priority, for example, the CDC. Such generative visibility tends, however, to erode over time as priorities shift, the company's activities become routine, and managers who were not party to the original political decisions take over. Conversely, for established state enterprises, changing circumstances and new policy initiatives may coincidentally bring them into the center of the political arena. Political salience may also be strictly derivative, as when the company's activities cause public scandal and draw unpremeditated government attention. Here Canadair is a classic example.

Finally, we observe that the nature of the state enterprise's commercial activities has important implications for the enterprise's relative autonomy from government controls. Diversification of corporate activities, particularly where they are carried out by indirectly held subsidiaries or affiliates, reduces political visibility. Similarly, the more the corporation relies on international markets, capital, and technology, the more difficult it becomes for the national government either to know about or to control operations that may take place beyond its direct jurisdiction. The tax-evasion tactics of CDC's subsidiary Polysar and of CN's affiliate Cast are illustrative.

If the ability of governments to use the commercial corporation as a policy instrument tends to diminish over time, it is certainly not because of any initial, inherent opposition between corporate and government purposes. Rather, it is because managers seek to enhance their relative autonomy and because outcomes derived from purely commercial considerations will not always be synonymous with the intentions of public policy makers. Yet in principle the relative autonomy of state enterprise managers should not create serious political dilemmas for governments that frame corporate activities within an explicit industrial or sectoral policy. Although rare, exceptional moments do exist when a government sets up and then directs a state enterprise to serve announced policy imperatives. In the next chapter we continue our investigation of the commercial corporation as a policy instrument by looking at just such state enterprises created to serve explicit policy objectives.

CHAPTER FIVE

The State in Business:
Beyond Profits

Can governments use commercial corporations to intervene in competitive sectors and yet orient corporate activities to meet goals that are not strictly commercial because socioeconomic benefits have been given explicit priority? In Canada many provincial governments have established commercial enterprises to promote regional economic development and thereby mitigate the problems of uneven economic development discussed in Chapter 2. Some governments have sought to exercise continued direction over these enterprises, which often are highly politically visible (many were created after contentious negotiations with multinational corporations whose behavior was seen to be at variance with provincial economic policy priorities).

To pursue our investigation of whether state ownership can be equated with state power, or the ability to control outcomes, we examine the experience of two provincial governments, Saskatchewan and Quebec, where public enterprises have been central to development policy. In each province in the 1970s the government took over ownership of profitable resource corporations (potash and asbestos). When asked to compete and produce for profit, we find, even those public enterprises directed by cabinet, such as the Potash Corporation of Saskatchewan, became subject to efficiency criteria and the standard commercial practices required to survive in transnational industries. Adaptation to the ground rules of corporate capitalism, in short, took precedence over industrial policy goals.

In seeking to explain the expanded economic role of provincial governments since the war, many observers focus on tensions within Canadian federalism to elaborate the theme of "province building." This concept is a miniature replica of the notion of nation building from the comparative politics literature of the 1950s. It refers to a state-led mobilization of resources to integrate society and economy designed to forge a sense of national (regional) identity.[1] For adherents of the province-building thesis, differences in political ideology among parties in power are less important to understanding the proliferation of government-owned enterprises than are the shared realities of economic necessity, nationalism, and regional class alliances which provincial state ventures can bolster.[2]

The themes of provincial economic nationalism and support for an incipient regional bourgeoisie appear frequently in expositions of the growth of the public sector in Quebec. In an analysis of the takeover of private hydroelectric companies in 1963 to form Hydro-Québec, Albert Breton argued that this public policy initiative was essentially an investment in nationalism, a policy tool used primarily "by the new middle class to accede to wealth and power."[3] Breton, an economist, sees the benefits from nationalization flowing predominantly to members of the then small but assertive middle class in the form of increased job opportunities—at the expense of lower-income Quebecers. Pierre Fournier has consistently maintained that the purpose of the considerable Quebec government intervention in the provincial economy was to promote the emergence and consolidation of a francophone bourgeoisie, as against the prevailing anglophone Canadian economic elite.[4] Though positively predisposed to the idea of Quebec nationalism, Fournier asks whether the substantial government enterprise sector has done anything for the Quebec population as a whole—anything, that is, beyond underwriting the establishment of a bourgeoisie that looked to government for assistance but, perhaps ironically, was as conservative on many important public policy issues, including independence, as its anglophone counterpart. Jorge Niosi, as noted in Chapter 2, identifies pressures from regional class alliances as one of three reasons for the growth of commercial Crown corporations across Canada. Looking specifically at Quebec, Niosi, like Fournier, believes that the Lesage government's decisions to establish a network of government enterprises after 1960 were part of a deliberate political project to consolidate an emerging francophone bourgeoisie.[5]

Literature on the changing role of the provincial government in western Canada is remarkably similar to that on Quebec. The focuses on province building to increase local economic control at the expense of external economic dominance—in this instance geographical (i.e., central Canadian) rather than linguistic—and on the burgeoning of a regional bourgeoisie that looked to the province for support are also dominant in John Richards and Larry Pratt's *Prairie Capitalism*.[6] They argue that a combination of frustration with federal resource policies, unhappiness with resource-based economies under considerable outside control, and, in Saskatchewan, social democratic ideology underlay the establishment of public enterprises by provincial governments. Looking at all four western provinces S. D. Berkowitz hypothesizes that "state elites operating under similar constraints would be likely, irrespective of ideology, to adopt institutionally similar solutions when faced with similar problems." The "problems" concerned are the developmental givens that the West has faced historically—isolation from major markets, high transportation and communication costs, dependence on staples commodities, and outflows of capital from the region. All of these factors have contributed to a sense of the West as a hinterland within Canada. The "solutions" are the twenty-one state enterprises created in Manitoba, Saskatchewan, Alberta, and British Columbia after 1970.[7]

Our explanation for the expanded role of provincial governments as producers and investors converges with the province-building thesis to the extent that we emphasize Canada's decentralized federal system as one of the limiting conditions of development—regional disparities incite competition between governments, and public ownership has become one of several accepted means of promoting regional interests. All provincial governments have seen the need for province building and been willing to use the Crown corporation as a vehicle to facilitate economic development. But some governments have more consciously regarded their enterprises as instruments to attain specific economic and social policy aims. Governments professing social democratic philosophies, such as the New Democratic party (NDP) in Saskatchewan, or explicit nationalism, such as the Parti québécois (PQ) in Quebec, have an announced intent beyond "growth," which is to harness government enterprises to advance broader objectives in social policy. Each sector has its special characteristics, and we look at two resource sectors where the role of provincial governments has become important in production. Both the potash and the asbestos sectors make it clear that although governments can intervene to establish commercial companies, their ability to move beyond merely running a business to meet broader developmental goals is very problematic.

Background to Intervention

The resource industries in Canada became especially attractive potential targets for state intervention in the 1970s. Provincial government decisions to participate directly in such important resource sectors as oil, gas, potash, asbestos, and uranium through ownership of competitive producing companies must be seen within the Canadian context outlined in Chapter 2—trade dependence in which exports of unprocessed resources are significant; high levels of foreign ownership of Canadian industry, notably in extractive industries; and uneven regional development that, within a competitive federal system, provoked governments to vie against one another on resource-related questions. The stakes were raised by the worldwide reassessment of the value of all natural resources which followed the OAPEC oil embargo of 1973.

The importance to the Canadian economy of trade in natural resources is indisputable. Canada is a major producer and exporter of many commodities. Since 1980 resource exports have annually been between 16 and 20 percent of total Canadian exports. In 1985 Canada was the world's second-largest producer of potash and of asbestos.[8] Approximately 95 percent of Saskatchewan potash is exported, with close to 60 percent of exports going to the United States and the remainder to offshore purchasers.[9] Exports of asbestos accounted for approximately 90 percent of production at the time of provincial takeover, mostly to the United States, the European Community, and Japan. Just as significant are the long-term Canadian reserves of both resources. Saskatchewan possesses reserves of potash estimated at 40 percent of world supply, while close to 35 percent of the world's asbestos reserves are in Quebec. This distribution of reserves gave both provinces critical strategic advantages in debates with the mining multinationals. The known Canadian reserves of both commodities, as well as the proximity of the prime market in the United States, meant that the companies could not readily find comparable production sites elsewhere.

Foreign investment in Canadian resource industries began in the nineteenth century and, as Chapter 2 noted, accelerated dramatically after World War II in response to U.S. concerns about secure supplies of strategic raw materials. By the late 1950s foreign-owned multinational corporations were prominent in virtually every extractive industry. Official figures on foreign ownership reveal that in 1970, 70 percent of the Canadian mining industry and 76 percent of the petroleum and natural gas industry were under foreign control; U.S. control accounted for 59 percent and 61 percent respectively.[10] The situations in potash and asbestos were quite typical. Although the social democratic government in power in Saskatchewan in the 1940s when potash was discovered wanted to develop the resource under public ownership, it possessed neither the technological nor the financial capacity to do so. Efforts to persuade the British and/or the Canadian governments to support provincial investment failed. Discouraged by the lack of cooperation from Ottawa and equally dismayed by the barriers to entry, the government invited private companies to develop potash, seeking to assure for itself only a share of the economic rents to be generated.[11] Of nine companies mining potash in Saskatchewan in 1975, when the government decided to intervene by taking over four existing mines, just two were wholly owned by Canadian-based multinational corporations. U.S.-owned or controlled mines produced approximately two-thirds of provincial output.[12]

U.S. companies had also been instrumental in developing the asbestos industry and, through mergers and takeovers, had come to dominate the sector. In the mid-1970s multinationals based in the United States controlled 66 percent of overall asbestos output outright and another 19 percent through majority interests and management agreements.[13] These large, vertically integrated producers shipped mined product out of Canada for processing. For example, the Johns-Manville mine, the largest asbestos mine in Canada, had only one manufacturing plant in Quebec but forty-six in the United States. The one foreign-owned producer whose operations were not vertically integrated was the Asbestos Corporation, which was 45 percent controlled by General Dynamics, and this company became the object of a takeover bid by the Quebec government. Asbestos Corporation, the province's second-largest producer, sold its output principally to a West German company for processing.

In the 1970s Canadian governments, like others around the world, began to reexamine the economic worth of their resources, the rates at which they were being exploited, and levels of long-term reserves. As a result, a more conservative perspective on resources came to prevail. This new attitude to natural resources and the higher prices that many commodities began to command in world markets translated into a determination to ensure that the public treasury received a larger return from extractive activity and a concern to exercise greater influence over the pace and pattern of resource development. Provincial governments began to talk of an "appropriate level of economic rent" accruing to the people of their province who, under the Canadian constitution, were the owners of the resources being extracted, and also of suitable regimes to manage resource development.[14] Some provinces evinced frustration over the behavior of multinational corporations that were reluctant to reinvest earnings in the provinces in which they were operating, refused to increase the processing of extracted resources within Canada, and would not divulge financial information about their operations. These provincial sentiments were quite quickly reflected in new policy initiatives that included elevated royalty rates, new taxation schemes, and in some provinces the creation of government-owned resource enterprises functioning in conjunction with or, in the cases to be examined here, in competition with private capital.[15]

In a federal polity characterized by strong differences of views between governments on economic policy questions, the federal government could not and did not remain uninvolved in issues of resource development. Intergovernmental rivalry on resources questions sharpened with the build-up of resource-based provincial economies, Prime Minister Trudeau's preference for a more centralized federation, and, after several decades of Keynesianism, an accumulation of social expenditures and federal indebtedness which reached critical proportions by the mid-1970s. Although provincial governments controlled access to resources within their borders, the national government also had important policy instruments, primarily taxation but also trade and commerce, which it could and did employ to affect the pace and character of resource development. On a number of occasions during the 1970s the federal government took policy posititions that heightened the intergovernmental conflict over resources. In 1974, for example, it altered the Income Tax Act to prohibit resource companies from deducting provincial royalties from revenues before calculating profits for federal tax purposes. It also participated with private capital in court challenges to the constitutionality of Saskatchewan legislation regulating the potash industry.[16]

Although Saskatchewan and Quebec are not the only provinces to have made deliberate use of their public sectors to confront the exigencies of uneven development, the decisions to nationalize significant portions of the potash and asbestos industries were taken by governing parties ideologically prepared to use public enterprises to achieve economic and social goals. Saskatchewan's New Democratic party premier expressed his government's attitude toward public enterprise in 1972: "let me make quite clear that this Government will encourage the continued operation and expansion of Crown corporations. We will develop our resources for the benefit of Saskatchewan people. When appropriate this will be done through corporations."[17] A Parti québécois statement on natural resources enunciated the principle that the owners of resources, namely the people of Quebec, should derive maximum benefits from them. Among the strategies suggested were increases in local processing of resources, the abolition of fiscal privileges to mining companies, and the development of mines by cooperatives and public agencies. "Therefore a Parti québécois government pledges to . . . ensure a majority control that is *québécois,* where Quebec enjoys a solid position in terms of international competition (asbestos for example)."[18]

Both Saskatchewan and Quebec had earlier been governed by parties that had consciously employed government enterprises as part of their development strategies. In Saskatchewan, CCF and later NDP administrations espoused social democracy and during previous tenures in office had created a variety of state-owned ventures.[19] All state corporations in Saskatchewan were (and remain) part of a centralized administrative structure designed to coordinate planning and ensure that state enterprises serve the policy purposes of the provincial government.[20] Since 1960 all governments in Quebec, Liberal, Union nationale, and Parti québécois, had perceived and consciously used governmental authority to strengthen local control over the provincial economy, as an agent of *rattrapage*, or overcoming its historical lag.[21] This process of conscious political promotion of economic nationalism, known as the "Quiet Revolution," both reflected and encouraged the emergence of two important social forces in Quebec: a new middle class of urban professionals looking for opportunities within the bureaucracy, and a burgeoning francophone capitalist class at first based primarily in real estate, finance, and the retail trades, which saw its possibilities for expansion into industry limited because of high levels of non-Quebec ownership. Quebec's emergent nationalism found institutional expression through the rapid development of the government sector. The first major undertaking was the 1963 nationalization of all remaining private hydroelectric producers in the province under the auspices of the previously small, government-owned Hydro-Québec. Thereafter government created Crown corporations in such strategic sectors of the economy as pulp and paper, mining, steel, petrochemicals, oil and gas exploration, agriculture, and finance. By the end of the 1970s provincial government investment accounted for close to 50 percent of all new investment in Quebec.[22]

In taking control over potash and asbestos capacity, Saskatchewan and Quebec established Crown corporations of considerable size: the Potash Corporation of Saskatchewan ranked 259th in the 1985 *Financial Post* listing of Canada's 500 largest firms, and the Société nationale de l'amiante (SNA) placed 388th.[23] But their size notwithstanding, it was evident almost immediately that a competitive international environment would limit their effectiveness as tools to reshape even segments of provincial economies. The characteristics of these international resource industries—their oligopolistic nature, uncertain markets, fluctuating demand, and the cost of mine development—which together with high levels of foreign ownership in both sectors were at the root cause of much of the provincial governments' decisions to intervene directly in production, combined to circumscribe the effectiveness of the new public enterprises as instruments of public policy.

THE POTASH CORPORATION OF SASKATCHEWAN

The November 1975 announcement by the government of Saskatchewan that it intended to intervene directly in the potash industry by acquiring the assets of producing mines dramatically altered the position of the nascent Potash Corporation of Saskatchewan. PCS, which had been created some eight months prior to the takeover announcement, was suddenly transformed from a small Crown corporation, charged with evaluating ways in which the provincial government might participate more actively in the potash sector, into a highly visible public enterprise, the world's second-largest potash producer.

The government did not set out to take over a segment of the potash industry; rather, by 1975 it saw itself with no alternative. A long and acrimonious battle with the industry had included industry challenges to provincial legislation, nonpayment of resource tax fees, refusal to submit financial statements, and postponed expansions of mine capacity despite rising demand for potash.[24] Underlying the conflict on the government side was growing recognition of the potential significance of potash to the provincial economy. The government was now determined both to influence the pace of resource development and to increase its share of the economic rents. Commenting on the takeover decision shortly after it was announced, Saskatchewan's premier Allan Blakeney made it very clear that his government's stance was a pragmatic one: "The reasons for the takeover are not any devotion to public enterprise. We simply must have control of production and the rate of return to the public treasury."[25]

Once the government had decided upon takeover, the immediate challenge was successful entry: Would state managers be able to run mines for profit in competition with established corporations in an oligopolistic world market? Economist Raymond Mikesell has argued that nationalized enterprises in the resource sector cannot successfully compete because they are at a distinct disadvantage compared to established multinationals with "downstream affiliates" and "worldwide marketing organizations."[26] The characteristics of the potash industry, however, make government ownership feasible—in contrast, as we shall see, to other resource industries, asbestos among them. Certainly the vulnerability of a nationalized company that takes control over only the resource extraction stage of the operations of multinational corporations is enormous in industries characterized by a high degree of vertical integration, especially where alternative sources of supply, or other inputs may replace those from the nationalized mines. If, in addition, proprietary technology prevents the government enterprise from keeping up with new techniques unless willing to pay the costs of licensing or engineering consultancy contracts, competition becomes very difficult.

None of these strictures applied in the potash industry. The processing of potash is relatively simple, and the techniques of both extraction and processing have not been subject to patents for some years.[27] Some potash is used in chemical production, but the primary end-use is fertilizer, and there is no known substitute for potash as one of the major components of fertilizer. Alternative sources of supply for companies operating in Saskatchewan were not readily available. Indeed, the corporate motive for investing in Canada was the depletion of U.S. reserves and the higher quality of Saskatchewan deposits; other major deposits were located in the communist world.[28] In sum, there were few alternative sources of supply, no substitution possibilities, stable technology, and insignificant vertical integration. A government corporation would therefore be in an excellent position to take its place among the oligopolists in international markets as long as it had the financial wherewithal and qualified personnel—which PCS did.

The NDP government did not focus immediately on policy innovations. Rather, its strategy was for PCS to become an established producer and to demonstrate that the government enterprise could run its mines in a businesslike manner. The potash takeover had resulted from revenue disputes, and so continued profitability under state management was essential to avoid political fiasco. One key decision ensuring a smooth transition to Crown ownership was the retention of experienced industry personnel. The government enterprise sought to keep all mine supervisory staff and plant managers as part of the acquisition package it negotiated with each of the multinationals. The conservative approach to management which PCS took was paralleled by its approach to industrial relations. Faced with an anomaly in which a social democratic government came to own a nonunionized mine, PCS made no effort to reconsider the results of a miners' referendum that had opted for a nonunion workers' association, nor did it deviate from wage scales prevailing in the private sector. In the transitional phase concern for the company's survival among the oligopolists clearly took precedence over experimentation with industrial democracy.[29]

Favorable market conditions and a growing demand for potash in the years immediately following the takeover also eased PCS's entry into the industry. The potash market in the mid- and late 1970s was characterized by rapidly increasing demand and escalating prices. For its first few years PCS did not have to face the oversupply and falling prices that had plagued the industry toward the end of the 1960s and would begin again in 1982.

By 1980 PCS had proved itself an aggressive operator in direct competition with five large corporations, all of them Canadian- and American-controlled multinationals, selling to the same North American and offshore customers. Although some multinationals refused to invest further in Saskatchewan and began to explore and develop potash deposits in New Brunswick and Manitoba, the larger private-sector producers gradually adjusted to a state-owned competitor, and some started investing to expand their output capacity.[30] PCS embarked on an ambitious marketing strategy to increase its share of North American sales and experimented with innovations in transportation to improve product delivery and reduce costs. It also joined Canpotex, the offshore marketing agency of the potash industry. From the outset, moreover, PCS moved to ensure that it had sufficient product available to augment its market share. The first phase of a several-billion-dollar expansion program was completed at three mines, increasing PCS's production capacity by one million tons annually and permitting a 23 percent increase in actual production. Completion of expansion projects in 1986 confirmed PCS's position as the largest potash producer in Canada and as a major player in the Western world.

The success of PCS in its first years of operation raised questions about its relationship to government and its tractability as an instrument of broader economic strategy. Like all NDP government ventures in Saskatchewan, PCS fitted into a coherent organizational structure that had been developed over more than thirty years. The key organization was the Crown Investments Corporation (CIC), itself a government corporation that acted as a financial holding company for seventeen commercial public enterprises and had responsibility for overseeing capital requirements for all twenty-two provincial state ventures. The CIC resembled the head office of a global corporation with its strategic responsibilities for long-term planning investments. CIC was accountable to its "shareholders"—the people—through the Committee on Crown Corporations of the legislature, to which it submitted annual reports on the operations of each statutory government enterprise. This holding company format set up a dialectic between autonomy and accountability for Crown corporations. It was intended to avoid politicians managing companies and managers playing politics. Basically, however, as a CIC report on Crown corporations made clear, government enterprises were seen as instruments of government policy:

> To the extent that Crown corporations resemble private corporations, they are given a large measure of independence. . . . The management is given wide scope to operate the existing plant and to initiate expansion proposals. However, in Saskatchewan the Crown corporations *are* a part of the government as well and the government accepts responsibility for broad policy matters and for finalizing the capital expansion program.[31]

Management had virtually complete decision-making latitude in operations (mining and marketing), but government did not intend it to have full autonomy.

Not only did public corporations fit into an established public sector through CIC, but the presence of cabinet members on the Board of Directors confirmed the NDP government's intention that public enterprises should serve broad public purposes. What objectives were served by the transfer of ownership in the potash industry from private to public hands? Because Canadian prairie soil does not require the main product of potash mining, fertilizer, in large quantities, the government expected the new enterprise to contribute in a more general way to economic development within the province. As Saskatchewan minister of mineral resources Jack Messer said, "we want to be certain there will be sufficient returns through the development of that resource going to the people of Saskatchewan. We also want to provide spinoffs from the development of that resource in the Province of Saskatchewan benefitting Saskatchewan people."[32] It was important, therefore, that PCS earn a surplus that government could use to provide social welfare benefits to the people of the province and that corporate strategy be oriented to provide spinoffs to the local economy.

The disposition of PCS revenue under the NDP was decided in four places: CIC, the Department of Finance, the legislature, and the cabinet. In the years immediately following the takeover, dividend payments were deferred; profits were plowed back into the corporation to finance mine refurbishing and expansion. From 1980 through 1982 PCS paid an annual dividend of $50 million to the CIC, which the holding company could use according to its own priorities, for example underwriting the development of other Crown corporations. PCS also contributed resource royalty payments, just as other potash producers did. Prior to the electoral defeat of the NDP government in 1982 there was considerable debate between PCS and the central agencies of government over the corporation's dividends and whether these should be paid so as to make them appear more dramatically a payment to the populace for Saskatchewan's resources. It can be argued that underwriting provincial economic development provides a general benefit to the people of the province. Decisions made under the NDP government with respect to the PCS surplus suggest, however, that the advantage to the citizenry in terms of social welfare expenditures was never directly demonstrated.

The NDP government argued that greater economic benefits for Saskatchewan flowed automatically from establishing the head office of a potash company in the province for the first time. The corporation produced a single product in a single province, thereby ensuring that capital would be reinvested in Saskatchewan and that jobs would be retained and created. Because PCS was part of an established public sector, one guided by social democratic principles, the cost-benefit calculations of enterprise managers included social considerations. The time frame for a return on investment could be longer than that of private managers, because enterprise managers were looking for the stable development of the industry rather than immediate profit maximization. Social costs they could regard as necessary capital costs because of government's sensitivity to its constituents, for example, farmers complaining of soil leaching due to the build-up of salt wastes that are the residue of potash refining. The five-year period between acquisition of PCS and defeat of the NDP government provides us with an opportunity to test the claim that a public enterprise serves provincial industrial development better than private companies, with their single-minded profit motive and international sphere of operations.

Government and PCS officials had little interest in pollution problems or local sourcing for machinery during the 1970s. Survival among the oligopolists absorbed all of their attention. By 1980, however, a change was evident. Both PCS budgetary priorities and public relations efforts focused on the future, with particular emphasis on research and development. The PCS board committed 1 percent of sales to R&D—management insisted it wanted an even larger figure—with special emphasis on innovations that could reduce the problem of salt storage or lead to new techniques of extraction that might avoid the creation of salt piles. To further the corporation's goal of diversifying product lines, the minister in charge of PCS announced the construction of a potassium sulphate pilot project at one PCS mine site.[33] The company also explored more ambitious possibilities for horizontal integration with an Alberta-based company interested in the joint creation of a plant to manufacture nitrogen-based fertilizer.[34] PCS executives placed heavy emphasis on local sourcing—the corporation centralized purchasing for its mines and aggressively sought to increase Saskatchewan content in various phases of its operations.[35] PCS spokesmen argued that the corporation established a standard in this respect which the multinational producers, anxious to be good corporate citizens, were endeavoring to emulate. The public enterprise did therefore appear to be playing a new role in industrial development, one that corresponded to the NDP government's broader development strategy.

To achieve all of the broader industrial development objectives it sought in Saskatchewan, however, the NDP required favorable market conditions. A government-owned enterprise, when compared with a foot-loose private multinational, looks particularly vulnerable, especially when it lacks diversified product lines and is exploiting a resource that does not generate forward linkages. In fact, just as PCS was completing its expansion program in 1981, world demand for potash fell precipitously. Prices fell from $142 to $100 per tonne in the 1981–82 fertilizer year, reflecting conditions well beyond corporate control: a worldwide recession and consequent reductions in both farm incomes and

Third World government budgets, as well as a new U.S. "payment in kind" program to reduce crop acreage. In explaining the corporation's poor performance, the PCS president spoke of depressed world commodity prices and the intense competition that the company faced from both offshore and U.S. producers in its major market, the United States. In 1982 potash production was 27 percent below what it had been the previous year; sales fell off 20 percent to the United States and 14 percent in the offshore market.[36] As a result of these unfavorable conditions, PCS net income dropped from $147.7 *million* in 1981 to $607 *thousand* in 1982. Intent on holding employment steady, management announced a "no lay-offs" policy in December 1981, thereby adhering to overall government policy to protect public-sector employees.[37]

The resounding defeat of the NDP in the spring 1982 provincial election precludes analysis of how this social democratic party might have reacted to continuing adverse market conditions. The Conservative government's strategy, although a far cry from its election promises to dismantle government-owned enterprises, signaled an abrupt turnabout in the position and direction of all Saskatchewan Crown corporations, PCS included. The principal changes involved revision of the administrative framework for directing government ventures and a new emphasis on profitability. With respect specifically to the Potash Corporation, immediately after the election the Conservative government directed it to halt production for four months because of decline in demand. PCS did what its private-sector counterparts had already done: lay off workers.[38] All but one of the mine expansion plans were canceled.

Despite radical differences with the NDP regarding formal doctrine, however, the Conservative party accepted the fundamental need for government intervention—albeit of a more limited nature—to insure that Saskatchewan made the transition away from an agriculture-based economy vulnerable to market forces outside the province. The corporation continued to invest in research and development, though with years of declining profit it could no longer adhere to the established guidelines of 1.5 percent of sales. Through continued expansion of its mines PCS provided both construction jobs for Saskatchewan workers and sales for material suppliers. Its 1983 annual report estimated that local sourcing for mine construction had reached approximately 70 percent of project total and that, overall, close to 80 percent of goods and services required to operate PCS mines were purchased locally. In short, the spinoffs for the local economy from potash production did increase despite adverse market conditions.[39] The corporation also announced that its long-planned demonstration plant for sulphate of potash, designed to produce a fertilizer compound not currently made in Canada, would commence operations in the spring of 1985 and that plans were under way to construct a commercial-scale plant with considerable annual capacity.[40]

In keeping with the theme of province building, then, we find the Conservative government intent on pursuing industrial spinoffs, but its ability to do so inhibited by the corporation's changing fortunes in the marketplace. The dubious financial picture for PCS and the specter of future uncertainty in the industry remind us of the heavy capital commitments and high risks involved in operating in volatile commodity markets. Although PCS enjoyed an overall profit on operations in 1984, its net income of $25.4 million represented an after-tax return on invested equity of only 4 percent. Moreover, the corporation's balance sheet showed that its debt : equity ratio was seriously out of line with its ability to generate cash, primarily as a result of weakening potash prices and excess capacity in the industry.[41] Reduced demand forced mine closures and long layoffs in 1985, and the corporation reported a record loss of $68.7 million. By 1986 prices for potash were at their lowest level since 1969, with little prospect of immediate improvement.[42] Moreover, the government enterprise faces considerable pressure from its competitors, both domestic and foreign. Within Saskatchewan, private producers have augmented capacity, and new mines are coming on stream in other provinces.[43] Foreign producers, including East Germany, the Soviet Union, Israel, and Jordan, have expanded production and now are entering markets in direct competition with PCS. It is clear, in short, that the profitability of PCS, and thus the provincial government's latitude to move beyond running a business to implement economic goals, will be dictated in large measure by international market factors—factors beyond the control of government officials and public enterprise managers.

Société nationale de l'amiante/ Asbestos Corporation of Quebec

The PQ government formally enunciated its asbestos policy on October 21, 1977. Major objectives included access to information on the industry to enable the government to evaluate its potential, improvement of working conditions in an industry long known for its poor health and safety standards, greater access to managerial positions for francophone Quebecers, and, most important, a dramatic increase in the local processing of asbestos fibers to create jobs. Although Quebec asbestos mines produced close to 30 percent of world asbestos output in the mid-1970s, only 3 percent of Quebec output was processed in the province before the state intervened directly in the industry; the remaining 97 percent was exported, primarily to the United States. Through its creation of a Crown corporation the Quebec government hoped to increase dramatically the quantity of asbestos processed within the province, to as much as 20 percent of mined product. Estimates of potential job creation varied from an anticipated rise in local processing to 10 to 12 percent within ten years, resulting in "thousands" of jobs, to an extremely optimistic 20 percent figure for local upgrading, which would have created some twenty thousand new jobs.[44] We argue that the Quebec government's objectives were both unrealistic and severely circumscribed by factors largely beyond its control. Although some expansion of processing was feasible, government projections about numbers of potential jobs ignored industry evaluations that anticipated far smaller increases in employment. Moreover, the Quebec government established its presence in the sector just as asbestos was going into a very serious slump, one brought on by weakening international demand and growing concern about the health hazards of asbestos use.

A recommendation that government intervene directly in the asbestos sector predated the 1976 election of the Parti québécois government under Premier René Lévesque and had its origins in a mining policy study that the Quebec Ministry of Natural Resources initiated in the early seventies. This review of the asbestos industry, the Alexandre Report, examined options to improve returns to the province from the industry and concluded with a recommendation that the government purchase an existing producer. The company considered the most appropriate candidate for state takeover was later targeted by the Parti québécois: Asbestos Corporation Ltd.[45] The Liberal government, in power in Quebec at the time, shelved the Alexandre Report.

Although resource questions were not prominent in the 1976 election campaign that brought the Parti québécois to power, in previous years the party had made very clear its position on resources: that from all resources maximum benefits should flow to the people of the province, and that the PQ would move to ensure majority Quebec ownership in those resource sectors where the province enjoyed a competitive position. Shortly after his party's victory Premier Lévesque discussed the resource issue at the Economic Club of New York. Business panic at the unexpected election of a separatist government was causing sudden outflows of capital from Quebec, and so the premier reassured his audience that the PQ's approach was pragmatic rather than ideological. He did not intend to launch any broad program of nationalization. In fact, only one industry was targeted for possible nationalization—asbestos.[46]

The symbolic importance of asbestos in Quebec politics reinforced whatever economic interest the new Parti québécois government had in the commodity. A highly emotional strike in the Quebec industry in

1949 gave the sector an unparalleled prominence in the minds of Quebecers. The confrontation at the mine site, which pitted mine-workers against companies that had the support of the provincial police, exemplified for many the close ties that existed between foreign-owned corporations and the Quebec government of the day, to the detriment of the working people of the province.[47]

The potash and asbestos industries shared certain structural similarities prior to government participation, as we have noted, the most important of which was the primacy of foreign-owned multinationals. But although foreign-owned firms were significant in both industries, vertical integration in the asbestos sector and the differences in requisite technical knowledge made asbestos much less feasible than potash as a candidate for state ownership. In other words, the differences in processing required by the two resources—relatively simple for potash, with a limited number of end-uses, in contrast to complex upgrading and a wide variety of end-uses for asbestos—both motivated and constrained the two provinces in their takeover strategies. With few end-uses for potash and relatively simple technology, the Potash Corporation could compete with private producers without significant difficulties, but then considerable investment in research and development became necessary to increase the spinoffs from potash extraction for the provincial economy. Asbestos, on the other hand, has extensive end-uses in the construction industry (asbestos cement pipe, sheet flooring, insulation and roofing products), in brake linings, in textiles, and in some paper products. This diversity of uses and the opportunities it provided for additional upgrading in Quebec, with a consequent increase in jobs, helped motivate the Quebec government to intervene directly in the industry. On the other hand, the vertically integrated nature of multinational corporations in the industry and their monopoly over processing technology, the lack of local research and development activity for new products, foreign tariffs on imported asbestos products, and transportation costs made barriers to entry formidable. As a result, public participation in the asbestos industry would quickly become a complex and costly undertaking.

The cornerstone of the Quebec government's policy was its intention to purchase a controlling interest in the Asbestos Corporation through a newly established government enterprise, the Société nationale de l'amiante.[48] If the parent company General Dynamics was not prepared to sell its subsidiary, then expropriation was a possibility.[49] Asbestos Corporation was the government's choice to enter the industry because it was a profitable company, possessed long-term reserves of product, and was not part of an integrated mining operation.[50] A takeover would enable Quebec "to talk on an equal-to-equal basis with giant companies like Johns-Manville."[51] Purchasing the company would also give the government access to information on the industry and a processing, marketing, and sales organization. Purchase of an existing producer was considerably cheaper and easier than establishing a new mine. In addition, the government intended to negotiate agreements with remaining private-sector producers to improve working conditions and to create a research unit for the industry.

The turnover announcement initiated a battle of words between the Quebec government and General Dynamics, a battle that was settled some two-and-a-half years later when the Supreme Court of Canada rejected an application by Asbestos Corporation for an injunction blocking expropriation of the company and refused to hear the company's appeal of a lower court decision upholding the province's power to expropriate.[52] At issue were the refusal of General Dynamics to sell its subsidiary, the multinational's test of provincial authority to expropriate embodied in Bill 121, and the price to be paid for the 54.6 percent share of the Asbestos Corporation owned by General Dynamics. The sparring parties obtained widely differing valuations of share worth: a market firm that the government used to determine a price suggested a value of $41 to $44 per share, whereas General Dynamics obtained an evaluation that recommended $100 per share.

While the dispute with General Dynamics was unfolding, the government moved quickly to implement its asbestos policy. Under the terms of Bill 70, passed by the Quebec legislature in May 1978, the Crown-owned asbestos company SNA is empowered to explore "for the development and exploitation of asbestos deposits, including the marketing of production as well as any activity of an industrial, manufacturing or commercial nature directly or indirectly relating to the processing of asbestos fibre."[53] The initial capitalization of SNA was $250 million. In May 1980 SNA acquired the capital stock of Bell Asbestos, the smallest producer in the province. This purchase included mining facilities and two small manufacturing plants, one in Quebec and one in British Columbia.[54]

The government enterprise had established or purchased ten asbestos-processing ventures by 1985.[55] These included a plant to manufacture asbestos felt flooring, a joint venture between SNA and a Montreal company to manufacture brake linings, and a $14 million plant in Thetford Mines which used asbestos residues to produce a magnesium compound.[56] Moreover, the government established its planned research center on asbestos, the Institut de recherche et de développement sur l'amiante, in June 1979 to improve and develop technology used in asbestos production and search for new uses and products; and an Asbestos Bureau that would, among other activities, oversee and direct negotiations with private producers in Quebec with respect to their long-term development plans. The scale of research activity, however, depended on industry profitability—the government committed itself to provide a million dollars annually over five years, but corporate contributions, fixed at 1.5 percent of annual sales, were variable.[57]

The key to Quebec's asbestos strategy remained the acquisition of the Asbestos Corporation, however. Negotiations on price resumed in April 1981 following the Supreme Court's pronouncement and the reelection of the PQ government. An agreement between the protagonists was reached in November 1981, and SNA assumed control of General Dynamics's 54.6 percent share of the Asbestos Corporation in February 1982.[58] The purchase gave SNA control of asbestos mines in Thetford Mines and Ungava, several mills, and a finishing plant in Nordenham, West Germany. So by early 1982 Quebec had successfully entered the asbestos industry and, through its state enterprise, had become a major producer. To what extent has government been able to use this corporate vehicle to achieve the goals that motivated its entry into a competitive international industry?

The Quebec government has put in place over the past decade a well-structured regime for controlling its numerous industrial and commercial ventures and for ensuring that they operate in conformity with provincial policy. Since 1980 each corporation has been expected to submit a corporate plan outlining projected activities and capital requirements, a plan that is then analyzed both by the responsible department and by the Department of Finance. Cabinet approval is necessary for any undertaking that requires a capital contribution by the government. Legislation governing most Crown enterprises authorizes the government and the responsible minister to issue policy directives to state corporations. Directives are issued sparingly, however; rather, the norm is communication among senior managers of state corporations, the directly responsible minister, and the minister of finance.[59]

The difficulties that the Quebec government encountered in attaining its goals for SNA did not emanate from weaknesses in this control regime. Unhappily for the province, the asbestos industry entered a decline that coincidentally began with Quebec's direct intervention. Demand slumped with the recession of the early 1980s and with growing concern about the health hazards of the product. Quebec now faces competition from new mines opened in Mexico and Greece, and health considerations have led to restrictions on, if not the complete banning of, the use of asbestos in manufacturing. Concern over negative health ramifications of contact with asbestos has particularly affected demand in Europe and the United States.[60] As a result, inventories are high, prices sagging. The quantity and value of Quebec's asbestos exports have dropped each year since 1979, and by 1985 they were only 50 percent of what they had been when the Quebec government entered the industry.[61] Despite inflation, SNA has not been able to raise prices; in fact, it is reported to have offered "substantial discounts to retain old customers and attract new ones."[62]

The slump in demand has clearly affected employment, which has declined in the sector annually since 1979. The number of employees in 1985 was less than half of the total six years earlier. The government-owned Asbestos Corporation, like other operators, has been forced to reduce, if not suspend, mining activity and lay off workers.[63] Reduced demand has also made it difficult to create jobs on the processing side of the industry. Some additional processing jobs, generously estimated at three hundred, have been created by the SNA acting alone or in cooperation with private capital. Another hundred or hundred-fifty jobs have been created in research. But so considerable has investment in SNA been since October 1978—some $94.8 million through March 1985, which figure excludes any payment for the acquisition of Asbestos Corporation[64]—that the cost per job created has been enormous.

These unpleasant realities were compounded by the revelation that government expectations in the late seventies were dramatically at variance with the predictions of a major study on the industry. This study, jointly done by Sorès Inc. of Quebec and Arthur D. Little of New York, saw little room for expanded asbestos processing within the province.[65] Of the fourteen asbestos products manufactured around the world, only five were suitable for manufacture in Quebec. Hundreds of new jobs appeared more likely than twenty thousand.

In short, government intentions to create employment by increasing local transformation of asbestos fibers have come to naught, and the prospects for future employment are bleak. Moreover, government has been unable to use its new position in the industry to encourage the remaining multinationals to augment their level of asbestos processing before export. Rather, Quebec governments have faced growing unemployment in the sector, with negative results for communities dependent on asbestos mining. They have also seen a successful effort by the major multinational in the industry, Johns-Manville, beset by multimillion dollar asbestos claims, to divest itself of its investment in Quebec. The prospects for continued operation of its mine are at best uncertain.[66]

That the Quebec government's asbestos venture has suffered serious losses since its creation is not surprising, because of international conditions in the industry. When the PQ decided to participate directly in asbestos production most producers, including Asbestos Corporation, were making substantial profits. By the end of the 1970s, however, the financial situation of the industry had deteriorated dramatically. Asbestos Corporation, SNA's major mine, has suffered continuous losses since 1981; so has Bell Asbestos, a smaller mining operation.[67] The Société nationale de l'amiante's total accumulated debt from 1979 to March 31, 1986, was close to $248 million.[68]

Complicating SNA's financial picture is the arrangement with General Dynamics for the purchase of Asbestos Corporation, which has cost the Quebec government $170 million. For an initial expenditure of $17.2 million in 1982, SNA took control of Asbestos Corporation by purchasing special voting shares in the General Dynamics subsidiary that owned 54.6 percent of Asbestos Corporation. That investment gave SNA a 51 percent interest in the subsidiary but only a 17.5 equity interest. Under a shareholders' agreement, General Dynamics could force SNA to acquire its remaining holdings in Asbestos Corporation at any time between February 1984 and February 1987 for a purchase price of $42 per share plus interest. It exercised this option at the end of November 1986—at a time when shares of Asbestos Corporation were trading at close to 5 percent of the per share cost to the Quebec government.[69]

SNA's performance on health and safety matters, also a high priority of the Quebec government, has not been impressive. The government enterprise owns mines that are among the more problematic in an industry beset with problems regarding the quality of working conditions: the Bell Asbestos operation, an underground mine, has had a very poor safety record, and the Asbestos Corporation mines were considered the most obsolete and dirtiest in the province.[70] SNA was expected to reduce the occupational hazards associated with asbestos production and to modernize production facilities to comply with provincial safety regulations, but in fact it has done little. In an industry under stress, expenditures to improve mine sites reduce the monies available for investment in other phases of the industry, particularly in further processing. The government's attitude toward health and safety issues suggests that it gave priority to balance sheet considerations. In contrast, and as a function of the emphasis on upgrading raw asbestos, since its establishment SNA has spent some $18.3 million on research and development.[71]

Government's response to economic adversity in the asbestos sector has been to rein in—to rationalize its various extraction facilities in an attempt to concentrate production and reduce capital demands. SNA closed its mining operation at Asbestos Hill in northern Quebec in late 1983 because the costs of extracting ore at less than 100 percent capacity north of the Arctic Circle made continued production unfeasible.[72] As a result, processing fell off at the one site acquired by SNA when it entered the industry, the plant at Nordenham, West Germany, which was dependent on product from Asbestos Hill; the mill was sold in June 1984 for the book value of the asset.[73] SNA has also examined various merger possibilities, first between its two remaining mines[74] and later between its facilities and some of the remaining private asbestos producers in the Thetford Mines area of Quebec. In March 1986 the Quebec government announced the formation of a limited partnership, Socom, between the two SNA mines, Bell Asbestos and Asbestos Corp, and two private mining companies. Socom is to operate the asbestos mining and milling plants of the four companies and rationalize them. Included in the rationalization plans is the 1987 closure of one Asbestos Corporation mine. SNA companies will together hold 45 percent of the new venture, which will be headed by a company executive from the private sector,[75] thus removing SNA one step from the operational side of the industry.

The immediate future for the asbestos industry and the Quebec government enterprise are no brighter now than in the recent past. The company sees its woes as part of the general crisis in the industry—a function of the foreign exchange problems of Third World countries and the U.S. Environmental Protection Agency's announced intent to ban major asbestos products. The latter consideration, health hazards, is more salient and less reversible. Both in the United States and in Western Europe, concerns about the health hazards of asbestos are not likely to abate, and efforts to find substitutes, more costly and less durable though they may be, are continuing.

Employment in the mining segment of the industry will fluctuate if not decline with efforts to make production more cost-efficient, and the new job opportunities expected from more forward linkages will not materialize. The optimism of entry has been replaced by the somber realities of operating a public enterprise in a depressed international industry. As Quebec's former minister of finance, a powerful figure in shaping economic policy for the Parti québécois, commented in 1985, "it was a mistake for the Quebec government to get heavily involved in the mining of asbestos. The health hazards of asbestos . . . had not been recognized early enough or acutely enough."[76] The government of Quebec, Liberal since 1985, is now trying to limit what has been described as "the financial hemorrhage" caused by SNA. It has sold two manufacturing subsidiaries, leased a third, and, as already noted, consolidated its mining operations. Other SNA processing subsidiaries have been targeted for sale, and research and development facilities will be rationalized.[77]

CONCLUSION

As the experiences of Saskatchewan and Quebec illustrate, governments in Canada can and do intervene in profitable industries in the

interests of their state-led development strategies. They can also successfully run commercial enterprises in competition with private companies.
More problematic is the ability of governments to insure the continued
profitability of their resource ventures in volatile markets and thereby to
garner the revenues they need to move beyond purely commercial goals.
The performances of the Potash Corporation and the Société nationale
de l'amiante suggest that government-owned enterprises have proved to
be less malleable tools of socioeconomic development than policy makers
had anticipated. Both provincial governments had expected to use their
resource corporations to achieve specific goals in social and industrial
policy. They soon discovered that the realities of the marketplace restricted their maneuverability. They were constrained from satisfying
their objectives within established oligopolistic industries by circumstances largely beyond provincial control, such as fluctuating demand,
and these circumstances resulted in a postponement of, or in the Quebec
case almost total inability to attain, stated goals. As well, government-
appointed managers quickly came to see the world very much as their
private-sector competitors did, as governed by considerations of market
and gain. Commercial goals, those involved in running a business, took
precedence over broader socioeconomic objectives.

Part III

NEW DIRECTIONS FOR STATE CAPITALISM

CHAPTER SIX

The State as Investor

There are many ways and means by which the state involves itself in competitive and even profitable industries in the mixed economy of the 1980s. Investment activity by governments—both federal and provincial—has expanded the scope of state capitalism well beyond the wholly owned state enterprise. Our investigation, too, must move in new directions beyond the classic questions of government–public enterprise relations if we are to understand why, how, and with what impact the state becomes a shareholder yet eschews outright ownership.

The role of the state-as-investor, whereby state capital and private capital combine in commercial undertakings and thus share both the risks inherent in entrepreneurship and the returns on investment, is not entirely a modern-day novelty. Some venerable state enterprises started in the interwar period as mixed public-private companies, and some retain private shareholdings: France's railways, the SNCF, Italy's AGIP, Britain's BP, and Canada's national airline, Air Canada. Only in the changing international political economy of the late 1960s, however, did it become common practice for governments in Europe to institutionalize the use of equity as an instrument of industrial policy by creating state holding companies and industrial investment funds. By the 1980s, under conditions of recession, most governments were opting to buy into, rather than buy out, private companies confronting financial crisis.

Canadian governments hold equity, usually indirectly through established Crown corporations, in at least four hundred "mixed enterprises."[1] Although governments may exercise greater influence over corporate behavior by guaranteeing large commercial loans than by holding a 2 percent interest in a private firm through a pension fund, recourse to equity rather than to loans, grants, or tax expenditures remains special. The acquisition of equity brings the state directly into the production process in collaboration with some elements of private capital and yet in competition with others. Whether it acknowledges it or not, the state thereby assumes partial responsibility for setting the terms of employment, production, marketing, and reinvestment of capital by the firm.

In other forms of government participation in corporate activities, such as the research and development grant, conditions may be negotiated. Equity, however, automatically confers special rights. First, ownership of common shares in a firm confers the right to vote for company directors and thus indirectly to take part in strategic decision making. Depending upon the percentage of shares held and whether the remainder are widely dispersed, the shareholder may obtain the right to nominate one or more members of the board and thus achieve direct decision-making power. Often, when shares are not publicly traded and the company is closely held, the initial subscribers grant themselves the right to appoint a specified number of directors or to veto key decisions stipulated in the articles of incorporation. Second, equity participation confers the right to subscribe for further shares in the event that capital stock is increased, making it possible to protect or enhance control. Third, equity confers the right to benefit from the distribution of assets in the event of liquidation. Fourth, equity confers the right to share in profits distributed through dividend payments upon the decision of the Board of Directors.[2]

Government, however, is not simply one more investor in the marketplace. Equity can be a highly discretionary instrument of policy if state capital is directed toward specific sectors, categories of firms, or individual companies. Certainly governments in most European countries have sought to use investment to redeploy factors of production, to enhance competitiveness, or to promote potential winners among private enterprises. Our analysis of the Canadian federal government's major investments suggests that Ottawa's use of equity has tended to be reactive rather than proactive—a problem-solving device of last resort. Despite the creation of a state holding company, the Canada Development Investment Corporation, intended to permit strategic investments, recession so inflated the scale of business failure in the 1980s that it became politically impossible for the government to refuse to salvage key companies. State capital was used to bail out companies in financial crisis, and the pattern of these bailouts, we argue, corresponded to the immediate needs of the commercial banks rather than to any preconceived investment policy. Several *provincial* governments have nonetheless devised purposive investment strategies. As we shall see, Quebec and

Alberta in particular have used portfolio investments both to generate revenues and to serve the goal of regional economic development. Their experience demonstrates that governments may be able to accumulate and target capital through the marketplace; but it also suggests that there are political limits to the state-as-investor in Canada.

HOW AND WHY THE STATE INVESTS

It is not entirely obvious what appeal public-private ownership through equity participation has for government. On the one hand, the potential for effective government control over the activities of mixed enterprises, unlike those of the wholly owned state enterprise, is inhibited by the presence of private-sector investors. The reasons are both legal (minority shareholders' rights) and political (the risk that private capital will exit). On the other hand, compared to alternative means of influencing private enterprise behavior such as loans or grants, equity is a relatively inflexible instrument of industrial policy. Shares cannot always be disposed of at will, and government as a co-owner cannot entirely deny responsibility for corporate mismanagement.[3] From a review of all known cases of investment by the federal government after 1970, we have distilled seven purposes ostensibly served by state investment in the mixed enterprise. Brief examples illustrate why and how the contours of state capitalism in Canada extend beyond the wholly owned Crown corporation. We focus here on equity investment (normally made by government or a government investment agency), leaving the joint venture (normally involving an established state enterprise) for scrutiny in Chapter 7.[4]

Return on Investment

In some instances the state purchases shares or securities with no purpose beyond the first-order objective of making money. Just as there are wholly owned state enterprises in Canada which run lotteries or sell liquor in order to permit government to increase revenues without increasing taxes,[5] so governments as investors manage pools of capital created by pension contributions or resource royalties simply to maximize the return on investment. The Crown corporation Canadian National Railways, for example, runs the CN Pension Trust Fund, which manages close to $5 billion and invests not only in bonds, mortgages, and real estate but also in oil and gas properties; it also holds shares in companies with a book value of over one billion dollars.[6] Some government loan programs to assist companies to adjust to international competition have included stock option provisions. The boards appointed to administer the Enterprise Development Program in the 1970s, for example, were authorized to exercise this option when "the value of the capital stock of the company has increased" simply so that the government would "benefit from the increased value."[7]

Security

The state in Canada often acts as an investment banker, usually through an established Crown corporation or industrial development program set out in legislation.[8] Here it undertakes a minority equity participation to provide insurance to creditors. Either the government-as-lender is insured against the frivolous use of its funds by gaining the right to monitor investment decision making, or the government's equity infusion reassures commercial lenders that a company's capitalization is adequate to permit term lending to high-risk borrowers (such as very small businesses). Officially viewed as passive and finite, such investments are excluded from the federal government's listing of its corporate holdings. In our view, the moment government appoints a member to the board of any commercial company the state acts as capitalist, however temporarily, in sharing both risks and some responsibility for investment decision making.

The Federal Business Development Bank (FBDB) is, for example, empowered to "purchase or otherwise acquire the whole or part of an issue of securities" of corporations which it "may" later sell.[9] Although the FBDB for a time acted primarily as a lender of last resort, it now vaunts its capability to "provide equity capital as well as, or in place of loans."[10] These investments, usually a significant minority position, have not normally involved FBDB in day-to-day management but allowed it to monitor activities, meet with management, and see all books. Yet, "in addition, the Bank might want to participate in all strategic decisions. . . . It will, therefore, generally ask for the right to have a representative on the Board of Directors of the company."[11] FBDB's role as investment banker was sanctified in 1983 when the government formally announced a shift in its mandate. Ottawa also approved funneling $90 million of bank funds over the subsequent three years to a new investment banking division, which has since enabled the bank to report an operating profit.[12]

Acquire a Good or Service

It is the further investments both of wholly owned Crown corporations and of established mixed enterprises which extend state capital to a wide range of competitive and profitable industries. Crown corporation subsidiaries and affiliates have in turn carried out yet other investments, many of them as part of the normal course of business—to secure a source of supply, to acquire a warehouse to facilitate distribution, and so forth. In 1982, for example, Petro-Canada purchased a 49 percent equity position in a Gulf Canada refinery for $95 million. Located in British Columbia, the investment enabled the state enterprise to deliver more petroleum to its expanded western sales outlets, just as its purchase of a 49 percent interest in Harvey's Oil of Newfoundland, a fuel oil distributor, allowed Petro-Canada to enter that province's retail fuel oil market.[13]

Incentives

When governments in Canada contribute capital to a new venture in the form of equity, that equity often serves, much like industrial assistance loans or grants, to facilitate economic activity by the private entrepreneur. All such discriminatory instruments favor some category of firms over others, perhaps on the basis of size, sector, or region, and thus reflect a more or less implicit economic development policy. Government chooses equity as the form of inducement either because the private investor insists upon a longer-term commitment by government to risk sharing or because the government insists on information sharing by way of board membership to ensure company compliance with the agreed criteria.

Thus when several Canadian and European companies agreed to develop the Nanisivik lead-zinc mine, located in the high Arctic, they made their decision contingent upon massive government assistance to create the infrastructure for a permanent mining community. In 1974 the federal government promised to construct a wharf and an airport as well as to pay for road construction. Ottawa then opted to take 18 percent of the equity in return for its contributions. (The holding would allow it to monitor the company's compliance with its conditions, which included employment of northern residents, a paced production schedule to stretch the mine's life span, and submission of environmental and technical studies.) The shareholder's agreement set up a monitoring committee to report to the minister of Indian and Northern Affairs every six months.[14]

Strategy

Only in the rarest of instances has the national government in Canada articulated a priori an investment policy, harnessing equity to an overt strategy of economic development. Two notable exceptions to the rule, the CDC (see Chapter 4) and Telesat, provide examples of mixed enterprises established to serve as instruments of explicit policy. Special legislation created Telesat Canada in 1969, in the tradition of "defensive expansionism" discussed in Chapter 2—satellite communications were deemed critical to national integration, and preemptive government encouragement was thought necessary to avoid U.S. dominance.[15] Telesat brings together thirteen Canadian telecommunications carriers (some private, some government-owned) and the government of Canada. Each contributed $30 million in capital. Unlike the CDC, Telesat shares have never been offered to the public at large, nor has the government been content to play a passive role as shareholder. The enabling act afforded government special privileges, such as veto power over the election of the company's president and cabinet approval for any common share transfers, and it gave the minister of communications the right to review procurement decisions and undertake any international negotiations.[16] Even though Telesat is subject to a regulatory body, the Canadian Radio-television and Telecommunications Commission (CRTC), the cabinet twice intervened to overrule the CRTC in favor of Telesat Canada's interests.[17] In principle, government might have resorted to a Crown corporation, as it did for international satellite communications (setting up Teleglobe). The mixed format, however, allowed government to mobilize the capital and know-how of experienced corporations and to assuage companies reluctant to use satellites by offering them a voice in policy, all the while gaining direct, decision-making participation.[18]

Problem Solving

Most frequently the government has been drawn into shared ownership of commercial ventures not as part of a carefully considered policy but by default, literally and figuratively. In numerous instances industrial assistance loans were secured by a government stock option that was then exercised when the company defaulted. In other instances, equity appears to have been government's last-resort solution to an immediate problem—that is, decision making by default. In the case of Ridley Terminals Inc. the creation of a mixed enterprise enabled several governments to solve a political dilemma and at the same time reduced the risk of large financial losses for the private companies implicated.

In 1981 it looked as if major projects under way to develop coal reserves in northeastern British Columbia were in jeopardy. Anxious to secure Japanese and Korean long-term contracts for coal, Canadian companies had brought new mines on stream. The committed amounts and delivery schedules required massive new infrastructure, including a new port at Ridley Island. But the private consortium that had undertaken port construction backed out when the rates it proposed to meet inflated costs were deemed unacceptable by mining companies that had fixed-price contracts with Asian buyers. Ottawa saw failure to meet delivery dates as having significant political ramifications: it could undermine future economic cooperation with Japan.

The federal government moved in to resolve the problem. Its Crown corporation National Harbours Board (NHB, now Ports Canada) would undertake some $48 million of infrastructure directly, but a separate legal personality was required to channel new funds. As NHB was precluded by legislation from establishing subsidiaries but not from making investments, Ottawa established a new mixed enterprise, Ridley Terminals Inc. (RTI), to build the coal terminal. NHB and Fed Com, one of the private consortium members, each contributed $23 million by way of preferred shares to capitalize RTI. A symbolic one million dollars of common stock was issued of which NHB subscribed 90 percent, allowing the new company tax-free status as a government enterprise. The federal government then insured another $185 million in loans to RTI from the private banks. To ensure completion on time, a supervisory committee headed by government officials monitored the entire project. The minister responsible saw the project as proof of "the high priority the national government attaches to facilitating major resource development . . . beyond the capacity of a provincial government or the private sector alone."[19] The good politician presents crisis decision making as strategy, of course, but here as so often we find government in Canada investing to resolve a private-sector problem that involves high political risks rather than advancing preordained public policy.

Toward an Investment Strategy? The cdic

Our review of Ottawa's investments leads to the generalization that the government most often made direct equity investments in mixed enterprises with private investors for ad hoc, reactive reasons.[20] This pattern of ad hoc investment by Canada's national government seemed to change radically with the establishment of the Canada Development Investment Corporation (cdic), a holding company modeled on European practice. The cdic describes itself as "a federal Crown corporation incorporated in 1982 to help manage in a commercial manner enterprises and investments assigned to it by government and to divest those enterprises and investments on commercial terms when the opportunity arises."[21] The political will to create an investment corporation that would follow cabinet instructions was generated in very particular economic and political circumstances. Several influential personalities interpreted these circumstances to mean that government must become more assertive to resolve urgent problems facing the state-as-investor.

Emboldened by their return to power in 1980 after a short-lived Conservative government, the Liberals put into place a highly directive economic development strategy.[22] Center stage was the National Energy Program (NEP), which has rightly been called "interventionist, centralist, and nationalistic."[23] In the name of energy security the NEP changed pricing, taxation, and exploration incentives for petroleum. To promote Canadianization it also assigned an expanded role to the state-owned enterprise Petro-Canada and set a target for 50 percent Canadian ownership in the oil industry. Industrial policy focused on "megaprojects" (involving investments over $100 million), usually in the energy field, which would serve as catalysts for economic activity.[24] Alongside these economic undertakings, the Trudeau government launched an all-out political mobilization to prepare for a new federal-provincial compact in order to "repatriate" the Constitution.[25] Both the economic and the political initiatives had the same aim—to secure the authority of the federal government as architect of "national" policy and to overcome the psychosis of fragmentation created by the election of the separatist Parti québécois in Quebec and by the combative economic policies of western provinces, particularly Alberta.

Several harsh realities, however, soon interposed themselves between an interventionist strategy and its application. Over 1981–82 all economic indicators plunged as, in James Laxer's words, "Canada experienced the most severe economic contraction of any industrialized country."[26] At the same time bitter objections to the NEP from both the multinational oil producers and the western producing provinces convinced the federal government to adjust ownership regulations and renegotiate pricing schedules. More important, with the drop in oil prices in 1982 companies committed in principle to megaprojects pulled back, leaving government either to provide the extra capital itself or to offer costly incentives to attract private-sector replacements. At this moment several crises for the state-as-investor came to a head: revelation of mismanagement at state-owned Canadair; impending bankruptcy of state majority-owned Consolidated Computer Inc; and appeals for refinancing by private enterprises whose loans had been guaranteed by government.[27]

The rising costs of its past investments and the rising incidence of corporate crises made it imperative, in the minds of advisers close to the prime minister, that the federal government not only reclaim control over state-controlled enterprises but forge an instrument of investment policy that could target placements and permit divestment prior to political scandal. Ottawa's inability to use the Canada Development Corporation (CDC) as such a vehicle for investment policy, despite its major block of shares, had after all been demonstrated twice over, first when the company refused to help refinance one of Canada's leading corporations, Massey-Ferguson, and again in 1981 when the Board of Directors resisted pressures to elect the government's candidate to its chair. Obviously, in the words of the former Liberal finance minister, "the CDC has ceased to be an instrument of public policy, and therefore you might as well recoup your investment."[28]

Disillusion with the CDC led to a divestment decision and concomitantly to the creation of the CDIC, presented in the first instance simply as a vehicle to hold the government's equity in CDC until such time as market conditions became favorable for its sale. The rapid evolution of the new company, moving within six months from a numbered company holding CDC shares, to a Crown corporation instructed to follow cabinet investment directives, to a holding company responsible for over $2 billion in assets, demonstrates the government's intent to fashion a more effective instrument for investment policy. It also attests to the influence of key personalities—in particular Maurice Strong, CDIC's first chairman.[29] After serving as Petro-Canada's first president and as a director of the CDC, Strong believed that the reactive approach to investment hitherto adopted by the federal government was irresponsible. Government's commercial holdings—direct or indirect—amounted to some $20 billion:

> The government is clearly the largest single investor in the private sector in Canada. But . . . it has come about through a series of ad hoc responses to policy needs that have arisen from time to time in respect of particular sectors of the Canadian economy, as well as cries for help from the private sector, rather than through any deliberate over-all policy of establishing the government as a major investor in the private sector.[30]

Strong saw no alternative to the federal government's "equity banker" role. There would always be market failures as well as projects of social benefit unable to attract adequate private capital. It was therefore essential not only to seek a commercial return on the government's investments but also to determine clear divestment criteria. The task of actually forging CDIC into this instrument of investment policy was taken on by Senator Jack Austin, who as deputy minister of energy, mines and resources had been instrumental in creating Petro-Canada. Promoted by Maurice Strong to become minister responsible for the CDIC, Austin was able to win backing from other cabinet ministers for political sleights of hand that would build up the new investment agency without the inconvenience of parliamentary debate.

The mandate and structures of the CDIC were never the subject of policy review, either within the party or in public. The CDIC was incorporated under the Canada Business Corporations Act in May 1982 by decision of cabinet ("order-in-council"), and its Articles of Incorporation were revised four months later by another order-in-council. Broad policy objectives were now stated: CDIC would "assist in the creation or development of businesses, resources, properties and industries of Canada" and could "invest in the shares of securities of any corporation" or in "ventures or enterprises" provided these were "related to the economic interests of Canada" or "likely to benefit Canada." Cabinet could determine corporate priorities directly—"the Corporation shall comply with any specific direction in writing that may be given to it by the Governor-in-Council [i.e., cabinet] in furtherance of any policy or policies of the Government of Canada." To avoid any repetition of the CDC experience, the important restriction was made that "any invitation to the public to subscribe for any securities of the Corporation is hereby prohibited."[31] Finally, cabinet directives in November 1982 transformed the CDIC into a holding company not merely for the shares of the CDC but also for major state-owned commercial enterprises—Canadair, De Havilland Aircraft, Eldorado Nuclear, and Teleglobe Canada—as well as for the $125 million in equity which the government had put into Massey-Ferguson. To fund the CDIC without recourse to budgetary appropriations that only Parliament could authorize, cabinet also directed the minister of finance to advance an interest-free, one-year loan of $500,000 to the corporation.[32]

What use did government actually make of this impressive new instrument of investment policy? The CDIC's first priority, which occupied virtually all of its board's time prior to the change of government in 1984, was neither investment nor divestment but the financial crises at Canadair and De Havilland. CDIC sought hands-on management and financial restructuring of these two government-owned aircraft manufacturers. The other two commercial state enterprises, Eldorado and Teleglobe, were transferred to the new holding company apparently less for any strategic reason than for the tactical necessity of finding funds to cover CDIC's operating costs until legislation regularized its status. At the time both were returning a profit. Cabinet agreed in principle to revise Teleglobe's legislation so that its profits would no longer revert to general government revenues but be put at the disposition of the CDIC. Meanwhile Eldorado was refinanced. The government converted its preferred shares, normally bearing a 20 percent dividend, to common stock, and the corporation reissued preferred shares bearing only 6 percent interest. In this manner the Crown corporation was decapitalized by $10 million, which became working capital for the CDIC.[33]

CDIC's second priority was to play a public relations role, assuring business and public that massive infusions of capital to troubled enterprises, both state and private, were not the wave of the future but part of a rationalization that would lead to a new, more businesslike management of government investments. Only in 1984, in the heat of an election campaign, did the government push for parliamentary consensus on legislation to legitimize the CDIC. Advocates sought to convince press and opposition that the holding company was an instrument for all parties. Senator Austin emphasized not only CIDC's purpose of enabling government "to perform as an active shareholder" but also its attraction as a vehicle for privatization, ready, as the corporation's objects now stated, "to effect divestitures of assets."[34]

Overall during the Liberals' tenure in office the CDIC acted, we believe, neither as a vehicle for policy, targeting new investments, nor as a vehicle for privatization, which remained a matter only of rhetoric. The CDIC served principally to rationalize state-owned enterprises in crisis in order to avert their financial collapse and divert political pressures by demonstrating new, "businesslike" management. In so doing, the CDIC prepared the way for the new Conservative government to launch a privatization policy in 1984 (a policy we examine in detail in Chapter 8). Second, the CDIC provided a convenient way of holding government shares in private industries in crisis—shares acquired as part of a political response to the exigencies of recession.[35] The CDIC was, for example, persuaded to take on responsibility for such new and doubtless money-losing propositions as the government's interest in the East Coast fishing industry. The CDIC minister confessed that "we did not make a recommendation. . . . Government decided we were the appropriate vehicle."[36] When we look to see where the state-as-investor undertook new commitments in the 1980s, we have to look not at the CDIC but at the dramatic series of corporate bailouts determined by cabinet.

BAILOUTS

It was not the political will to use state investment as part of a purposive industrial policy, to which the formation of the CDIC attests, but instead the high drama of corporate rescue packages which captured headlines in the 1980s. In a recession the scale of threatened business failure made it politically imperative for government to attempt to resolve or at least to defer crisis. In trying to understand why the state in Canada takes on the risks of a shareholder, we find several common characteristics that distinguish these bailouts from the state's earlier salvage operations. The companies in question were not market failures in the classic sense of the term but had overextended (encouraged by the banks) in a world of easy credit.[37] They needed government backing not to finance losses as such but to *refinance* debt burdens that had become impossibly onerous with the jump in interest rates over 1980–81. In certain cases it was not the company itself but its Canadian bankers who first appealed to government, out of concern either for unsecured loans or for loss of face with the international lenders within loan consortia. Rather than remain arms-length creditors, the banks in some rescue packages stipulated conditions for refinancing which included their taking an equity position and a seat on the company's board of directors. One major rescue package, in the fish-processing industry, illustrates the pivotal role that the commercial banks played in the timing, terms, and conditions of bailouts. The circumstances that led to an unintended policy outcome—government ownership by way of bailout prompted by financial crisis—produced a typical array of the dilemmas facing the state-as-investor in the recessionary 1980s.[38]

In November 1983 the Parliament of Canada passed the Atlantic Fisheries Restructuring Act—a package of grants, loans, and equity authorizing the federal government to commit $138 million to help rationalize virtually the entire offshore industry, which involved companies employing 44,000 people in 45 processing plants and 129 vessels across four provinces. The act's stated purpose was "to facilitate the development of viable Atlantic Fisheries that are competitive and privately-owned through the restructuring of fishery enterprises." To achieve this goal the minister was empowered to "acquire . . . shares, debentures or other securities of . . . any fishery enterprise."[39] Clearly this was no spur-of-the-moment decision. Two years earlier, upon learning of the likely bankruptcy of three of the five major deep sea fishing and processing companies based in Newfoundland and Nova Scotia, both federal and provincial governments had had to face the prospect of enormous social and economic dislocation. More than 25 percent of the region's population still lived in fishing villages, thousands of which were single-industry communities. At the same time fishing was a significant national industry—after the legality of claims to a two-hundred-mile "exclusive economic zone" was established in 1977, exports of seafood rose to make Canada the world's leading exporter in 1979. The broad economic and social interests at stake made a case-by-case response to company problems inadequate. The prime minister set up a task force on the Atlantic fisheries in January 1982. Its report, submitted by year's end, became the basis for complex negotiations with the interested companies, banks, and provincial governments. The result was a complete restructuring of the offshore industry, now dominated by two "super-companies," each partially owned by the federal government.[40]

Social policy and commercial policy vied with each other throughout the subsequent two years of restructuring. The task force had introduced the hard facts of indebtedness and gross margins with elegiac references to the place of the sea in the Canadian soul. Nonetheless the bottom line, as the report bluntly put it, was that "the fish processing industry on Canada's Atlantic coast is in financial crisis."[41] The proximate cause of crisis, beyond the perennial problems of labor costs, foreign competition, and the like, was the debt crunch: "Increased interest costs—well above any level that could be associated with a normal growth in the scale of business or with inflation—were a major cause of the rapid deterioration in the financial condition of the industry during the past two years."[42] The immediate need, therefore, was a refinancing accompanied by restructuring through mergers and plant closings to ensure the industry's future "economic viability." In the trade-off between "employment maximization" and "economic viability," cabinet respected the task force recommendations and emphasized the latter.[43] This focus on financial and commercial criteria placed the banks, particularly the Bank of Nova Scotia, which held most of the outstanding loans, in a powerful position to influence outcomes for each company. In Newfoundland the banks' cooperation made possible Ottawa's acts of force majeure in restructuring the industry against the preferences of both the provincial government and a key corporate player. In Nova Scotia the banks acted as arbiters, selecting among contending proposals for refinancing.

The federal and Newfoundland fisheries ministers had agreed in the spring of 1982 that the best basis for restructuring the industry would be to merge the assets of the three leading companies after forgiving commercial and government debts. The provincial cabinet, however, could not accept Ottawa's insistence on purely commercial criteria to dictate plant closures. Faced with Newfoundland's recalcitrant defense of social welfare considerations, the federal minister boldly announced a unilateral restructuring decision in July 1983: Ottawa and the Bank of Nova Scotia would become co-owners of the new supercompany. Government would contribute $75 million in capital, the bank would convert $44.1 million of its debt to equity. Negotiations with the affected companies to carry through the deal confronted an unexpected obstacle, however, when the major shareholder of the largest firm, Fisheries Products, balked, wanting a higher price and a bigger management say in the new company. This shareholder was Ottawa's "own" mixed enterprise, the Canada Development Corporation, which only embittered the dispute. At this point the Bank of Nova Scotia unexpectedly called in its $67 million in loans, forcing Fisheries Products into receivership.

According to the bank, new capital for the company was crucial, and thus "we had to move to protect our investment in a going concern and to make sure there was no disruption of operations which might have led to the loss of vital U.S. markets."[44] The company contested its receivership in the courts and sued the bank, the federal government, and the head of the task force for conspiracy to defraud company shareholders. The receivership, the company claimed, was intended simply to pressure Fisheries Products into participating in the restructuring plan favored by the bank. Ultimately, political compromises were made, and the provincial Supreme Court rejected the aggrieved company's claim, allowing the two governments to announce their shared goals and the creation of a new company jointly owned with the Bank of Nova Scotia.[45] This company, Fisheries Products International Inc., would have a board of five directors appointed by the federal government, three by the province, one by the employees, one by the Bank of Nova Scotia, and a jointly appointed chairman. It was "the objective of both governments to return the business to private investors in the shortest possible time," while affording the bank (and each government) the "right to veto any such sale."[46]

On the heels of the Newfoundland settlement came a related large-scale bailout in Nova Scotia. Here in September 1983 the federal and provincial governments, together with the Bank of Nova Scotia, agreed to buy most assets of H. B. Nickerson & Sons, including its controlling share of Canada's largest fishing company, National Sea Products ("NatSea"), and to transfer some assets to the new government-controlled company in Newfoundland. The federal government was to contribute new capital whereas both the bank and the province were to convert approximately half of their debt instruments into equity. Private shareholders were to retain a minority interest in NatSea and the right to approve the deal. Federal and provincial policy makers were at pains to emphasize "that it would be completely wrong to characterize restructuring as nationalization of the offshore fishery" and to underscore that "both governments are committed to divest their equity interest to the private sector as soon as the long-run commercial viability . . . is assured."[47]

The Bank of Nova Scotia (BNS), with as much as $75 million owing from NatSea and a majority ownership interest in the new company through its consortium with the federal government, was in a key position to play broker in what turned out to be nearly six months of contention over financing and ownership. Thus in January 1984 BNS, along with other creditors, the Toronto Dominion and Royal Banks, telexed the fisheries minister that the first private investors' proposal was unacceptable. Shortly thereafter a second proposal by Nova Scotia businessmen was eliminated when the BNS refused to extend the negotiation deadline for the forty-eight hours needed to secure federal government financing. The bank stipulated a new deadline three weeks thereafter for the company's board to find an acceptable proposition, or it would call the loans. Its president explained that although "the Bank of Nova Scotia would prefer long-term private control . . . the more immediate problem is how to stabilize the debt-ridden industry."[48] NatSea's directors were able to meet the zero-hour threat when a private investment consortium raised additional capital and convinced the Toronto Dominion Bank to pay off the BNS in return for preferred shares, thus avoiding the threatened foreclosure. Vociferous objections from the provincial government and the Halifax press regarding excessive interference from outside Nova Scotia convinced Ottawa to separate its joint holding with the Bank of Nova Scotia formally, so that the federal government had 20 percent ownership and three directors on the board while the Bank of Nova Scotia retained a 14 percent shareholding and could name one director. In March 1984, at the annual shareholders' meeting, an agreement was approved giving control to private investors.[49]

The fisheries bailout involved the restructuring of an entire industry and generated a major debate within cabinet as to the appropriate policy instruments. Cabinet gave serious consideration to creating new wholly owned Crown corporations, as the preliminary version of the task force report had suggested, and indeed it used a takeover to reorganize part of the Quebec industry.[50] A special subcommittee of cabinet met frequently during 1982–83 and continued to debate the appropriate mixture of loans, equity, and government ownership in the Atlantic fisheries.[51] The mixed enterprise format seemed best suited to financial viability and eventual reprivatization. To avoid full-scale nationalizations the federal government required the participation of the banks, not simply to convert debt to equity but to provide a private-sector presence. The banks benefited from having their loans resecured through infusions of new state capital, or, in the bailouts of the petroleum and farm equipment industries, by government loan guarantees. Difficult negotiations over refinancing then placed the banks in a better position than either the affected companies or the provincial governments to exercise political brokerage.[52] The nuances differ across cases, but the pattern is clear: in major new commitments of equity after 1980 Canada's national government responded not to the clarion call of an industrial strategy but rather to the exigencies of financial crises in a time of recession.

PROVINCIAL STATES AS INVESTORS

In contradistinction to the federal government, several provincial governments have recently forged state investment strategies as part of a broader framework of economic development objectives. Why does the state-as-investor play a more directive role at the provincial level? Historically in Canada, as we saw in Chapter 2, the combination of regional disparities and provincial state autonomy has tended to inhibit Ottawa's ability to carry through its national economic policies. Much provincial government intervention, moreover, especially after 1960, has been explained not just by new opportunities for economic growth—particularly in the resource sector—but also by the political will to overcome the handicaps of uneven regional development in Canada. (This development we discussed as "province building" in Chapter 5.) The competitive nature of Canadian federalism was exacerbated in the 1970s by the often preemptive policies of the Trudeau government. In the view of one provincial government, "the intention was to reassert the federal presence right across Canada: to attempt to bypass the provinces wherever possible and to centralize power in Ottawa."[53]

Not all provincial governments, however, have institutionalized a state investment capability. Three factors seem to favor a more active government-as-investor: economic opportunity (e.g., windfall profits in a resource industry); intergovernmental conflicts of interest (e.g., federal regulatory, pricing, tariff, or taxation policies that adversely affect the provincial government's revenues); and strong political leadership (e.g., a party or an individual highly committed to regional development and having the electoral mandate to absorb the political costs). It has been in Alberta and Quebec where policy makers have most consciously sought to target investments to advantage the regional economy.

Alberta

The oil-rich province of Alberta reaped tremendous benefits from the jump in world oil prices following the 1973 OAPEC embargo. Even though domestic prices in Canada were negotiated with the federal government and kept lower than world prices, increased production and royalties generated revenues beyond the immediate needs of the provincial government. This windfall in turn prompted two political concerns: first, to find an investment strategy that would optimize the use of these funds, and second, to find ways to overcome the vulnerability of a regional economy tied to the fortunes of a volatile commodity. In this context the Alberta legislature passed the Alberta Heritage Savings Trust Fund Act in May 1976. The preamble explained that

> *Whereas* substantial revenues are being received by the Province from the sale of non-renewable resources owned by the people of Alberta; and

Whereas there is a limited supply of non-renewable resources and therefore revenues from the sale of those resources will ultimately be reduced; and

Whereas the Legislature of Alberta considers it appropriate that a substantial portion of those revenues be set aside and invested for the benefit of the people of Alberta in future years . . . [the Fund is enacted].[54]

The broad development strategy to be served by the fund derived from the Janus-like philosophy of a Conservative government that vociferously promoted free-wheeling free enterprise while exercising a very directive role over economic activity in the province.[55] Although government considered several options to state-directed investment, the obvious alternative, further tax reductions, was deemed inflationary. It was also likely to attract unwanted immigration from other regions of Canada while missing the opportunity to create future sources of revenue from capital invested. Most telling, however, was the positive argument that, in the words of the province's deputy treasurer, "by directing investment into certain sectors of the economy and into specific projects there would be an opportunity to affect the direction of growth of the Alberta economy to reduce its dependence on conventional oil and gas production as Alberta's reserves decline."[56]

The Alberta Heritage Fund was created to serve as an instrument of investment policy linked to regional development strategy; this becomes clear when we consider its decision-making structures and the types of investments permitted by its legislation. The fund was authorized to invest up to 30 percent of revenues from nonrenewable resources in one of four ways: (1) capital projects, intended to "provide long term economic or social benefits to the people of Alberta" but probably not earn any return, limited to 20 percent of the fund's assets; (2) loans to other governments in Canada, limited to 15 percent, later 20 percent; (3) investments that would "tend to strengthen or diversify the economy of Alberta" at the same time as they yielded "a reasonable return or profit," and (4) all residual funds in debt instruments such as debentures or bonds of other governments, banks, and blue chip corporations. In keeping with a free market philosophy, the enabling legislation authorized no equity investments, but as we shall see this thinking would alter. Additionally, a fifth division of the fund was created after amendments to the legislation in 1980 to encourage spinoffs and horizontal integration for an economy still reliant on oil and gas. This Energy Investment Division could undertake unlimited investments to "facilitate the development, processing or transportation of energy resources within Canada," provided they yielded "a reasonable rate of return or profit."[57]

Clearly cabinet has determined what constitutes an investment to strengthen the economy or an investment likely to earn a profit—a cabinet, moreover, responsible to a legislature dominated by the same party and until 1985 presided over by a high-profile premier. The act did authorize the Legislature to direct the fund (by way of resolution), and it also created a standing committee of the Legislature to consider annual reports on the fund's activities. The effective authority in practice, however, has proved to be the Heritage Saving Trust Fund Investment Committee, consisting of cabinet ministers. This committee must approve and may direct investment decisions by the designated administrator of the fund, the provincial treasurer.[58]

Intergovernmental conflict reinforced the provincial government's commitment to a directive investment policy. The burgeoning fund gave Canadians elsewhere the impression that the "blue-eyed sheiks" of Alberta were benefiting from the international oil crisis at their expense.[59] From an initial $1.5 billion in assets, the fund climbed to over $10 billion by 1981.[60] This accumulation of petrodollars in a national economy by then deep in recession provoked adverse reaction from other governments in Canada. Yet Albertans were convinced, particularly after the second rise in oil prices in 1979, that their province was in effect subsidizing manufacturing and jobs for central Canada by respecting a price ceiling below world levels. Even a federal *Conservative* government— briefly in tenure in Ottawa—could not convince the province to recycle petrodollars through new national energy funds in exchange for higher oil prices. From the Albertan perspective, federal energy policies stymied provincial development goals. By using its Crown corporation, Petro-Canada, to enter the industry, the federal government had effectively circumvented the constitutional restrictions that allocate rights over resources to the provinces. By giving incentives in its National Energy Program to companies that shift production to the north or "Canada Lands," which are within federal jurisdiction, Ottawa reduced Alberta's future royalty and tax share. The Alberta Heritage Fund's annual report attacked the NEP, which, it claimed, "had a direct and negative effect on the provincial economy and on our non-renewable resource revenues."[61] Albertans overwhelming supported their government's militant stance on oil prices, returning the Conservative party to power in 1981 with 75 of the 79 seats in the provincial legislature.

Alberta itself conducted a vigorous internal debate on the role of the state-as-investor, centered on the appropriate strategy for investing the fund's resource revenues. The key issues concerned the balance between economic development and an immediate return on investment, the acceptability of government equity investments in the market economy, and the trade-off between "savings" through the fund and social expenditures. Many supporters of the fund, inside and outside government, felt that fund management was simply too conservative and had not achieved the rate of return that could justify its mandate. In the view of the deputy provincial treasurer, "it was not fully anticipated by anyone just how difficult it would be to find a sufficient volume of investments that would meet the twin criteria of the Alberta Investment Division, namely investments that would provide a source of income to the Fund while tending to strengthen and diversify the economy of Alberta."[62] Most of this division's investments were in the debentures of Crown corporations. As for the residual monies, several billion dollars invested by the Market Securities Division, all were in fixed-income securities, whereas, the *Financial Post* noted, a typical pension fund would have perhaps 50 percent of its monies invested in equities.[63] Such criticisms inspired a 1980 amendment to the fund legislation creating the new Commerical Investment Division, intended to yield "a commercial return or profit to the Trust Fund."[64] Henceforth the fund could purchase shares in private enterprise.

This resolved the issue of the rate of return on fund investments, but it did so by raising a broader question about the expanded role that the provincial government was playing in the marketplace. The fund already held shares in two mixed enterprises, Syncrude and the Alberta Energy Corporation (AEC), interests originally held by government and only recently transferred to the fund for portfolio management. Although "a principal object of AEC is to operate at a profit" and although no single shareholder other than the government may own more than 1 percent of the voting shares, the Alberta government had kept at arm's length by appointing three businessmen to the Board of Directors in lieu of exercising its formal right as shareholder to vote.[65] The decision to allow the fund to make equity investments was inspired by strictly fiduciary motives, but it nevertheless agitated observers ideologically committed to the free market. As a result, no placements were actually made for several years. Only when recession reduced the provincial government's revenues was the fund instructed to begin making some equity placements to increase its return. Its subsequent foray into the market, buying the beer, liquor, and newspaper companies, rekindled objections to government participation in competitive businesses. To soothe ideological sensitivities, cabinet set guidelines that restricted shareholdings by the fund to 5 percent of any one company; no single investment could exceed 10 percent of the division's total portfolio. The fund would not seek membership on the boards of companies.[66]

The third issue shaping the fund's first decade concerned the proper trade-off between collective "savings" and immediate consumption. With the softening of world prices for oil and the downturn in investment in Canada, Alberta experienced its own recession after 1982, resulting in budget deficits and a jobless rate that at 11 percent surpassed the Canadian average. Recession made more persuasive those who had consistently argued that government activity to "benefit the people of Alberta" could in moral terms define "people" only as the current generation and not project into the future.[67] Government, worried less about moral issues than about budget crises, skimmed off the cash. After 1982 the fund no longer received its quasi-automatic transfer of 30 percent of nonrenewable resource revenues but was reduced to 15 percent for two years, with the percentage thereafter to be determined annually by the Legislature. Furthermore, the fund no longer retains its net earnings to reinvest; these monies now revert to the general government treasury.[68]

Economic recession and the dynamics of politics have thus reduced the resources available for investment by the Alberta Heritage Fund. These are, however, "conjunctural" limits to the provincial state-as-investor and are susceptible to change in future. It is perfectly possible, for example, that the restructuring of Canada's petrochemical industry in favor of gas feedstocks, now under way, will bring new monies to the fund. It is also conceivable the Albertan government will find that its efforts to diversify the regional economy require a more interventionist stance.[69] If so, an institution with $12.5 billion in assets is in place and amendments to its legislation now permit the fund to be used by the government of the day (directed by the cabinet), either as an instrument of development policy or as an investor taking equity positions in the marketplace purely for profit.

Quebec

The conscious use of state capital to advance industrial development in Quebec dates from the 1960s, when, as we saw in Chapter 5, Quebec's new nationalism took institutional expression through an array of state-owned enterprises in the hydroelectric, steel, petroleum, and mining industries. In this same historical transition period the Quebec government set up the two agencies that today serve as formidable vehicles of investment policy—the Société générale de financement (SGF) and the Caisse de dépôt et placement du Québec. The Caisse now manages $22 billion dollars in assets, ranking eighth among Canada's top financial institutions, and it has bought into some of the major Canadian, as opposed to Quebec-based, corporations. The SGF, now an industrial holding company with just over $1 billion in assets, ranks 130th by sales among Canada's top 500 industrials.[70]

Both companies were created, the SGF in 1962 and the Caisse in 1965, as instruments to enhance provincial autonomy. The SGF was originally set up as a mixed enterprise, with government representatives in a minority position on the board. Its primary objectives, as stated in its legislation, were to promote new commercial ventures that would restructure the economic base of the province and encourage the mobilization of Quebec savings for the purpose. The SGF could take shares in or take over an enterprise.[71] As for the Caisse, the very creation of an agency to manage pension contributions in Quebec was a political triumph for the province, which had emerged from fractious federal-provincial negotiations in 1964 as the only jurisdiction in Canada to have independent control over such funds. In the view of the interministerial committee that had prepared government policy on the issue, pension funds were a pool of capital not locked into established business interests, and control of the funds would give the provincial government a freer hand to advance its economic strategy. For one member of the working group set up to draft the actual legislation, "it went without saying that the Caisse should bias its activities in favour of francophone controlled financial institutions in order to contribute to correct a historical imbalance."[72]

If the reasoning behind the establishment of the Caisse and the SGF in the 1960s placed the two investment agencies within broader economic development goals shaped by nationalism, the fit was very loose indeed. For the first decade or more neither institution can be said truly to have served as a tool for government to apply specific industrial or investment policies. Nor did their activities dramatically extend state capitalism in the sense of bringing the state into competitive private enterprises as a direct participant in production, exchange, and investment. The Caisse held bonds and mortgages, and sometimes took minority equity shares, but was regarded primarily as a fiduciary agent and as underwriter of the established public sector. It could make unlimited investments in government or Crown corporation bonds, but funds invested in new ventures could not constitute more than 7 percent of its portfolio.[73] The SGF was quickly "captured" by its predominantly business board and acted to salvage family-owned firms, thereby transmuting a private-sector elite into a public-sector enterprise elite.[74] Only since the late 1970s have the Caisse and the SGF been reoriented to target provincial investment to those sectors or specific firms that matched evolving government priorities in industrial policy. We focus on the Caisse, Canada's largest equity investor with its $6 billion portfolio of shares held in more than 350 companies.[75]

The special characteristics of the Caisse can best be appreciated in comparison with the Alberta Heritage Savings Trust Fund. In terms of the *source of funds*, the Alberta Heritage Fund depends on revenues from nonrenewable resources that vary according to industry fortunes and tax or royalty regimes. An annual political decision determines just what share of these revenues will be transferred to the Heritage Fund. The Caisse relies on contributions to pension, retirement, health, and automobile insurance schemes. These are automatically managed by the Caisse, so that its fortunes are broadly determined by demographic and employment trends. Also it may, as the Alberta Fund once could, retain the earnings from its investments. The Caisse's assets, however, are in a sense liabilities, that is, they are owed to the contributors. In terms of *policy direction,* the Alberta Fund is overtly guided by political criteria. Cabinet must approve all decisions, while legislation dictates the general conditions of profitability for different categories of investments. The Caisse is formally independent of government and until the 1980s did not divulge details of its holdings. Government direction thus comes through an informal, interpersonal path and by way of management and board appointments that insure compatibility of objectives. In terms of *control* over the state's role in business, the Alberta Fund is bound by legislation to place the major portion of its funds in capital development or sociopolitical projects; investment in private enterprises is a residual. The Caisse is also bound by law in the distribution of its investments: no more than 30 percent of its assets can be invested in common shares. Alberta guidelines at the moment restrict the fund's equity holdings to 5 percent of an individual company, whereas the Caisse's statute is more liberal, placing the ceiling for a shareholding in any one company at 30 percent. This 30 percent limit is an ambiguous figure. It conforms to the notion that the Caisse should remain a passive financier, but in today's corporate world it is a proportion that often translates into control.[76]

Does the Quebec government deliberately impose direction on the Caisse's investment policy, or do the size and market clout of this state agency automatically give political visibility to investments made primarily to improve earnings? The degree of Caisse autonomy remains controversial. Certainly the Parti québécois prior to its election in 1976 had made clear its intention to reorient the Caisse in order "to underscore its role as supplier of capital for industrial development and particularly its share-holdings in enterprises likely to contribute to balanced regional development in Quebec."[77] Pierre Fournier's report, solicited by the government in 1977 to evaluate the effectiveness of state enterprises in advancing public policy, argued that the government should appoint managers more sympathetic to its aims and exercise greater direction over Caisse policy so that the agency could better fulfill its responsibility for industrial development. Improved coordination among the Caisse, SGF, and the government's small business finance company SDI was required to maximize state direction over Quebec's economic development.[78] A review of the Caisse's performance over the first five years of PQ governance, however, leads Stephen Brooks and Brian Tanguay to see only a broad coincidence between Caisse investments and government policy. They note that the share of Caisse investments in private enterprises never exceeded 20 percent. In those instances where the Caisse named representatives to boards of directors, moreover, it does not appear to have exerted control over their activities. Overall, "there is little evidence that the investment policy of that agency [the Caisse] is influenced in a direct and systematic way by the political project of the PQ government."[79]

The new management appointed by the PQ government in the late 1970s was, we believe, more responsive to government priorities. The new government certainly induced the Caisse to make several investment decisions. At the same time the distribution of Caisse investments and the limits on its equity investments suggest that the Caisse continues to act primarily as a fiduciary agent. The principals' own interpretations of their roles are clear. In the 1981 Caisse annual report Jean Campeau, newly appointed president by the Parti québécois government, explained that the Board of Directors of the Caisse had agreed to give greater priority to one of its original purposes—Quebec's economic development. To pursue this objective, the Caisse intended to increase the share of its investments going to Quebec-based companies and to target specific companies—judged "strategic"—where it would buy up blocks of shares to achieve a "substantial" holding. Campeau insisted that this reorientation of investment policy simply conformed to the Board of Directors' independent desire to reduce holdings in fixed-return debt instruments, which were no longer prudent in an inflationary economy.[80] For Jacques Parizeau, then minister of finance responsible for the Caisse, the investment agency "gradually evolved into the kind of lever that successive governments had looked for in a broad collection of Crown corporations." Although as minister he could not issue outright directives to the Caisse, his relations with the president were "special," with frequent informal exchanges of information. Whenever government policy and the Caisse's view of its mandate diverged, the directors of the Caisse prevailed. And yet, Parizeau wryly observes, "as their term of office expires . . . changes can be brought to bear."[81]

Two examples of the Caisse's new strategic investments cited by its president illustrate the market clout and increasing visibility that the state investment agency acquired.[82] When the government chooses to use the Caisse, as in the case of the natural gas industry, it has at its disposal a very powerful instrument of intervention. When the Caisse targets equity, as in the pulp and paper industry, it can pursue and win a hostile takeover bid, although at the cost of generating major controversy.

In December 1980 Gaz Métropolitain of Montreal, in which the Caisse was the largest shareholder, and Gaz Inter-Cité Québec, controlled by a Winnipeg company, each applied to the provincial regulatory board for the right to distribute natural gas in the province. The decision on allocations was delayed while, as the Quebec minister of natural resources later explained, the government put in place its energy-sector policy, which included state control over gas distribution. In the intervening months a shareholder's agreement was reached which enabled the Caisse to vote 56 percent of Gaz-Metro's shares even though technically it remained a 30 percent shareholder, as its legislation required. Shortly thereafter the state enterprise Soquip, responsible for oil and gas exploration, was authorized to purchase 20.2 percent of shares in Gaz-Metro and then make a takeover bid for rival Inter-Cité (where the Caisse also had a minority holding). As a result two state agencies, the Caisse and Soquip, acquired a combined controlling interest of 50.2 percent in each of the "rival" natural gas distributors.[83]

The most dramatic move by the Caisse was the takeover it coordinated with the SGF of Domtar, a giant pulp and paper corporation in 1981. Domtar ranked thirty-sixth among Canada's industrial corporations, with vertically integrated operations that ranged from sawmills to the production of fine papers. The Caisse had held over 20 percent of Domtar stocks for several years. In August 1981 a surprise announcement informed the public that the Caisse and the SGF held 22 percent and 20 percent of Domtar's stock respectively and had signed a shareholder's agreement to vote their combined 42 percent shareholding as a block. In consequence the Domtar board was being enlarged to permit the two state agencies to name directors who would also become members of the company's Executive Committee. The exact motives for the takeover remain unclear, but the government had designated pulp and paper as a priority sector; SGF had been counseled to anchor its operations in a major money-making investment to stabilize earnings; and, according to journalist rumor, the minister of finance had been outraged by Domtar's recent decision to move the headquarters of its salt-mining subsidiary outside Quebec.[84] The business community's reaction to the takeover was hostile, especially after hearings before the Ontario Securities Commission determined that the Caisse had bought up blocks of shares indirectly through trust companies and then had transferred them to SGF to avert negative reaction to a "state takeover." Minority shareholders were also aggrieved, because no public offer had been made. Debate over whether a state enterprise was obliged to file "insider reports" prompted the Quebec government to commit its corporations in future to respect established stock market practices, but the Securities Commission nonetheless barred the Caisse from trading on the Toronto Stock Exchange for over two years.[85]

The reorientation of the Caisse into an aggressive player in the marketplace shows that provincial governments, unlike the federal government, can target investments to shape industrial development. The response to the Caisse's activism, however, reveals political and ideological limits for the provincial government-as-investor, limits similar to those we saw in the Alberta Trust Fund case. In Quebec itself many considered that the Caisse had transgressed the boundaries of its mandate. Even the francophone business community, in theory the beneficiary of state policy, was ambivalent. According to a 1983 survey of senior officers of companies operating in Quebec, French-speaking executives overwhelmingly judged the Caisse to be insufficiently independent of government (81 percent said so) and were reluctant to see the Caisse engage in joint investments to take control of private companies. Although they deemed Caisse membership on a board of directors perfectly appropriate, only 23 percent considered it a good idea for the Caisse director to sit on a board's executive committee.[86]

Outside Quebec the Caisse's new high profile loosed a counter-reaction.[87] In particular, investigation into the Domtar case by the Ontario Securities Commission kept Caisse activities in the limelight, giving the business press plenty of occasion to articulate its opposition to state intervention. The president of Canadian Pacific, in which the Caisse had a 9 percent holding, was emboldened to refuse the Caisse's request for membership on his Board of Directors. He then lobbied the federal government to preclude what he argued would be state control of a pan-Canadian company in the interests of Quebec nationalist aims. Ottawa, motivated as much by an opportunity to assert federal powers over the expanding economic role of the provinces as by the need to comply to pressure from a powerful corporate sector, took up the cause by introducing Bill S-31, "An Act to Limit Shareholding in Certain Corporations." The specific prohibition proposed in this November 1982 bill was that "no government shall hold or beneficially own more than ten per cent of the shares of any class of shares of a corporation." To avoid the irony of such a proposal (the federal government itself, through the CDC, for example, had a multitude of such investments), a clause permitted the federal cabinet to make any exemptions it chose for individual companies or for classes of firms.[88]

In a detailed analysis of the Senate Committee testimony Allan Tupper identifies a coincidence of interests behind Bill S-31: "For corporations, the Bill provided a bulwark against provincial government influence in profitable, nationally significant firms. For the federal government, S-31 promised to curb provincial government investment strategies, enhance federal control over such strategies, and strengthen federal jurisdiction over transportation."[89] But the attempt by Ottawa to curtail the provincial governments' investments by way of S-31 inevitably failed. Extensive hearings unleashed two special interests that opposed the federal government's own role in the economy. First, corporate testimony attacked not just the Quebec government's strategy but state intervention in general. It called for the rollback of all government investments, Crown corporations, and regulatory interference in corporate affairs. Second, other provinces, regardless of the conservative ideology of some, unanimously denounced federal encroachment on the right of provincial governments to use whatever tools they might choose to invervene and direct regional economic development.[90] As for the Caisse itself, it may have avoided provocative takeovers since the debate over S-31, but the chairman's report in 1985 betrayed no intent to modify its role. On the contrary, given its growth, "the Caisse can now start to act effectively in the world of financial and industrial giants where billions are the measuring unit and fierce competition between enterprises and countries is now a standard strategy."[91]

CONCLUSION

Governments in Canada now have extensive investments in enterprises other than wholly owned corporations. For the federal government, despite its 1982 initiative in fashioning a state holding company (CDIC) reminiscent of European practice, the use of equity has not conformed to any explicit investment strategy. When economic recession created new exigencies calling for government intervention, investment—not outright ownership—appeared an attractive way to resolve the immediate problems faced by companies in crisis.

The autonomy of the provinces, on the other hand, allows some governments to devise development strategies and establish investment agencies to carry them out by channeling resources to targeted sectors or projects. Here the limits to state capitalism, which may be permissive or restrictive, are defined by a political dynamic. In Alberta, diminishing resource revenues generated pressures to divert funds away from investment toward immediate government expenditures. The provincial government now goes to the market primarily in search of a profit on its equity investments. In Quebec, those business interests offended by government's aggressive investment policy could appeal to other jurisdictions. At the same time the withdrawal of federal legislation to restrict provincial investment and the support afforded Quebec by other provincial governments shows that the nature of politics within the Canadian federal system may make the limits on the role of the state-as-investor very permissive indeed.

CHAPTER SEVEN

Collaborating with Private
Capital: Joint Ventures

The deepening recession of the late seventies and early eighties obliged policy makers, in Canada as elsewhere, to reassess the optimal ways to promote economic activity. Recession made collaboration with the private sector increasingly attractive to governments in search of investment capital, know-how, and new markets that might generate both revenue and employment. In joining forces with other investors governments in Canada have extended state capital into a variety of profitable industries and thereby altered established patterns of production and competition.

Joint ventures are a specific form of the mixed enterprise discussed in the previous chapter. They are partnerships not between individuals but between two or more entities—governments, state enterprises, private companies—to undertake a specific project or activity. The pooling of resources that occurs is *de nouveau*. Each of the partners has an equity participation in the venture which is not readily transferrable and thus a voice in policy, although actual management arrangements vary.[1] (We, of course, are principally interested in those joint ventures where the state collaborates with private capital whether Canadian or foreign.) Recourse to a joint venture implies that (1) there is a project or activity government wants to see carried out; (2) private-sector resources—capital, for example, or technical marketing or expertise—are required so that 100 percent state control is not feasible; and (3) factors exist that preclude the private enterprise from going it alone, whether these inhibitions stem from the perspective of the firm (high risk, for example) or of the government (e.g., national ownership targets).

The joint venture appeals to governments for several reasons. Participation in a joint venture looks to be an effective tool to promote economic development. Because investment capital is pooled, governments can spread their dollars across several projects and thus have a greater overall impact on economic activity within their jurisdiction than if they poured the same sums into a single state venture or diffused it through general incentive programs. Where risks are perceived to be high, as they so often are for resource development projects, government participation may induce private firms to invest in a given location or industry. By placing equity and gaining a voice in the running of companies together with experienced private-sector firms, governments expect to gain access to technical information, draw on proven technological capabilities, and in general better appreciate the operations of a particular industry. Finally, the government, through its established state enterprises, may take part in a joint venture to guarantee itself either a share of output or negotiated market shares.[2]

Joint ventures are not totally new in Canada. As early as 1978 economists at the Foreign Investment Review Agency (now Investment Canada) were observing a "rapid growth of joint ventures between foreign investors and Canadian governments or government corporations,"[3] and as our profile of state capitalism in Chapter 3 suggested, joint ventures by Crown corporations accounted for most cases of provincial government investment. In this chapter we explore three new developments that explain why in the 1980s the joint venture has become a prominent form of state capitalism. First, because provincial governments have remained reliant on the revenues generated by resource development and continued to depend in part on foreign capital and technology, established Crown corporations have expanded the scope of their joint ventures in the resource sector. Second, provincial governments that earlier had disclaimed any desire to intervene directly in production—such as Ontario and Nova Scotia—have set up new enterprises to undertake joint ventures, particularly in energy. Third, governments have made a new, albeit tentative, effort to act as venture capitalists by using joint ventures to promote new technologies. This chapter examines these three developments in turn.

Joint Ventures in the Resource Sector

Most joint ventures undertaken by the state in Canada cluster in the resource sector and involve provincial governments. This bias expresses the conditions that limit Canadian economic development—a weak manufacturing base that continues high reliance on resource exports, and a federal system wherein provincial governments focus their growth strategies on their regionally specific comparative advantage. Like the wholly owned state enterprises discussed in Chapter 5, joint ventures in the resource industries have been established primarily for purposes of province building—to stimulate exploration and development of mineral deposits which will, in turn, create jobs and generate revenues. A second related reason for their proliferation was the rise in oil prices and concerns for energy self-sufficiency. Although in the late 1960s Quebec created a state-owned energy venture, Société québécoise d'initiatives pétrolières (Soquip), as part of its explicitly nationalist development strategy, most other provinces would follow the Quebec example only in the late 1970s and early 1980s. The mandate of Nova Scotia Resources illustrates the dual purposes of province building and energy independence: the corporation is empowered to "propose, negotiate and manage" Nova Scotia's investments in petroleum, mineral, and energy projects to promote energy self-sufficiency. It should also "accelerate development" of the province's energy and mineral resources and "maximize benefits to Nova Scotians" from the exploitation of their resources.[4]

At the same time there are sector-specific reasons why the joint venture has become government's preferred vehicle for investing in resource industries. Even at the federal level the three Crown corporations that account for most joint ventures are all in the resource sector—Petro-Canada, Eldorado Nuclear, and the Cape Breton Development Corporation. Through its more than thirty subsidiaries Petro-Canada in particular has used joint ventures to do business.[5] The nature of risk, both economic and political, as perceived by large private corporations helps explain the increasing resource to joint ventures between state and private enterprises.

For mining multinationals, investment experience in newly independent Third World countries since the 1960s has made the joint venture both frequently unavoidable and accepted as an alternative to wholly owned subsidiaries. Thus, at a major conference on industry trends in 1980 the president of the American multinational Amax Inc. explained that joint ventures allowed his company "to benefit from the experience of our partners, reduce our financial exposure and reduce the potential political risk."[6] The same considerations motivate Canadian and foreign-owned firms to participate in joint resource ventures with governments: shared investments mean shared risks, which is particularly appealing because of the capital requirements of resource projects, the long time frames before returns may be realized on investments, and the economic and political uncertainties attendant on resource extraction. Moreover, the likelihood that mining companies will cooperate with provincial governments is very high, for the Canadian constitution attributes the ownership of natural resources to the provinces. The exploration permits issued by provincial governments thus control terms and conditions of entry.[7]

Joint ventures with governments are attractive to investors who must overcome regulatory barriers to foreign ownership. For example, the federal government imposed tight control over the uranium market during World War II because of the mineral's strategic importance and wrote this control into law in 1946. All uranium properties and plants must be owned by a company incorporated in Canada, and foreign equity in new uranium ventures is now limited to a maximum 33 percent.[8] Because these provisions for Canadian ownership must be satisfied before mining can begin, foreign-owned companies anxious to invest in uranium must find Canadian partners. As our discussion of the Saskatchewan Mining Development Corporation (SMDC) will reveal, foreign investors, both state and private, have joined the corporation in the search for and production of uranium.

Investment incentives may also induce private capital to seek state partners. To further the federal government's goal of 50 percent Canadian ownership and control of the country's oil and gas industry, announced in the 1981 National Energy Program (NEP), Ottawa instituted an exploration and development incentive program designed to favor firms with significant Canadian ownership. The NEP further restricted exploration permits for Canada Lands, those areas under federal jurisdiction including the Arctic islands and the offshore, to companies with at least 50 percent Canadian ownership.[9] To avail themselves of the NEP's tax provisions, many multinationals farmed out some of their lands to Canadian firms, including state-owned corporations, and formed new exploration partnerships, many of them with Crown corporations.

In sum, the joint venture has appeal to both the private sector and governments in Canada as a vehicle for investment in resource production. This section focuses primarily on the experiences of Saskatchewan and Quebec with joint ventures in the resource sector. It highlights *collaborative* relationships between private capital and government enterprises, which stand in marked constrast to the confrontational behavior of these same two provincial governments during their takeovers in the potash and asbestos industries analyzed in Chapter 5.

The Saskatchewan Mining Development Corporation, which operates one of the largest exploration programs for uranium and hard rock minerals in North America, was established in 1974 to engage in all phases of the mineral industry from exploration through to the development, production, and sale of all minerals found in Saskatchewan (except potash and sodium sulphate, both produced by other Crown corporations). SMDC was one of several wholly owned commercial corporations created by the New Democratic party (NDP) following its election in 1971.[10] Initially SMDC invited private corporations prospecting for uranium or other minerals to approach it to participate in joint ventures. Within a year voluntary participation had become compulsory. After March 1, 1975, all companies undertaking mineral exploration in Saskatchewan to the value of $10,000 or more in any one year were required to offer SMDC up to 50 percent of the project. Following the election of the Conservative government in the spring of 1982, mandatory state participation in all new mineral ventures ceased; nonetheless, SMDC has continued to play an active role in the province's mining industry.

Successive Saskatchewan governments dating back to the late 1940s recognized the potential of the uranium industry and were anxious to promote it both to diversify the province's resource base and to create a new source of revenue. The province offered a variety of development incentives, including road construction, loans, and prospecting grants, but the NDP government was dissatisfied with industry investment in uranium. The energy crisis of the early seventies generated concern about the province's energy supplies and increased the strategic value and price of uranium,[11] and in this context the private-sector reluctance to participate in the industry prompted government to search for new ways to encourage investment.

The immediate catalyst to the formation of SMDC was an offer made to the province by a group wishing to sell a one-third interest in a uranium project (an offer made after efforts to find another private-sector partner had come to naught). This project, then in the earliest exploration phases, would become the Key Lake uranium mine, now the world's largest producing uranium site. The province found the proposal attractive and created SMDC to take advantage of this specific opportunity as well as to promote the government's larger objectives in the uranium and mineral sectors. Crown reserves held heretofore by the Department of Mineral Resources and mineral properties acquired by the Department of Northern Saskatchewan under various provincial exploration programs were transferred to the new government enterprise. SMDC's purposes are quite clear: to sponsor and stimulate mining activity within Saskatchewan, to act as a window on the mining industry in general and on the uranium industry in particular, and to provide the province with a direct source of revenue from the exploitation of mineral resources.

Within a few years of its establishement SMDC had become a major player in the Saskatchewan mining industry, spending one of every three dollars for exploration in the province.[12] SMDC has concentrated on projects in areas of proven mineral deposits or with access to existing mining facilities. Its holdings represent approximately 40 percent of Saskatchewan's total known reserves of uranium. Among its properties is the Cigar Lake site, confirmed by exploration as the world's largest high-grade uranium ore body.[13] This project, an international joint venture with French and Japanese investors in which SMDC is the majority partner, reputedly has ores many times richer than those of average uranium mines and the capacity to become even more productive than Key Lake.[14] SMDC's exploration and development have, in the words of its board chairman, placed "Saskatchewan firmly on the international stage as a world-class developer and exporter of another high-quality resource."[15] In a decade the corporation had a 50 percent share in the world's largest producing uranium mine, significant ownership of another producing site, and various interests in uranium reserves in Saskatchewan. SMDC now produces 6.5 percent of the Western world's annual output of uranium.[16]

SMDC's major producing investments in the uranium sector are in two mines, Key Lake and Cluff Lake. Both now extract, refine, and market "yellowcake" (semiprocessed uranium). The Key Lake mine is a joint venture between SMDC (50 percent ownership), Germany's Uranerz Exploration and Mining (33.33 percent), and Eldor Resources, a subsidiary of the federal Crown corporation Eldorado Nuclear (16.67 percent). As an equity partner, SMDC contributed proportionally to complete exploration, determine the feasibility of mine construction, and bring the mine into production—costs that totaled more than $500 million.[17] In the Cluff Lake mine SMDC holds a 20 percent interest, which it purchased in 1979 for $66.9 million from Amok, a French-owned mining firm.[18] Because the Cluff Lake project had started before SMDC was authorized to make joint venturing mandatory, and because the legislation did not allow for back-in participation, the state entity could join the venture only through a buy-in. The mine is operated by Amok. Participation at Cluff Lake attracted SMDC for several reasons: it would provide SMDC with experience with a producing mine, experience that would be useful with respect to the Key Lake project (then in an earlier stage of development); participation would allow SMDC to diversify its sources of uranium, enabling the corporation to offer its customers greater security of supply; it would further permit SMDC to gain experience in the marketing of uranium; and finally, as a matter of principle SMDC wanted a part of all operating uranium sites and certainly the new and promising Cluff Lake mine.[19]

SMDC's partners over the years have been many and varied, including Canadian and foreign firms as well as other state enterprises. As we have seen, the federal government is a partner with SMDC in the Key Lake mine as well as in ongoing exploration projects, through Eldorado Nuclear. French, German, and other European investors have been active joint venturers with SMDC almost from the outset; Japan is a more recent participant in the uranium sector. Some of these foreign companies are owned wholly or in part by their government: Cogema Canada is a subsidiary of the French Atomic Energy Commission, Uranerz Exploration and Mining is a subsidiary of Uranerz-Bonn of West Germany, and AGIP Canada is controlled by the Italian state. Participation with SMDC allows foreign entities, whether state or private, to comply with established provincial government and federal restrictions with respect to foreign ownership of uranium ventures. It also ensures these countries secure, long-term supplies of ore for their nuclear generators, now an increasingly important source of electric energy.

SMDC has, in recent years, farmed out some of its uranium and other mineral projects to Canadian and non-Canadian investors. From SMDC's perspective, farmouts of uranium properties to foreign utilities were particularly encouraging since they demonstrated both the utilities' long-term commitment to nuclear power and their confidence in SMDC as a secure source of supply.[20] Although some private-sector mining companies initially expressed reservations about a government-owned company, their relationship to SMDC has seen much less conflict than that between the Saskatchewan government and private companies in the potash industry. The reasons behind successful collaboration include the relatively less developed stage of the uranium industry; the availability of capital from SMDC, which reduced partners' explorations costs; and the involvement of foreign-owned companies that were themselves either state-owned or accustomed to dealing with state enterprises.[21]

SMDC began to generate revenue for the province when it sold its first yellowcake in 1981.[22] Through the end of 1985 the government corporation had paid dividends of $18 million on net earnings of $46.3 million. In addition, over the same period SMDC paid provincial royalties and taxes of $12.6 million. These sums as yet represent only a small return on the province's very substantial investment. However, such mines as Key Lake and Cluff Lake are expected to generate considerable revenue for Saskatchewan over their lifetimes. Most of SMDC's sales, on its own or by its joint venture partners, are to foreign, among them American, utilities on long-term contracts.[23] These long-term contracts help insulate the corporation from fluctuations on the spot market for uranium. Nonetheless, a recently soft market for ore has had an adverse effect on earnings. Although nuclear power accounts for a growing percentage of the world's electricity generation, the uranium industry currently suffers from overproduction and high inventories.[24]

As a holding company with a wide mandate, SMDC has been able to shift its activities over time, thereby helping diversify the province's economic base. During the early years when uranium exploration in Saskatchewan was extensive and joint venturing compulsory, SMDC concentrated exploration dollars on uranium and participated in over 250 joint ventures. It was also the sole operator of a number of uranium exploration projects. The cessation of compulsory joint venturing in 1982 coincided with a weakening in international uranium markets and a concomitant change in SMDC's level of exploration. The corporation then narrowed the focus of its investments, reducing the number of its uranium joint ventures to fewer than thirty so as to concentrate on projects with the greatest development potential.[25] Recognizing that diversification was and would continue to be essential for a successful mining company and to hedge against the continuing decline in the uranium sector, moreover, SMDC began to devote a larger percentage of its total exploration budget to develop base and precious metals, not only in Saskatchewan but also in Manitoba and British Columbia.[26] Although it is now corporate policy to concentrate only on intraprovincial exploration and development (extraprovincial ventures have ceased), some of these investments were made because SMDC's partners in uranium ventures approached the corporation to participate with them in other mining activities.[27] Among SMDC's current partners in its efforts to diversify are companies with which it already has investments in uranium. Of more than thirty non-uranium joint ventures in which SMDC is involved, the most promising are in gold. SMDC expects its joint ventures to produce the company's first gold in 1987.[28]

From among Quebec's many state enterprises empowered to undertake joint ventures with private capital, we have selected two in mining and petroleum, Société québécoise d'exploration minière (Soquem) and Soquip, for discussion.[29] Both companies were established during the 1960s as part of the government's policy to enhance the public sector's role within the Quebec economy and to increase the participation of francophones in key industries. In the eyes of the Quebec government, collaboration with private capital in the high-risk mining and oil and gas sectors became ever more attractive as a way to exploit provincial development opportunities in the 1970s, following the energy crisis. The federal government's National Energy Program offered inducements to non-Canadian companies to join with provincial enterprises such as Soquip to benefit from the Petroleum Incentives Program (PIP) grants. In the provincial government's view, financing of projects through joint ventures would promote Quebec-based private enterprise, thus increasing provincial value added and local employment in a manner that did not involve massive amounts of government funds. More immediately, participation with private-sector partners would subject provincial government enterprises to the discipline of the bottom line, a significant attraction in circumstances of fiscal restraint.[30]

The charter of Soquem, a wholly owned state enterprise established by special act of Quebec's National Assembly, authorized it to carry out mining exploration by all methods and to prospect for, develop, mine, and process all mineral substances (except iron ore and asbestos). The corporation is enjoined to be profitable.[31] Soquem can undertake exploration on its own or in partnership with the private sector. In a recent five-year-period, 1981–85, Soquem was engaged in 147 exploration projects; 51 or approximately 35 percent were undertaken jointly. For the first three years of the period, Soquem's partners contributed close to 25 percent of exploration expenses incurred on these projects. In the 1984–85 exploration year, however, their contribution rose to 70.7 percent, reflecting the success of the state enterprise in attracting investment funds into the mining sector.[32] Soquem can and does embark on research and exploration on its own. To move beyond exploration, however, Soquem must form partnerships.[33] In effect, although Soquem may cover a greater proportion, if not all, of exploration costs on a mining site, development costs are shared.

Soquem's investments in production are more diverse than those of SMDC. They are also on a smaller scale, with the bulk of their output sold in North America. Soquem owns an interest in five operating mines; three extract gold, the fourth niobium, and the corporation has become the sole owner of a fifth, producing commercial rock salt. The gold mines, all joint ventures with Canadian mining companies, have been producing for some years and, despite fluctuating international prices for the metal, have been profitable, making a significant contribution to Soquem's overall financial position. Niobec Inc., the only North American producer of niobium (columbium), a metal used in the manufacture of steel, is a joint venture between Soquem and the Teck Corporation. Soquem discovered the mineral deposit near St. Honoré in the Saguenay–Lac Saint-Jean region of Quebec in 1968, and the mine became operational some eight years later. Its partner, Teck, is a Canadian-controlled company with approximately 20 percent of its shares held by Metallgesellschaft of West Germany.[34] This joint venture supplies about 15 percent of the world's columbium requirements, all in the form of concentrates, and is the world's second-largest producer of the commodity.

Although Soquem is directed to develop minerals deposits only in concert with private-sector partners, its experience testifies to the evolutionary character of joint ventures. Arrangements that begin as joint ventures sometimes evolve into wholly owned undertakings and then as the state undertakes partial divestment, subsequently may assume mixed enterprise status again. Soquem's Mines Seleine Inc., a mine producing rock salt, illustrates such changes in corporate ownership. It began as a joint venture, but Soquem acquired all of the assets following difficulties among the partners. The salt mine's poor financial performance led to an unsuccessful attempt by Soquem to sell all or a portion of the mine's shares. The public offering of Cambior's shares (discussed below) raised enough money to clear Mines Seleine's debt. At time of writing Soquem continues to operate the mine.[35] The history of a Soquem subsidiary, Société Minière Louvem Inc., is similar. Created in 1968 as a joint venture to develop copper and later zinc deposits, the partnership did not last. Soquem became the sole owner of Louven, which produced copper until 1975. Since then Louvem has explored and evaluated ores in various parts of Quebec, concentrating on the search for gold. In 1984, to obtain additional working capital, Soquem was authorized to sell some of its mining properties in northern Quebec to Louvem and permit the subsidiary to go public through a stock offering. Soquem's share of Louvem stood at 34 percent at the end of 1986. With the monies obtained through the share offering Louvem was able to embark on new exploration and development.[36]

In addition to establishing partnerships to develop mineral deposits, Soquem has been permitted to purchase shares in operating mining companies and thereby both intensify its participation in mining exploration and encourage Quebecers' entrepreneurship in the resource industry. Between 1980 and 1984 Soquem, through its wholly owned subsidiary Soquemines, bought 32.7 percent of the capital stock of the Sullivan Mining Group of Montreal, a company active in the production of nonferrous and precious metals in Quebec and elsewhere, and 34 percent of the stock of Odyno Minière Inc. It also created Resources Aiguebelle Inc. in conjunction with local prospectors to develop gold and limestone deposits.[37] As a result of its diverse exploration and production activities, Soquem has collaborated with more than twenty partners, the vast majority of them privately owned Canadian enterprises. Included are some of the largest Canadian mining companies, such as Noranda, Falconbridge Copper Corporation, and the International Nickel Company of Canada, as well as enterprises owned by other governments and smaller Quebec-based companies.

Overall, Soquem has, despite the statutory injunction to make a profit, acted to underwrite exploration by large corporations and to recapitalize small Quebec-based companies. Because it has given priority to exploration activities intended to promote new development in the province, Soquem, unlike SMDC and Soquip, registered substantial deficits on operations over the five years ending in 1985. For a provincial government deeply concerned about budget deficits, this poor financial performance generated questions about Soquem's future. Soquem was among the first Crown corporations designated by the Liberal government (elected in December 1985) for sale, although the company was not to be privatized totally. A new subsidiary, Cambior, was formed to take over

Soquem's most attractive mining assets (i.e., excluding the money-losing rock salt mine) and to offer 69 percent of its shares to the public, thereby becoming a mixed enterprise. The sale raised sufficient funds to retire Soquem's debt. Soquem will retain its 31.8 percent interest in Cambior and continue as a government-owned mining exploration company.[38]

Soquip, the first wholly state-owned oil company in North America, was established by the Quebec government in late 1969 and began its operations in January 1970. Its purpose was to explore for oil and gas in Quebec in order to reduce the province's dependence on offshore energy supplies. (At that juncture Quebec met some 75 percent of its energy needs by oil, 80 percent of it imported from Venezuela and the Middle East.) Although its charter gave Soquip a mandate that encompassed all facets of the petroleum industry—exploration, production, refining, and distribution—the Quebec government made it clear that Soquip's priorities would lie in exploration. Like Soquem, Soquip could move beyond exploration only in collaboration with the private sector.[39] Soquip's legislative mandate stipulated that the company should undertake joint ventures with other corporations or individual investors but that such ventures, as well as any share purchases, would require government authorization.[40] Exploration was to be undertaken wherever possible in partnership with companies already active in the petroleum sector.

For the first few years of its existence Soquip concentrated on the search for oil and natural gas in Quebec, until it became clear that an important energy discovery within the province was improbable. In fact, Soquip's extensive efforts resulted in only one discovery of natural gas in commercial quantities, not far from Quebec City. For this reason Soquip diversified its exploration activities both within Canada and offshore. In the words of a leading Quebec cabinet minister, Bernard Landry, "I'm not saying we've abandoned our search for gas or leases held in Quebec, but Soquip, which is mandated to explore for hydrocarbons, is simply looking for a good investment."[41] As a result, the corporation's Quebec-centered operations have come to focus primarily on research and development with respect to natural gas, for example, the promotion of natural gas as a vehicle fuel and new techniques for transporting and storing gas.[42]

In September 1980 the Parti québécois government enunciated a new energy policy for Quebec. One key element was a broadened mandate for Soquip. The original legislation was amended in 1981 to empower the agency "on a profit-making basis to purchase, import, transport, cause to be refined, market or sell hydrocarbons."[43] With a considerable increase in its working capital Soquip diversified. It moved into natural gas distribution by acquiring a majority interest jointly with the Caisse de dépôt et placement du Québec in Gaz Métropolitain and Gaz Inter-Cité

Québec Inc. in March 1981. It also started offshore exploration in Hudson Bay and off the east coast of Canada. Exploration and production in western Canada and exploration in the estuary and gulf of St. Lawrence were also intensified. These activities were undertaken in partnership with other investors "in order to combine resources and expertise, share risks and give the Company more scope than if it acted independently." Within five years of receiving this new mandate Soquip was describing itself as "a diversified [energy] company" that together with "its associates [has] assets of more than $1 billion."[44]

By heavy extraprovincial investment in energy Soquip has acquired oil and gas properties that will guarantee the company's attractiveness to the private sector as a potential joint venture partner. Through its subsidiary Soquip Alberta, created in 1984, the government enterprise engaged in exploration for and production of conventional oil and natual gas in the four western provinces and the Northwest Territories but primarily in Alberta. Soquip's partners in western Canada include Dome Petroleum and some smaller Canadian oil companies. Soquip obtained its initial gas removal permit from the Alberta government in 1983; this has been amended in subsequent years to enable the company to send natural gas to new markets in Quebec. Together with its partners, Soquip now supplies some 12 percent of natural gas consumed in Quebec.[45] To augment its Albertan stores of natural gas, Soquip purchased the Canadian assets of the Denver-based Sundance Oil Company in December 1984, after having quietly acquired a 10 percent share through private deals. These assets it then transferred to its Alberta subsidiary.[46] The Sundance acquisition increased Soquip Alberta's landholdings and gave the government company knowledge of and the opportunity to participate in much of the expected exploration activity in western Canada. Soquip Alberta has now become "a medium-sized oil company" whether one gauges size in terms of production or of revenue.[47]

Petroleum exploration off the east coast of Canada became a Soquip priority once the area's hydrocarbon potential was confirmed in 1979. Soquip's strategy was to take up positions in regions that had the most promising prospects and were most likely, over the medium and longer term, to add substantially to the enterprises's oil and gas reserves. To achieve this objective, in 1983 Soquip formed a joint venture, PAREX, with two other companies, Aberford Resources and Denison Mines, both Canadian-controlled companies with some foreign shareholders; each participant owns an equal share in PAREX.[48] Because PAREX had a high degree of Canadian ownership, it was eligible for petroleum incentive grants provided by the federal government under its Petroleum Incentives Program. Again federalism influenced state capitalism as federal legislation made it both attractive for private-sector companies to seek state partners and economically feasible for state corporations to participate in costly exploration ventures. Indeed, Soquip, through its subsidiary Exploration Soquip Inc., proved to be the seventh-largest recipient of PIP grants.[49] Beyond its own exploration PAREX signed farm-in agreements with companies already engaged in offshore exploration to enable it to participate in areas where drilling was under way. Among the companies linked with PAREX are Petro-Canada, Bow Valley Industries of Calgary (a major Canadian oil and gas firm), and Esso Resources Canada.[50] With the decline in oil prices and the March 31, 1986, termination of the Petroleum Incentives Program, Soquem and its partners in PAREX are concentrating their activities in areas where discoveries have already been made and undertaking only that drilling required by farm-in agreements.[51]

Despite uncertainties in the energy market, Soquip and its subsidiaries continued to diversify. To augment revenues derived from crude oil, in 1985 Soquip Alberta helped establish CanPet Marketing, a company whose purpose is to market crude oil and natural gas liquids in North America on behalf of independent oil producers. In early 1986 Soquip and three partners, including Gaz Métropolitain, formed the Soligaz consortium to explore the feasibility of, and later construct, a natural gas liquids fractionation plant in Montreal, which would supply markets in Quebec, eastern Canada, and possibly the northeastern United States. The project would also help maintain and further develop Montreal as a petrochemical center. Finally, through a 1985 agreement with Petro-Canada to provide technical assistance to Morocco's oil sector, Soquip has moved into financially remunerative international consulting and training.[52]

Quebec's Soquem and Soquip provide a contrast in terms of size and degree of internationalization, yet both illustrate the importance of joint ventures as a means of attracting investment capital when government revenues are limited. Established to promote the development of Quebec's fuel and nonfuel mineral resources, both companies have participated in joint ventures with large numbers of partners, private-sector and state, thereby injecting millions of dollars into the Quebec economy directly through exploration and development expenditures and commodity sales and indirectly through revenues from oil and gas sales. Whereas Soquem has concentrated on the search for base and precious metals within Quebec and has remained a province-centered enterprise, Soquip, its mandate enhanced under Quebec's energy policy, has gone beyond the regional economy to become a significant player in the national oil and gas sector. The purpose is provincial, but (like Hydro-

Québec, discussed in Chapter 3), the mandate has come to be defined in terms of extensive extraprovincial activities undertaken primarily, but not solely, in conjunction with other investors.

New Energy Ventures

Quebec created corporations and joint ventures as part of a long-standing commitment to use the state to further development. Other provincial governments were prompted by the new exigencies of the energy crisis and the new incentives of the National Energy Program to look to joint ventures despite their traditional preference for market solutions. Provincial investments in the energy sector reveal three significant features of Canadian state capitalism in the 1980s: the state is determined to participate in major resource industries and will collaborate with a variety of partners to achieve its ends; provincial governments have structured their energy corporations to take advantage of federal incentive programs and to comply with federal regulations; and private capital has been prepared to accommodate itself to government partners to accord with legal regimes and ensure eligibility for exploration grants. Two examples, Nova Scotia Resources and the Ontario Energy Corporation, demonstrate how new realities in the energy field galvanized governments to become direct investors by way of provincially owned holding companies.

Nova Scotia Resources Ltd. (NSRL), created in 1981 as part of that province's energy plan for the eighties, is empowered "to acquire and manage, *in partnership with the private sector*, participating interests in projects to develop petroleum, energy and minerals and related industrial activities." Directed to operate under "private sector rules," the company is to seek investments that will have a positive impact on Nova Scotia's industrial development, achieve a balanced and reliable cash flow from diverse sources, and acquire technological expertise that will enhance provincial capabilities.[53] Since its inception NSRL, alone or through its subsidiaries and affiliated companies, has engaged in offshore exploratory ventures and established for itself an asset position in the significant oil and gas fields off the provincial coast. Gas produced offshore was intended for both Canada and the United States—in 1985 NSRL and its partners in the Venture Gas Project applied for permission to export gas to the northeastern U.S. market.[54] Among NSRL's partners in exploration are major firms in the Canadian petroleum industry such as Shell Canada, Mobil Oil, and Petro-Canada. To conduct its offshore oil and gas activities NSRL, like Soquip, established a taxable subsidiary that was eligible for and received PIP grants from the federal government covering as much as 80 percent of its exploration expenditures on Canada Lands.[55] With the termination of PIP, Nova Scotia Resources is seeking alternative financing to permit it to continue its exploration and develop promising offshore hydrocarbon sites.[56]

In addition to its exploration interests Nova Scotia Resources formed a joint venture with TransCanada Pipelines to design, construct, and operate a natural gas pipeline from the offshore (Sable Island) gas fields to potential markets in Canada and an export point on the Maine border. The conditions under which the joint venture was established illustrate the aggressiveness of governments with respect to participation in the energy sector: although NSRL holds 50 percent of the nominal shares in the new gas transportation company, Sable Gas Systems, its partner is responsible for funding all activities up through completion of the necessary regulatory hearings that precede the granting of permission for pipeline construction and operation; should NSRL exercise its option to acquire up to one-half of the equity of the Sable Gas Systems it would then, upon project certification, reimburse its venture partner for its share of precertification costs.[57]

Although its major focus has been on hydrocarbons, NSRL has diversified to include coal production and the search for gold and other minerals. Novaco, established in 1970 as a Crown corporation to extract coal, became a subsidiary of NSRL in 1982 and operated a coal mine until 1985. Since then it has restricted its activities to land reclamation and the evaluation of further coal production. Through its subsidiary Canadian Offshore Resources Ltd., itself a joint venture established with Inco in 1983, NSRL agreed in 1984 to participate in its first on-land activity—a province-wide mineral exploration consortium, SCOMINEX. SCOMINEX, managed by Inco, is committed to expend a minimum of $3 million on mineral exploration over the years 1985 to 1987, primarily, though not solely, on prospecting for gold.[58]

Finally, like many state enterprises in the resource industries, Nova Scotia Resources combined the search for energy sources with sophisticated research and development. Its first activity, in fact, was participation (with a 19.5 percent interest) in a consortium, Scotia Coal Synfuels, to examine the technical and economic feasibility of liquefying Nova Scotian coal. Consortium members included two federal enterprises, Cape Breton Development Corporation and Petro-Canada, and two senior private-sector companies in the Canadian petroleum industry, Gulf Canada and Nova Corporation. Close to half the costs of the consortium's research were borne by a fund set up jointly by the Canadian federal and provincial governments (the Federal/Provincial Oil Substitution Fund) to underwrite the search for alternative energy sources.[59]

As Canada's most populous and industrialized province, Ontario is a major consumer of energy, most of it imported from outside the province. When energy prices rose dramatically in the 1970s, Ontarians felt the change. To pursue secure sources of energy for the future the province, under a Conservative party that downplayed direct involvement of government in the economy, established the Ontario Energy Corporation (OEC) in 1975. Mandated to cooperate with the private sector to explore for new energy sources and to invest in energy-related (including conservation) technology, the OEC grew into a major actor on both sides of the energy equation. A decade after its establishment the OEC had assets of over $700 million and twenty-four investments (of which twenty-three were with private-sector partners) in energy technology and oil and gas explorations.[60] The bulk of these assets were accounted for by the company's 1981 purchase of a 25 percent interest in Suncor Inc., the Canadian subsidiary of Sun Co. Inc. of Radnor, Pennsylvania. The decision to acquire this interest generated enormous controversy within the province, and within the Conservative party, over the reasons for the purchase, the cost of the shares, and the public policy effectiveness of a minority interest in the company.[61] Both partners saw advantages in the government's investment in Suncor; it gave OEC a "window" on the oil industry as well as a stake in an integrated petroleum company, and it allowed Suncor to become sufficiently "Canadian" to qualify for federal incentive payments that would help defray the costs of exploration on frontier and offshore territory.[62] By creating a taxable subsidiary (Ontario Energy Resources) to hold its share of Suncor, the Ontario government enterprise enabled Suncor to tap federal grants.

Through a subsidiary, Onexco Oil and Gas, the Ontario Energy Corporation took part in exploration and development of energy fields at sites in western Canada and southern Ontario. In 1985 Onexco participated with various Canadian oil and gas companies in eighty-one wells, of which forty-three were completed as discoveries.[63] Frontier exploration, its major exploration focus, was carried on through Trillium Exploration Corporation, a joint venture established in 1982 and owned by Onexco (66.67 percent) and Suncor Inc. (33.33 percent). Once again the forming of a joint venture accommodated the interest of both parties: Suncor wished to supplement its Canadianization, already under way, to take maximum advantage of federal PIP funds and thereby to continue the high level of exploration on lands it owned in the frontier areas; OEC wanted to enhance its holdings in Suncor as well as to support directly the search for new oil and gas sources in Canada.[64]

Trillium participated in drilling in almost every frontier area—the Arctic islands, the Beaufort Sea, and the Northwest Territories, as well as offshore Nova Scotia and offshore Newfoundland. Although Trillium's working interest in many of these exploration sites was small, it managed to negotiate farm-in agreements with leaseholders that included Esso Resources Canada, Chevron Resources Canada, Shell, Suncor Inc., and Petro-Canada.[65] In 1984 Trillium purchased a 5 percent equity interest in Panarctic Oils, thus gaining a share of that company's drilling program as well as its oil and gas reserves in the Arctic.[66] Because Trillium and, therefore, Ontario Energy Corporation were heavily dependent on federal incentive payments to defray exploration costs (Trillium recovered the maximum 80 percent of the $75 million it spent on exploration in 1984 and 1985), the announced termination of the Petroleum Incentives Program rendered future frontier exploration uncertain. A change of government in Ontario in May 1985 occasioned a reexamination of OEC's role and a decision to dispose of the company's assets.[67] At the same time the government recognized the difficulty of withdrawing from the industry, particularly from frontier energy investments. Trillium's strategy had been to focus drilling expenditures on reserves that could be developed into producing wells within five to ten years.[68] Depressed oil prices at the end of 1986 made it unlikely that the government would find buyers for its conventional oil holdings. As a result OEC's subsidiaries will probably survive, at least for the short term.

The extensive provincial investment in fuel and nonfuel mineral joint ventures suggests that this new mode of state investment in production has held a substantial attraction in the 1980s for both government and private-sector partners.[69] Joint venturing in the resource sector is by no means the sole focus of current state participation with private capital, however. The state as venture capitalist has also spread the risks of development for private capital by creating state enterprises to promote new industries, particularly those involving high technology.

THE STATE AS VENTURE CAPITALIST

As part of the effort to stimulate particular sectors and to promote new industries able to compete in the changing international division of labor, provincial governments moved to equity participation in nonresource industries. Many provincial development corporations were established in the 1960s to attract private investment through public relations and, more important, by making debt capital available on favorable terms. The new provincial enterprises, by contrast, are more directive from the outset, frequently demanding from corporations they assist financially both an equity position and representation on the Board of Directors. Although the Liberal provincial government decided in its first year of office, 1986, to privatize its high-technology ventures, Ontario's experiences illustrate both the opportunities for, and the difficulties in state promotion of "sunrise" sectors. We first discuss the Ontario Energy Corporation's venture capital subsidiary, Ontario Energy Ventures (OEV), because it was one way in which Ontario moved from the energy sector into sunrise high-technology areas.

Ontario Energy Corporation's investments in energy research and technological development numbered seventeen at the end of 1984 and were focused in five priority areas: energy from waste, energy management, enhanced oil recovery technology, oil substitution, and transportation. Many were joint ventures, whereas others took a more traditional form, underwriting private-sector research and development through loans. OEV's partners were diverse, including Ontario-based companies, an Alberta venture capital fund, and American and Canadian oil and gas companies (among them Panarctic Oil and Petro-Canada).[70] Although most of OEV's investments were in the development stage when the Ontario government decided to wind down the activities of its parent company, Ontario Energy, some had developed a reputation for innovation—for example, in the transit industry and in computer technology. With the 1986 decision Ontario Energy Ventures began to rationalize its investment portfolio and divest itself of investments.[71]

The province of Ontario created two other corporations that invested in high-technology industries through joint ventures or on their own, the IDEA Corporation (Innovation Development for Employment Advancement) and the Urban Transportation Development Corporation (UTDC). The legislation creating the IDEA Corporation in 1981 enunciated three major objectives: to promote technological innovation by involving universities, research groups, individual inventors, and private corporations from all regions of Ontario; to bring together the research capabilities of the public sector with those of the private sector; and to enhance economic growth and employment throughout Ontario.[72] To fulfill this mandate IDEA was to target government capital for joint investments in two ways: *preventure capital,* in which IDEA would provide equity capital to research projects in very early stages to help them to the point where other investors might participate; and *venture capital pools,* in which IDEA would participate with other investors to establish a significant venture capital group prepared to invest in technological innovations at more mature stages of development.[73]

IDEA Corporation had an Ontario government commitment of $107 million in funding over the five-year period ending in 1987, with expectations of becoming financially self-sustaining thereafter.[74] Monies were expended through five specifically designated and incorporated technology funds (biological and medical, chemical and process, information, machine and automation, and microelectronics) as well as through two other funds, the IDEA Research Investment Fund Inc. for projects at a very early stage of commercial development and the IDEA Innovation Fund Inc. for investment in projects that the technology funds could not easily accommodate. The five technology funds were designed to be attractive to pension funds, insurance companies, and other capital pools that had not yet invested heavily in innovation and that would be prepared to work with a government agency. Through partnerships with diverse investors the enterprise aimed to maximize the number of potential investments through a careful distribution of government funds. In this way IDEA Corporation could obtain considerable leverage in the marketplace and link its investments with the financial community. In return for its investments, meanwhile, the IDEA Research Investment Fund could acquire full or part ownership of the research or participate in licensing or other arrangements to obtain a return on its monies.[75]

A review of IDEA's short record confirms that the pursuit of growth through investment in innovation is uncertain and requires a long time frame for a return on capital. IDEA's chairman recognized this, noting in the corporation's annual report that "encouraging new ideas and building commercial successes from them is no easy task."[76] IDEA provided seed monies to investors and participated in venture capital funds; by 1986 it had made some fifty-eight investments, thirty-seven in new firms and twenty-one in other innovations, ranging from software to hardware, from medicine and pharmaceuticals to microelectronic companies, for a total commitment of $41.5 million.[77]

More controversial than its direct investment in precommercial technology was IDEA's participation in venture capital pools. IDEA made financial commitments to three syndicated ventures through its specific technology funds and was joined in two of these investments by such Canadian capital sources as pension funds, life insurance companies, and banks.[78] In theory the corporation's participation in capital pools was to enhance opportunities for technological innovation, but in practice this was not always the case. Questionable investments together with criticisms of corporate style led the Liberal government to reexamine the corporation's activities and decide to phase it out in 1986.[79] In announcing this decision the Ontario treasurer noted "that while the original concept of providing preventure capital to accelerate the development of technology-based innovation was valid, the IDEA Corporation has proved to be an inappropriate vehicle to deliver these services to the public."[80]

Less industrialized provinces that attempt to follow the same techniques to promote innovation face rather different problems. In 1983 the Alberta Heritage Savings Trust Fund was directed to finance a new venture capital company, Vencap, to encourage private initiative and thereby assist the province to move beyond its resource dependence. A $200 million loan from the fund made Vencap the largest venture capital company in Canada. Vencap has a nine-member Board of Directors composed entirely of businesspeople and can issue shares to the public. Although it has turned a profit on its investments, Vencap's true entrepreneurial activity has been limited—just four joint ventures with private investors as of early 1985 and eighteen by the end of the year. In this case the obstacles that hinder development through joint ventures appear to be structural rather than ideological: the small population and fragile industrial economic base of Alberta do not bring forward many viable proposals for funding over Vencap's minimum $1 million capitalization.[81] Vencap has begun looking beyond Alberta for investments, provided these will "enhance the economic future of Alberta."[82]

In contrast to the relatively small-scale efforts of IDEA Corporation and Vencap to promote high technology through joint ventures was Ontario's UTDC, which by 1985 ranked 268th in terms of sales and 240th in terms of assets on the *Financial Post* list of the largest Canadian industrial corporations. In a decade UTDC had become a vertically integrated enterprise capable of undertaking the complete range of activities related to the design, development, testing, manufacture, and sale of mass transit systems. In its memorandum of understanding the Ontario government exhorted the corporation to "operate in a totally commercial manner including technical development and sale of transit products" and indicated that it might "compete in both the Canadian domestic and international marketplace."[83]

The establishment of UTDC in 1973 coincided with a new provincial transportation policy for Ontario which emphasized mass transit over automobiles.[84] Having opted for public transport, the government of Ontario undertook to ensure that research and development of transportation technology would unfold in a way linking the state and private sectors. Speaking at the official opening of the UTDC Transit Development Centre in September 1978, James Snow, Ontario's minister of transportation and communications, recognized that the costs associated with new transportation technology were such that private capital was unwilling to incur them without significant government assistance: "The private sector in Canada is capable but often too limited to venture into development and commercial production of advanced technology unaided by an equal commitment from the governments."[85] UTDC's objectives—which included the establishment of a research and development capacity in Canada so that "there would be domestic production facilities for Canadian municipalities" and the exploration and marketing of "the results of the R&D programs through the private sector in Canada"—

reflected this linkage between public and private sectors as well as the importance of ensuring production within Canada.[86]

The corporation's early activities concentrated heavily on research and development of pioneering rapid transit technology, including a magnetic levitation transit system acquired by licence from a West German firm and design of small rapid transit vehicles running on guideways and powered by linear induction motors. UTDC then shifted focus somewhat, stressing the sale of more commonplace transit equipment and systems such as street and subway cars while continuing its research into new technology. Rather than design systems and vehicles that relied totally on new and thus untested technology, UTDC emphasized upgrading the quality and operating performance of existing technology. The corporation also reoriented its marketing efforts to sell entire systems rather than replacement vehicles.[87]

Although UTDC began life as a wholly owned enterprise, its corporate structure eventually included four wholly owned subsidiaries, two joint ventures, and their respective subsidiaries. Of particular interest here are the joint ventures linking the state and private capital. One, Rail-Trans Industries of Canada, a joint venture between UTDC and Hawker Siddley Canada Inc., became the vehicle-producing facility of the UTDC group. Established in 1984, this company purchased the assets of Hawker Siddley's train and streetcar plant as well as shares in the plant previously created by UTDC to manufacture and assemble light rapid transit vehicles. With this joint venture UTDC acquired the capacity to produce both light rail vehicles and heavier equipment used for commuter traffic and subway systems. RailTrans itself participated in joint ventures, joining with one private-sector competitor to bid on new trains for Canada's rail passanger system and with a second to produce a new model of streetcar.[88] UTDC's second joint venture, Metro Canada International Ltd. (MCIL), formed in 1982, linked the Ontario government enterprise with a Canadian engineering company with worldwide experience, Lavalin Inc. (which would buy UTDC in 1986). MCIL's mandate was to market products and services that ranged from planning and feasibility studies to complete turnkey transit systems on the Pacific Rim. MCIL concentrated on China and Thailand, assisting UTDC to form joint ventures with Chinese companies to bid on projects.[89] Though not a joint venture, UTDC's American subsidiary, UTDC (USA) Inc., warrants mention because the variety of its activities in the United States since it was established in 1980 underlines the relative speed with which the corporation began to expand its horizons and became internationally competitive. UTDC (USA) had contracts to provide transit systems and/or street and subway cars for a number of American cities and has also participated in joint ventures with U.S. firms to bid on transportation contracts.[90]

UTDC appeared to be a profitable enterprise for the government of Ontario, with revenues in 1985 of $251.4 million, assets of $22.7 million, retained earnings of $21.7 million and long-term sales contracts of $1 billion.[91] The provincial Liberals' decision to privatize rekindled debate over the wisdom of a government high-technology enterprise and its ability to translate innovations into commercial success.[92] UTDC was in fact able to generate new technology in the transportation sector but encountered difficulties in completing projects and securing markets in a highly competitive international environment. The corporation's president saw little choice but to expand into manufacturing and contracting: "We couldn't commercialize the technology without taking responsibility for it."[93] Private companies were prepared neither to take the risks of production nor to provide the performance bonds required by transportation system buyers. When UTDC was sold to Lavalin Inc., the Ontario government retained 15 percent ownership of the corporation and a 25 percent share in future pretax profits. The province also agreed to retain responsibility for completion of seven previously negotiated contracts, some of which may not be profitable.[94]

The UTDC case suggests that the provincial government-as-investor can enter a new industry and use the know-how acquired through joint ventures to extend into new markets. Other governments have been less successful, however, as a federal government corporation created to promote the commercialization of new technologies in the energy sector shows. Here, in attempting to play a venture capitalist role, the state provoked so many objections about unfair competition that Ottawa chose to dissolve the company.

In 1980 the federal government, as part of its National Energy Program, established a new Crown corporation, Canertech, to provide financing, including equity, to companies developing alternative energy (e.g., solar) or conservation technology.[95] Petro-Canada, the state-owned oil company, was directed to incorporate a subsidiary, which the government intended to purchase at cost once it was bringing in revenues and then set up as an autonomous state enterprise. Twenty million dollars capitalized Canertech.[96] Enthusiastic management quickly engaged Canertech in investments and joint ventures, many through its subsidiary Canercom. For example, the state company took a majority position in Mechron Engineering Products, which installed energy-efficient electrical generating systems, and a minority share in Pacific Enercon, a British Columbia insulation manufacturer; and it combined with Ontario's OEC in a joint venture, Omnifuel, to develop wood gasification technology.[97]

Although the government in its National Energy Policy UpDate paper, highlighted Canertech's role and recapitalized the company with another $35 million in 1984, Canertech provoked objections from companies not chosen as potential winners and from competing companies that claimed unfair competition. In response, Canertech's president made a forthright appeal to business logic: "If we are to fulfill our mandate to commercialize innovative technology and expand the market for innovative products and processes, it seems to me that competition is inherent."[98] The political heat was turned on, however, when the consultancy engineering association submitted a brief to the federal government, objecting particularly to the selective financing offered by Canercom's joint ventures. Moreover, a lawsuit in Alberta charged unfair competition with a local mineral wool insulation company. Once falling oil prices diminished the urgency of alternative energy development, and in the face of bureaucrats' dislike for the high-flying but money-losing proposals of Canertech's management, the minister of finance appointed a new chairman of the board to report directly to him on the company's operations. The likely outcome became a certainty with the election of a Conservative government in 1984—Petro-Canada was directed in December to dissolve Canertech.[99]

CONCLUSION

Collaboration rather than competition with private capital is the norm for joint ventures, because both the state and the private sector expect to benefit from partnership. Joint ventures have proved to be a flexible method of investment, allowing the state in Canada to participate in fuel and nonfuel mineral extraction as well as in sunrise or high-tech industries, all in the pursuit of economic development. At the same time, partnerships with the private sector are not always successful, and the state may find itself in full possession of a company it once owned only partially or withdrawing from a joint venture that has become unattractive or controversial. The experiences of Ontario and the federal government suggest that state investment in high technology can engender difficulties that make the venture too costly to retain. It is this dynamic character of joint ventures, particularly as such ventures are normally undertaken indirectly by Crown corporations, which makes them an attractive way for government to intervene. Project-specific investments can be made, incentives can be proffered to a large number of private companies, and divestment can be undertaken or monies written off without the same political visibility and without recourse to the bureaucratic procedures that tend to constrain the wholly owned Crown corporation.

For the private investor, joint ventures are often appealing because they permit the sharing of risk; but there is also an element of necessity involved, because often in Canada companies find themselves with no alternative to partnership with government. Statist interests frequently dictate the terms of joint ventures, as we have seen in this chapter. In the case of the uranium exploration and development in Saskatchewan, for example, both federal restrictions with respect to ownership of uranium mines and provincial mining regulations compelled companies to seek out joint ventures with the state. Similarly, the federal government's National Energy Program made joint venturing unavoidable for non-Canadian oil and gas companies that wanted access to Petroleum Incentives Program grants. In effect, the NEP served statist objectives at two levels of government, because the program reduced the costs for provincial governments to enter or to become more active in the energy sector. Thus the interplay of federal priorities and provincial interests combined to oblige and entice capital to join with the state in exploration and production. The NEP example, however, also shows that some of the incentives for joint ventures are time-bound—PIP grants were based on the assumption of rising oil prices and were phased out after 1986. Again, the joint venture format is appealing precisely because it permits the state to get into or out of activities rapidly in response to changing markets.

The activities of the state-as-investor and the state-as-joint-venturer make it clear that state capitalism in Canada extends well beyond the wholly owned state enterprise. Once recession and budgetary constraints had pushed governments in Canada and Europe to look beyond Keynesian political economy, many governments also began to question the scale of their commitment to the state enterprise sector. It is quite logical to expect state investment to focus increasingly on vehicles other than the traditional public enterprise, which ties up large sums of state capital and which often faces statutory limits on activities and investments. The new direction for state capitalism points, rather, to more flexible forms of investment. Governments will intervene in production through holding companies, subsidiaries, joint ventures, and mixed enterprises, which they create not only by buying into private concerns but also, and increasingly, by the partial sale of shares in state enterprises.

CHAPTER EIGHT

Looking Ahead:
State Capitalism in Question

The challenge for our closing chapter is to consider the evolution of state capitalism. By the 1980s the expanded role of the state as producer and investor in competitive industries was being challenged by new political coalitions engaged in a broader debate about the viability of the Keynesian welfare state. We can see this reexamination of the state in business as part of a search for an economic strategy that might rekindle growth and recapture international competitiveness. In Canada the election of a Conservative government in 1984 introduced a policy of privatization inspired by neoconservative principles (business rather than government must be the engine of investment) and backed up by pragmatic assessments (tight budgets no longer permit the subsidization of money-losing public enterprises). But in comparative perspective it becomes evident that in Canada, as in most West European countries, privatization serves not to dismantle the public enterprise sector but to rationalize state holdings.

Whether motivated by ideology as in Britain, Germany, and Holland, or obligated by fiscal constraints as in Italy, Sweden, and Spain, governments in Europe have announced they will "denationalize," "privatize," or "rationalize" their corporate holdings.[1] Immediately following its election in 1979 the British Conservative government led by Margaret Thatcher proclaimed its intent, within a monetarist economic policy, to "reduce the extent of nationalized and state ownership and increase competition by providing offers of sale." In Germany the return to power of the Christian Democrats brought promises to reduce the role of the state in industry and a list of privatization candidates. In Holland an interministerial commission presented a sweeping privatization plan to the government in 1985. Social democratic governments, although continuing to reject denationalization in principle, nonetheless encouraged their state holding companies to divest. The Italian government appointed a new chairman in 1983 to reorient IRI, and thirteen state companies were permitted to issue shares on the stock market. Spain's socialist government, after two years in power, instructed its holding company, INI, to get the state out of industries that could not survive in international competition—"The stance INI is taking is that of seller."[2]

In this universal search for policies to overcome recession in the highly competitive world economy of the 1980s, the most extreme positions, which we examine in detail as alternative models, were taken by Britain and France. The Thatcher and Mitterrand governments propounded diametrically opposed doctrines on the proper balance between public and private sectors and on the feasibility of using state enterprises to promote industrial development. Their concerted efforts to put these doctrines into practice attracted international attention and shaped debate elsewhere over the role of the state. Our analysis of nationalization in France and privatization in Britain—what were the policy proposals and how far could governments go in implementing them?—defines the outer boundaries of state capitalism in the mixed economy.

THE FRENCH EXPERIENCE

When the French left swept to power in May–June 1981 after the election of a socialist president, François Mitterrand, and a Socialist party majority in the National Assembly, they brought with them a long-promised program of nationalization. Shortly after the formation of a Socialist-Communist coalition government the prime minister put forward draft legislation to extend state control to the large industrial groups and banks first targeted in the Common Program that had bound the two parties together in 1972.[3] With the final passage of the Nationalization Law on February 11, 1982, Mitterrand repaid a political debt and demonstrated his ideological rigor. The French president also consolidated the most significant public enterprise sector in Western Europe, a sector that his government promised to use as the cutting edge of an industrial strategy to bring France out of economic recession.[4]

By its nationalization law the French state acquired 100 percent ownership (with compensation) of thirty-nine banks, two financial institutions, and five major industrial groups. Included in the industrial groups were France's top-ranking companies in electrical equipment, chemicals, glass, and aluminum.[5] In addition, through a series of negotiations with individual companies the Socialist government extended state control to several strategic sectors. It acquired a 51 percent ownership position in two privately held, highly successful French companies in the defense field—Matra (armaments) and Dassault (military aircraft)[6]—and took control of the subsidiaries of three foreign multinationals in computers, pharmaceuticals, and telecommunications.[7] Finally, in the steel industry, conversion of government loans to Usinor and Sacilor, responsible for 80 percent of French production, had already made the state a minority shareholder; the Socialist government merely continued the process, becoming a majority owner.[8]

These acquisitions not only expanded the size of the French public sector but shifted the composition of the government's corporate holdings in favor of competitive, high-tech industries. In some sectors nationalization introduced the state-as-producer for the first time. Thus state ownership jumped from a nonexistent to a significant share of industry turnover in synthetic textiles (75 percent); office automation and data processing (35 percent); industrial glass (35 percent); and electrical equipment (26 percent).[9] The expanded role of the state in industry is truly impressive when we recognize that after 1982 the government controlled thirteen of France's twenty leading industrial groups, representing half of the country's largest enterprises (those with more than 2,000 employees). State enterprises accounted for half of all research and development expenditures by French firms. Many French state enterprises were already engaged in international competition, notably in energy, aeronautics, and automobiles, and the new nationalizations dramatically reinforced this trend. The five industrial groups nationalized in 1982 were diversified, competitive corporations with multinational operations. Typically, the St Gobain group controlled some 105 companies in France or abroad, with industrial plants in seventeen countries, and marketed its products in more than a hundred countries.[10]

The new French government sought to center its public enterprises in an industrial policy intended not simply to spur investment but to direct it into those activities which would recapture international competitiveness. After nearly a decade of recession, with private-sector investment in decline, French industry's shares of both home and world markets were shrinking. In defending nationalization before the National Assembly, government speakers made it clear that economic recovery was the overriding objective of Socialist industrial policy.[11] The new "industrial public sector" would provide a powerful policy instrument. Government intended to direct nationalized firms to invest so that French industry would reconquer the domestic market; generate spinoffs for private industry by subcontracting in France; and become centers of technological innovation. A secondary objective was to set a new standard in industrial relations, including mechanisms for worker participation in a companion Law on Democratization.[12]

Letters of instruction sent to the chief executives of all newly nationalized industries in 1982 specified responsibility for advancing these industrial policy objectives. After assuring the executives that they had complete autonomy to pursue their company's best interests, as long as they respected the broad lines of government policy, the minister of industry charged: "You will look first for economic efficiency by continually improving your competitiveness." In so doing, he insisted, "the usual criteria for management of industrial enterprises apply." That is, the government expected that all activities would result in "normal rates of return to capital invested." Only then were the firms asked to set an example in industrial relations by promoting information sharing, safety, and retraining. Overall, the letters concluded, company strategy "should contribute to reaching the three principal objectives of the government's industrial policy," which are "job creation . . . modernization through renewed investment . . . [and] long-term viability of French industry in home and international markets through innovation and enhanced competitiveness."[13]

France, after two years of Socialist government, presented an extreme case of state capitalism both in terms of the extent of state control and in terms of the purposiveness of policy. Could policy makers carry through their ambitious program? Ultimately, of course, the limit to their success was the election of a center-right coalition in 1986 committed to reprivatization. Yet it is the Socialists' own modifications to their ambitious plans to use state enterprises as policy instruments which reveal the limits of state capitalism in the mixed economy.

The Socialist government attacked its principal objective—to restructure industry and restore France's competitiveness—by executing a series of sector plans. The result was an impressive rationalization and realignment of activities among firms in the steel, chemicals, nonferrous metals, electronics, shipbuilding, and machine tool industries.[14] State-owned enterprises were the dominant players in the first four sectors. An equally complex restructuring had taken place under the Pompidou government in the late 1960s and early 1970s, but now the government used its position as shareholder to promote or in some cases impose rationalization. Despite an announced policy of restraint for the 1983 budget year, the minister of industry, Pierre Chevènement, convinced his cabinet colleagues to contribute capital to the nationalized industries after having extracted agreement from the eleven major state enterprises, in their new "plan contracts," to make the requested investment or divestment decision.[15] St Gobain, for example, was forced to give up its electronics interests in favor of Thomson. The state-owned steel companies were obliged to take on some of the steelmaking operations of

Creusot Loire when the government bailed out of this major French private enterprise.[16]

The state in France was clearly not a passive shareholder but sought to use its extensive corporate holdings to implement an industrial policy that would rationalize and modernize French industry.[17] The Socialist government's ambitions for its nationalized industries, however, changed radically during 1983 and 1984. Three factors coalesced to induce the Mitterrand government to abandon dirigisme in its approach to the industrial public sector and adopt a hands-off "business logic": the international political economy, budget restraint, and elections. The change in approach to nationalized industries derived from a shift in France's macroeconomic policy away from a neo-Keynesian expansionary strategy to a full-scale austerity program after March 1983. Because of the high U.S. dollar, high interest rates, and continued recession, France could not go it alone while its European partners were pursuing deflationary policies. Faced with a ballooning deficit and public debt, as well as a deteriorating balance of trade and payments, the government was forced to devalue the French franc three times. The third devaluation coincided with losses for the Socialists in municipal elections, and Mitterrand adopted the austerity measures being promoted by his more conservative ministers.[18]

With new economic policy priorities, the approach to nationalized industries had to change. If the budget deficit and public borrowings were to be reduced, the share of government expenditures going to the public-sector enterprises could not continue to rise—they were already up from 4.8 percent in 1980 to 6.9 percent in 1982.[19] A large portion of the subsidies went to the older public enterprise sector. Indeed, nearly two-thirds went to the state railways (SNCF) and the coal mines, and half of that was just to cover the costs of pension funds. These hard-core expenditures made it all the more important to turn the commercial enterprises around. Yet the two state steel companies alone sucked in half of the new capital contributed by the government—capital that appeared to be investment but in fact made up for losses. Overall, the self-financing capability of the industrial public sector was declining rapidly, dropping from 45.4 percent to 16 percent over 1981–82. Worse from the point of view of a balance of payments policy that aimed to strengthen the French franc, much of the borrowing by public-sector enterprises was in international currencies, 50 percent or more of the debt held by the SNCF, Air France, and the Atomic Energy Commission (CEA).[20] Recessionary conditions could be blamed, because the earnings of private industry were also undercut. But when 1982 results showed only one of the newly nationalized groups with positive returns, the business press mocked the government's strategy, asking "how to invest when you're propping up 425 billion [francs] in debts?"[21]

In October 1983 Prime Minister Laurent Fabius formally set before Parliament the new orientation for state-owned enterprises. He explained that there was no point in going back over the original goals of nationalization. The urgent questions was whether these enterprises should be used for illusory defensive purposes, such as retaining a declining industry, or for an offensive long-term strategy to restore France's international competitiveness? The government had chosen: it would confirm its commitment to the second strategy. Two consequences followed. First, in the competitive sectors the government abandoned a statist industrial policy. The prime minister enjoined industrial groups to do whatever it took to get out of the red, to balance their books by 1985—a deadline that indicated the belief that financial returns reaped election returns. The government intended, according to Fabius, to respect the fundamental prerequisite for corporate success in the marketplace, "managerial autonomy." Second, in the declining sectors, such as steel, the answer was to abandon job creation or protection in favor of maintaining a "global level of employment" across the industry and terminating noncompetitive product lines.[22]

The application of business logic to the industrial public sector in France may be illustrated in different areas: government controls, investment, divestment, joint ventures, and financing. A regime of government controls created a tight network of information and personnel linking the older nationalized companies and the ministries, but from the outset, the newly nationalized industries were excluded by law from this regime. No state financial comptroller sat in industry offices or attended board meetings, nor were budgets submitted to government. The "plan contract" being a multiyear document, few actions require government authorization in the interim unless a company seeks state subsidies. In the area of investment, all French firms, private or state, required ministerial approval for overseas investment above a specified amount. But no controls were exercised over the reinvestment of funds generated abroad. Yet by 1983 each of the newly nationalized groups had at least 50 percent of turnover from sales abroad. Management, therefore, had much discretion to locate investment according to the company's worldwide strategy.[23]

What of the divestment decision—could a Socialist government permit the transfer of public assets to private hands? Legally only the parent companies of the five industrial conglomerates had been nationalized (to avoid the costs and delays that lawsuits in many countries could have entailed). Yet the Constitutional Court had determined in 1978 that subsidiaries of public enterprises constituted public assets and could not be disposed of without government approval. Recognizing that such strictures were unacceptable for competitive companies, the government turned a blind eye to divestments undertaken in the normal course of business. It prepared a *Loi de respiration* ("breathing law") to legalize what had become standard practice. Thus in 1984 Pechiney sold forty of its plants and offices in the United States and used the proceeds to construct a new smelter in Canada. Meanwhile St Gobain's plastics subsidiary sold its subsidiary to a private French company. Although nationalism had colored the Socialist industrial policy, initially the state-owned industrial groups in fact pursued the cross-investments and joint ventures now typical of leading international firms in order to appropriate new technologies and spread the risks of innovation. By no means were foreign partners always excluded. For example, Rhône Poulenc's subsidiary in agrichemicals went in 50-50 with a small U.S. corporation to create a genetics engineering company; CEA's investment subsidiary took a minority interest in a new venture controlled by the Norwegian state-owned group Norsk Hydro to produce plastic optical fibers.[24]

To keep the state budget under control, the government had to find alternative means of investment financing for its nationalized industries. A new category of shares was legislated, the "titre participatif," which in effect was a preferred share conferring no ownership rights but entitling the holder to a fixed dividend on half the sum invested and a variable return on the other half. Well before the electoral defeat of the Socialist government, Renault and four of the five industrial groups nationalized in 1982 had issued these shares both to state banks and to the general public. Some state enterprises went further. St Gobain consolidated seven subsidiaries under the aegis of one, St Gobain Emballage, and offered 15 percent interest to the public through the stock market.[25]

These modifications of economic strategy and of government's relationship to the public enterprises provoked cries of betrayal from the left and gleeful calls for denationalization from the right. Increasingly on the political defensive, the Socialist government allowed the minister of industry to disclaim any fixed "religion" on nationalization, suggesting that the state could conceivably reduce its role in business.[26] The way in which the industrial public sector was managed in France after 1983 suggests that business is politics in liberal polities; even socialists in power had to adapt their industrial policy to economic and fiscal constraints as the pincers of political pressure were closing from left and right. They opted for business-as-usual and by so doing allowed the conservative alliance victorious in the March 1986 elections to put privatization at the center of its program of economic liberalization. Despite some procedural tussles with President Mitterrand and initial doubts as to whether the French stock exchange could absorb large flotations, by year end 1986 the Chirac government had taken several striking initiatives, notably general legislation that authorized the sale not just of recently nationalized firms but of sixty-five state-owned banks and companies.[27]

Our aim is not to speculate on the future of privatization in France but to look back at the Socialist program of nationalization as an indicator of the outer boundaries of state ownership in competitive industries.[28] The real story, it seems to us, is not so much about dogmas as about a necessary reconciliation between state capitalism in a mixed economy and the exigencies of international competition and international finance. The nature of the enterprises nationalized in 1982—industrial conglomerates fully involved in internationalized networks of production, trade, and finance—made this reconciliation inevitable.

The British Experience

Britain in the 1980s presents a state capitalism in sharp contrast to that of France under the Socialists. The Thatcher government has demonstrated that the state in capitalist society can radically reduce its role as producer and investor in industry. As Whitehall described it, "in 1979 the UK Government embarked on an ambitious program of returning state-owned corporations to the private sector. Privatization, as this policy is known, ranks among the most radical reforms of the UK's economic and industrial structure since 1945." Although pragmatic considerations such as reducing public-sector borrowing requirements certainly made such divestments attractive, the expanding scope of British privatization policy derived from a neoconservative ideology that rejects the premise that state intervention is required to ensure investment and growth. Here, the Thatcher government claimed, its experience offers a model for others: "Though many features of the UK scene are unique, the reasons for privatization are likely to be the same, whatever a country's experiences: the desire to increase competitiveness and efficiency; and the belief that the powers of the free market place can achieve this better than state control."[29]

That a Conservative party in Britain should proclaim denationalization central to its electoral program is scarcely surprising. Since the war the alternation of political power between the Labour and Conservative parties has meant an oscillation of rhetoric, promoting nationalization and denationalization respectively. Two developments, however, *were* surprising. First, the Thatcher government carried out its threat to denationalize, selling off state assets to an extent unprecedented under any previous Conservative government. Since the reversal of Labour's decision to nationalize steel in the 1950s, Conservative party rhetoric had usually given way to realpolitik. Thus despite election promises, Edward Heath's Conservative government (1970–74) sold only some minor state holdings in the travel business and indeed nationalized a major industrial corporation, Rolls Royce. Second, the Thatcher government turned from a reactive concept, "denationalization"—the undoing of what the opposition had nationalized—to an open-ended, programmatic concept, "privatization," which made the sale of public enterprises part of a grand strategy to recast the balance of public and private power in Britain.

Within its first three years in office the Thatcher government had introduced twelve pieces of legislation which either sanctioned the sale of state holdings in commercial enterprises or liberalized their statutory monopolies to permit progressive privatization. The first targets were companies in competitive industries which had been nationalized during the 1970s, often under the direction of the Labour government's creation, the National Enterprise Board. The government sold the NEB's holdings in some thirteen enterprises, including its 25 percent interest in International Computers, its half-interest in Ferranti (electrical engineering), and its 24 percent interest in the British Sugar Corporation. Shares in some directly held corporations were issued to the public while the government retained a major interest— thus ownership in British Aerospace, nationalized over bitter Conservative objections three years earlier, and Cable & Wireless, the international telecommunications company, was reduced from 100 percent to just under 50 percent. Other companies were sold outright, among them the National Freight Co. (road haulage) and Amersham International (radiochemicals). Where poor performance precluded immediate sale, as for British Leyland, British Rail, and British Steel, revisions to legislation permitted disposal of some activities—such as the hotels and laundries run by British Rail— and encouraged joint ventures.[30]

Impressive as this list may appear, these denationalizations alone could scarcely have made Britain into an alternative model of state capitalism. Rather, they streamlined its industrial public sector—getting rid of dubious ventures, bringing in instant cash, and demonstrating the government's ideological rigor while a controlling state interest was retained in major corporations. The Conservatives' legislative agenda, however, went much further. It proposed the eventual sale, after restructuring, of companies in the energy and transportation sectors, which European governments usually deem strategic, and the liberalization of state monopoly in such service industries as telephones and gas distribution, which are elsewhere presumed sacrosanct to the public and hence untouchable by elected politicians.

Proposals are one thing, implementation another. Yet despite major debates in Parliament and some embarrassing snags in the marketplace, most of the proposals were implemented once the Conservative government was reelected with a massive majority in 1983. State ownership in British Petroleum was reduced to 32 percent; the North Sea oil production and exploration interests of BNOC were hived off and a majority of the shares sold; and the North Sea interests of the British Gas Corporation were totally divested. British Airways and the transport docks were transformed into public companies, and both eventually sold. The government legislated an end to the monopolies on gas sales by the British Gas Corp. and on the provision of telephone services and equipment by British Telecom. The critical test of investor acceptance of privatization was passed in 1984, when the largest share issue in British history—some U.S. $6 billion for shares in Telecom—was well oversubscribed. After this turning point the government could put forward the sale of British Gas Corp. and other public services such as the water authorities. Furthermore, partial privatizations were completed as, for example, the government sold its remaining shares in British Aerospace. By the close of its second term in 1987 the Thatcher government had dismantled much of the public enterprise sector, both traditional and competitive, built up in Britain since World War II.[31]

From the outset Conservative party ideologues drew a causal connection between privatization and Britain's economic decline. No one disagreed on secular trends. Not only was Britain affected by the Europe-wide process of deindustrialization as the share of employment in manufacturing fell dramatically after 1970, but productivity gains did not compensate for the fall. The share of overall output for which manufacturing accounted actually dropped. The dramatic decline in Britain's share of trade in world manufacturers and its deteriorating balance of trade had of course much to do with the end of empire, but at the same time foreign manufactures increased their penetration of the home market.[32]

The neoconservative analysis of economic decline, however, came closer to a political vendetta than a strategy. Sir Keith Joseph, perhaps the minister initially most closely identified with Thatcher, diagnosed the "poisons" responsible for economic decline: "High state spending crowds out enterprise and threatens freedom"; "high direct taxation coupled with egalitarianism . . . encourages the lazy"; nationalization precludes profitability because companies have "immunity from fear of bankruptcy."[33] Besides this ideological-symbolic motivation for denationalization—show a commitment to "get the state out of business"—the Conservatives put forward another, purely pragmatic purpose. The first sales were rationalized primarily on the grounds that unacceptable budget deficits and consequent public-sector borrowing levels could be reduced by bringing in cash from asset sales and by placing the new mixed enterprises in the public accounts category of "private sector." So, for example, when the chancellor of the exchequer pledged to cut state borrowing in two, he foresaw half the savings from reduced spending and the other half from selling corporate assets.[34]

After reelection in 1983 the Conservatives ridiculed their critics. "We are accused," said minister John Moore, "of sacrificing the nation's assets . . . of selling the family silver to pay current debts. Nothing could be further from the truth. The Government's privatization strategy is justified on economic and business criteria. . . . If the present momentum is maintained, it will help provide a remedy for some of the ills that have beset UK industrial performance in recent years." The accelerating pace of denationalization expressed the political momentum of the Thatcher team once experience demonstrated it could be done and that the vague slogans of neoconservatism could be forged into an internally consistent ideology centered around the concept of privatization. "Privatization," as Moore, minister responsible for the program, explained, "is a key element of the Government's economic strategy. It will lead to a fundamental shift in the balance between the public and private sectors."[35] Four components of the privatization program were intended to free productive assets from bureaucratic constraints and reintroduce competition in key sectors of the economy. Denationalization or the sale of corporate assets was only one; the others were contracting out services to private firms, transferring some government services to the private sector (while introducing user fees for services still provided by the state), and liberalizing former monopolies.[36] British observers see the expanding scope of privatization policy, from reactive denationalizations to strategic pretensions, as inseparable from the crisis of the Keynesian welfare state in Britain. Privatization was part of a shift in Conservative party thinking as "its adherence to the post-war Keynesian interventionist consensus had been successfully challenged by monetarism and by the revival of support for the free market as a more reliable instrument than elected governments for securing economic goals."[37]

In seeking to substitute its free market culture for Keynesianism, the government added a populist appeal in 1984 to its earlier rationales for privatization. The appeal was to an "impossible dream, a "people's capital market." The influx of some two million new investors enticed by the privatization of British Telecom set off this new theme, which served both to divert attention from drastic unemployment levels and to preempt Labour calls for renationalization at the next election.[38] Decrying the undue influence of financial institutions that held large blocks of shares, the government asked people to join the "new army of capitalists" mobilized to create a truly "free enterprise culture." In some instances the government went over the heads of Labour's traditional support, the large trade unions, and offered preferential terms for share purchases to workers in nationalized industries. In the case of Telecom, despite a union call to boycott the offer, over 200,000 employees purchased shares.[39]

At first glance the only limit to privatization seems to be that final arbiter, the next election.[40] Britain under Thatcher is an extreme case of the state-as-capitalist withdrawing from its role as producer and investor in industry. Yet the government did confront two limits to full-scale privatization: the external constraint of the marketplace, and the self-defined limit set by strategic interests. Marketplace constraints on privatization stem first from the simple fact that as vendor the state has to attract a buyer. In the manufacturing sector, notably the state-owned companies for steel, automobiles, shipbuilding, and aircraft engines, structural deficits made it implausible to privatize immediately. The government in each case appointed new chief executives whom it instructed to turn the companies around, regardless of lay-offs. In 1986 British Steel, for example, achieved its first profit since 1975, but only after relentless cutbacks; the company had 54,000 employees, compared to 228,000 a decade earlier. In restructuring the companies managers were permitted to hive off certain activities and focus on profit centers while continuing to benefit from government investment financing. Thus in 1984 British Leyland, the state-owned automobile company, made its first operating profit in four years and its luxury car subsidiary, Jaguar, could therefore be fully privatized.[41] (Ironically, the Conservative government has demonstrated that the state can run companies according to business norms even though it has castigated public-sector enterprises as inherently bureaucratic and inefficient.) In some sectors, particularly energy, where companies were profitable, buyers became discouraged by changing market conditions that diminished the attractiveness of the government's offer. In 1982, for example, the attempt to sell 51 percent of Britoil flopped when news that Saudi Arabia might undercut current prices brought all oil stock prices down. London underwriters rather than the government were left with the one-third of shares unsold.[42] In all such cases marketplace constraints in effect delayed rather than aborted privatization projects, but time is not an inexhaustible resource for elected governments.

Another feature of the marketplace, that anyone is in principle free to enter, sets the second limit on privatization: the recognition of national interests that require some state control over market forces. In the case of British Leyland, when first Ford and then General Motors came forward as prospective purchasers in winter 1986, strong objections from Tory backbenchers to a foreign takeover obliged the government to pull back from its original terms of sale. New conditions, such as a minority ownership ceiling for the profitable Land Rover division and guarantees of British content, scuttled the deal.[43] In tendering its offer to sell 100 percent of Enterprise Oil, a highly profitable company that had spun off the North Sea oil activities of state-owned British Gas Corp., the government stipulated special conditions from the outset. The company should remain "independent", that is, have widely dispersed ownership rather than come under the control of special interests. To ensure this independence the government held onto one special share, allowing it to veto any takeover attempt until 1988, and the prospectus precluded any buyer's taking up more than 49 percent of shares. When Rio Tinto Zinc (RTZ), a multinational resource giant based in the United Kingdom, bid for 49 percent, the energy secretary exercised the government's special rights by restricting RTZ to a 10 percent holding, much to the chagrin of city investment brokers who were stuck with an undersubscribed issue.[44]

In fact, many "privatized" companies are, like Enterprise Oil, subject to government directives or, more often, prohibitions, usually exercised through the mechanism of a special or "golden" share. The official explanation for golden shares is that "to secure matters of essential national interest . . . the Government has retained specific powers over the future ownership or control or conduct of a privatized company."[45] The golden share does not represent any equity ownership but is a purely political means of intervention in corporate decision making on stipulated issues. In the cases of Amersham International, Cable & Wireless, and Jaguar the articles of association prevent any single investor or investment group from controlling over 15 percent of equity, while the government's veto power through its golden shares ensures no revision to the articles. In the case of Sealink, the channel ferries previously operated by British Rail, the sale to a subsidiary of an American firm became acceptable only after the government specified that its golden share would impel the company to put its ships at the service of the British government should war break out. As for British Aerospace, foreign ownership was limited to 15 percent in the first round of privatization in 1981. At the time of full privatization in 1985 government retained a special share to maintain this foreign ownership ceiling as well as the nationality of directors (who must be British citizens). It also claimed the right to appoint one director because of Britain's commitment to its European partners in the Airbus consortium.[46] Such decisions to assert control in specified areas suggest political limits to the complete withdrawal of the state from production. Even a neoconservative government in capitalist society retains statist interests that may require direct intervention in corporate decision making.

NEW DIRECTIONS FOR STATE CAPITALISM

In the British and French experiences we see two alternative models for the future of state capitalism. Mitterrandism presents a social democratic option: extend the competitive public enterprise sector to maximize state direction over industrial deveopment. Thatcherism, on the other hand, is a neoconservative option: privatize public enterprises, even traditional monopolies, to minimize direct state intervention in favor of private-sector initiative. We use the term "model" in a qualified manner, since neither case could readily be replicated. The determination with which the two governments put their respective nationalization and privatization programs into practice derived from nationally specific constellations of political factors and the idiosyncratic personal qualities of the leaders. Nonetheless, France and Britain indicate the frontiers of state capitalism—just how far the state can go in assuming the function of producer in competitive industries or in retracting its direct investment in production.

The French experience demonstrates that even after the state undertakes extensive nationalization of successful firms in leading sectors, its ability to achieve industrial policy objectives remains circumscribed by an international system of production, trade, and finance. Moreover, the imperatives of budget management and electoral survival preclude the spending of scarce state funds on purely social objectives without regard for commercial returns. This Socialist government saw itself obliged to observe "sound business principles" by cutting back subsidies to money-losing enterprises, closing down uneconomic plants, downplaying job protection, and allowing managers to invest or divest principally on the criterion of international competitiveness. The familiar dilemma of social democratic regimes in a capitalist economy reemerged, much exacerbated by internationalization of production: the Socialist government in France stabilized the economy while losing crucial political support from the left. Other social democratic governments, in fact, have not sought to imitate the French. Rather than extend state ownership, they have tried to adapt their established public enterprise sectors to the exigencies of fiscal restraint and a changing international division of labor.

In socialist Spain the state holding company, INI, undertook 17 percent of the country's total industrial investment in the early 1980s through its majority interest in 66 firms and controlling interest in another 187 companies with 642 affiliates. The high losses and heavy indebtness of many state enterprises inspired the hard-line stance that INI's chairman took after 1982. A rationalization program has since streamlined operations. It aimed first at getting out of traditional sectors unable to meet international competition—steel, textiles, shipbuilding, ball bearings—or converting plants to concentrate on more specialized products. Union militancy forced compromises, as in shipbuilding where closures had to be staggered and conversion to ship repair work tried in order to preserve jobs. The second objective of rationalization in Spain was to promote industries presumed able to compete, such as electronics, by way of technology transfer agreements and joint ventures. Financing through foreign equity participation is now encouraged. At the same time the government has not desisted entirely from extending state capital. It recently nationalized Spain's power grid, but it did so by creating a state-controlled holding company with participation by private firms.[47]

The reorientation of Italy's state holding companies has likewise focused on international competitiveness and profitability. The losses incurred by IRI's more than six hundred companies and the consequent demands on the state budget prompted a turnaround. Adopted in 1982, this strategy aimed at reducing losses, rationalizing operations of noncompetitive industries, and bringing in private-sector funding. IRI explained to failing companies that "the era of rescues is past. We have neither the resources nor the desire to take them on."[48] The state has cut back on losers, especially in the steel industry where some plants were closed and the overall work force reduced. Although companies have been sold, however, full-scale privatization is not the point. Making money *is*, as for the thirteen state companies authorized to offer shares on the stock exchange. In these cases the state maintains a controlling interest while an inflow of some $600 million (U.S.) takes the pressure off the state treasury.[49] In the favored high-tech industries, clearly, Italy no longer aims to maintain 100 percent ownership or to preempt foreign participation. Instead we see the state-owned energy engineering firm, Saipem, selling a 20 percent interest, much of which was subscribed by foreign investors, while the electronics group STET negotiated three joint ventures with IBM for microchips, automation, and telecommunications. In the chairman's view, "the need for state participation does not mean total state ownership of companies."[50] Characteristically, then, in the 1980s social democratic governments have both modified their rhetoric and rationalized their corporate holdings in an adaptation to fiscal restraint and to the new patterns of international competition.[51]

British experience demonstrates that given favorable political circumstances, there are few limits to the withdrawal of the state from direct production which cannot be crossed. Where limits were set, they were defined by the government itself, usually to protect statist interests such as national security. The ultimate limit to the rollback of the state in Britain was political. It took the form of a backlash against Thatcherism as the accumulated social costs of a harsh austerity policy came to be seen, even within the Conservative party, as responsible for drastic levels of unemployment and business failure.[52] Elsewhere in Europe the implementation of privatization programs reveals no serious disciples of Thatcher's policies. Behind the symbolic language of the "free market" it is not denationalization but rather a rationalization of state holdings which is typical of center-right governments.

In West Germany, for example, privatization has taken the form of reducing rather than disposing of government interests in eleven industrial, banking, and transport groups. The center-right coalition government formed in 1984, unlike government in London, lacked both the electoral mandate and a leader as forceful as Thatcher. As a result proponents of privatization confronted a real political struggle. Objections came not only from the social democratic opposition and unions but also from nationalists. Thus Franz-Josef Strauss's Christian Social Union, part of the ruling coalition, did not wish to see so large a reduction of government ownership in the national airline, Lufthansa.[53] In a federal polity where state (Länder) governments hold substantial shares in mixed enterprises, regional interests also prompted resistance. The Länder governments foresaw bargaining with private investors (likely to dominate the representional boards that characterize German companies) rather than with Bonn. They worried lest strictly bottom-line considerations preclude the usual political bargaining over special regional considerations. Although the finance minister reintroduced privatization in 1986, the initiative behind the rhetoric turns out to be very tentative indeed. Some equity has been sold, most notably reducing the state share of the holding company VEBA from 43 percent to 25 percent. If such partial sales add monies to the treasury, they do not change the substantial role of the state in the German economy. As the London *Financial Times* saw it, "Bonn's control over, or interest in, some 900 enterprises is virtually unaltered."[54]

European experience in the 1980s suggests that all governments are searching beyond Keynesian economics to find a way out of recession. In this search, parties with divergent doctrines are questioning not only the general role of the state in the economy but also its direct role as producer and investor in competitive industries. Yet in looking for alternatives, formal ideology—whether socialist or neoconservative—has been chastened by the need to adapt any economic strategy to the two exigencies of advanced capitalism in the 1980s. First, nationally based industry must compete within an international division of labor radically altered by a decade of recession and industrial restructuring. Second, governments, to survive in power in liberal polities, must scramble for scarce resources in a political struggle much intensified by a decade of fiscal constraint. How does Canada compare?

CANADIAN STATE CAPITALISM IN QUESTION

The election of a Conservative government to Ottawa in September 1984 sharpened the debate over the viability of the Keynesian welfare state in Canada and introduced the policy of privatization of state-owned enterprises. As the minister of finance succinctly put it, "Crown corporations with a commercial value but no ongoing public policy purpose will be sold."[55] Privatization fit within a broader political agenda for the Conservatives, who saw their impressive mandate as an expression of Canadian exasperation at the Liberal legacy of "soaring government deficits and rising unemployment; of expansive, intrusive government and sluggish, uncertain economic growth." The new government's official priorities therefore were to reduce the public debt, to foster new investment and competitiveness, and "to redefine the role of government."[56] With characteristic flourish the minister of industry, Sinclair Stevens, announced that all holdings of the Canada Development Investment Corporation (CDIC)—commercial companies and equity interests with a combined book value of about $2 billion—were up for sale. Their privatization, the minister explained, would ensure that the "discipline and vitality of the marketplace will replace the often suffocating effect of government ownership."[57]

In its broad formulation, the Canadian government's privatization policy reflects neoconservative ideology everywhere, which sees public enterprises as symptomatic of an intrusive state and accepts as axiomatic the benefits to be derived from their transfer to private ownership. The chairman of the government's Ministerial Task Force on Privatization heralded these benefits—privatization, by reducing the role of the state in the economy, Robert de Cotret argued, "will improve market efficiency and the allocation of resources; it will improve firm efficiency through market discipline."[58] In addition to ideology, however, there was a strong pragmatic element in the Conservatives' privatization policy. Rather than being explicitly linked to programs with an impact on market structures, such as deregulation, the sale of Crown corporations was initially presented as just one in a series of initiatives to "realize further cost savings through more efficient management across the entire federal government."[59] The common aim was to reduce the federal deficit, whether by eliminating programs or by bringing in revenues.

In their first year in office, the high opportunity time for any government, the Conservatives served both ideological and pragmatic purposes with their "for sale" list. On the one hand Ottawa signaled to business its advocacy of the free market by soliciting bids for a small number of highly visible Crown corporations—specifically the aircraft manufacturers Canadair and De Havilland, the uranium mining and refining company Eldorado Nuclear, and the international satellite telecommunications company Teleglobe. On the other hand ministers satisfied the urge to show instant "balance sheet" results by unloading several smaller companies with low visibility and ready market value, such as Northern Transportation Company Ltd., a profitable marine transport company operating in the Northwest Territories.[60] This sales list was not entirely original, since the previous Liberal government had officially targeted some of these companies for privatization.

In the absence of programmatic aims connected to a militant neoconservative economic strategy, such as those which developed in Britain, Canadian privatization in practice could be highly selective.[61] The seriousness of purpose of the Conservative government was nonetheless manifest in the open-ended nature of its privatization policy and in the creation of government machinery to carry it out. Privatization statements by individual ministers were sanctified as policy in the November 1984 Economic Statement, which called for "a careful review" of the objectives and performance of all Crown corporations in view of their economic impact and the level of government financial commitments.[62] After a confused six-month period marked by interministerial jockeying for control over privatization, the government formalized the process through a task force in May 1985.

The task force's mandate, composition, and modus operandi made it a powerful instrument of privatization policy. Created and instructed by a letter from the prime minister, the task force was unique in being composed solely of cabinet ministers. Asked to advise the prime minister, it bypassed the normal process of submissions to Treasury Board, which otherwise has statutory responsibility to approve any measures with financial consequences to government. All commercial corporations came within its purview, and the burden of proof was on responsible ministers to demonstrate why a particular corporation should *not* be sold. In summer 1986 Prime Minister Brian Mulroney went beyond these exceptional measures to name a minister of state for privatization and to institutionalize policy-making advice within the bureaucracy. In the new minister's view, virtually all Crown corporations were potential candidates for the auction block.[63] What does the record show?

The results of the federal government's privatization policy, as of early 1987, are not unimpressive, as Table 4 demonstrates. This scoreboard makes the Conservatives appear to be carrying out a more significant retraction of the state from direct production than any government

Table 4. Privatization Program (Book Value[a] of Assets in $ Million at Financial Year End 1983/84)

Identified for sale
Eldorado Nuclear ($719.5)

Sold
Canada Development Corporation (shares) ($241 market value)
Canadair ($257)
Canadian Arsenals ($88)
De Havilland Aircraft Canada ($252)
Northern Transportation Company ($75.1)
Pêcheries Canada ($19.7)
Teleglobe Canada ($510)

Dissolved
Crown Assets Disposal Corp. (0)
Uranium Canada[b]
Società a responsibilita limitata Immobiliare San Sebastiano[b]
CN (West Indies) Steamships ($0.9)[b]
St. Anthony Fisheries ($1.5)[b]
Loto Canada Inc. ($15.4)
Canadian Sports Pool Corp. ($11.3)
Canagrex ($0.3)[c]

Functions being absorbed by a government department
Canada Museum Construction Corp. ($15.5)

Transfer to another level of government under negotiation
Northern Canada Power Commission ($270)

SOURCE: Book value figures from President of the Treasury Board, *Annual Report to Parliament on Crown Corporations and Other Corporate Interests of Canada, 1983–84* (Ottawa: Minister of Supply & Services Canada, 1985), pp. 6–7, Table 1.
[a]Book values provide a standard of comparison to overall government holdings but should not be equated with either market value or actual sale price. Northern Transportation Company, for instance, sold for $27 million, considered to be a fair approximation of market value given its outstanding debts.
[b]Company inactive when dissolved. In several instances, despite legislation authorizing dissolution, the companies still technically exist according to companies law: e.g., CN Steamships, St. Anthony Fisheries.
[c]Act in the process of being repealed; company dissolved.

in Canada has done since the Social Credit government in British Columbia in the late 1970s.[64] According to the federal government, in 1984, when privatization became policy, its Crown corporations represented some $50 billion in assets, but the combined assets of corporations sold or at the bidding stage by March 1987 had a book value of just $2.2 billion, 4.4 percent of the total.[65] Several companies sold or targeted for sale are important, particularly the four under the CDIC's aegis, but the others are minor players. Until privatization is extended to such major players as Petro-Canada, Air Canada, and Canadian National, which have extensive subsidiaries and affiliates, and numerous other commercial corporations such as the Cape Breton Development Corporation, Canadian Saltfish Corporation, and Atomic Energy of Canada, Canada will retain a very substantial state enterprise sector.

What inhibits full implementation of the federal government's announced program of selling off its commercial holdings? Looking more closely at Ottawa's program, we find that divestment revealed contradictions within "the business community" and that urgent demands for new state investment generated controversy for a Conservative government obliged to extend rather than simply retract state capital. These contradictions and countertendencies, illustrated below, highlight the complexities that obstruct any straight and narrow path toward privatization.

The divestment of federal government's shares in CDC, representing 46.8 percent ownership, had already been approved by the Liberal government and ought to have been a straightforward affair.[66] Instead, competing interests within the private sector emerged, making it clear that privatization could have as many political costs as benefits for an elected government. Because the federal government was unwilling to forego entirely the original "Canadianization" purpose attributed to the CDC, it discriminated between Canadian and foreign capital, limiting all foreign subscriptions to 25 percent. Later, after completion of the share offering, the pattern of acquisition showed a significant interest in the hands of several affiliated companies of one conglomerate, the Brascan group. A privatization program claiming to enhance competition had the appearance of favoring corporate concentration. Although the revised legislation for CDC had sought dispersal of ownership by limiting any single Canadian shareholder to 25 percent, the permissive definition of affiliated companies (only those where another company held over 50 percent of shares) had enabled the Brascan group to make coordinated purchases. The parliamentary committee hearings required to revise CDC's legislation generated unwanted publicity when CDC management tried to change the guidelines to avert what was beginning to look like a hostile takeover.[67] It turned out that several members of the divestiture committee put in place by the state holding company, CDIC, were officers or directors of the Brascan group of companies, and the minister of industry found himself in the political hotseat, grilled by the opposition and contradicting statements by the chairman of the CDC board. Financial analysts castigated the government for bringing down the value of CDC's shares, and when all was said and done, the federal government remained a shareholder.[68] It retained 14 percent ownership and appointed five of the twenty-one directors.

The sale of Teleglobe, the highly profitable Crown corporation responsible for all overseas telecommunications by satellite, clearly raised multiple policy issues. Government underestimated the complexity of the issues, greatly delaying the timetable for privatization and bringing sharp criticism from business. The government's immediate interest in marketability implied maintaining Teleglobe's monopoly position, but this clashed with its commitment to competition, which implied liberalization. Meanwhile, lower rates from the United States had already inspired many corporate users to bypass Teleglobe entirely, with the effect of eroding its market share. Other state-owned enterprises were well established in the telecommunications industry also, and so Crown corporations were themselves among the bidders. In addition, Teleglobe's membership in international organizations such as Intelsat prompted the government to specify a limit on foreign ownership. When policy guidelines were eventually published, not everyone was impressed: as a business press headline put it, "Teleglobe Canada's Sale is 'Act First, Think Later.'"[69] Indeed, a full year after receiving bids for the Crown corporation, Ottawa was obliged to rethink its objectives in privatizing Teleglobe and recommence the bidding process.[70] Such are the pitfalls of privatization. Capital is, of course, not a single constituency but an aggregation of contending interests.

A countertendency to privatization also emerged during 1985 when, despite energetic opposition from within its own party, the government approved Petro-Canada's purchase of Gulf Canada's refineries and service stations in western Canada. This $886 million investment turned the state-owned oil company into Canada's largest gasoline retailer. Government authorization came as part of an effort to facilitate a larger takeover and is a classic case of Canadian state intervention to support private capital in a sector with high levels of foreign ownership. Chevron's takeover of Gulf in the United States provoked a private investors' group to seek to purchase the Canadian holdings. For a Conservative government in Ottawa these developments created a legitimate opportunity to "Canadianize" through the marketplace. If only Petro-Canada would buy those assets not required by the private investment group, the deal would become feasible.[71] The government nonetheless had great difficulty in reconciling formal ideology with practice. The energy minister insisted that "we have always maintained that Petro-Canada should act like a private sector corporation. . . . It has done that by seizing a sound commercial opportunity." The dismay within the Conservative caucus was considerable. As one member of parliament lamented, "we spent all last fall talking about getting the government out of business and then we turn around and allow a Crown corporation to do something like this."[72]

The impact of any privatization strategy emanating from Ottawa is necessarily reinforced or undercut by the policies adopted by provincial governments. Here we observe a tendency similar to what we noted in

Europe: the streamlining of government investment in production, involving some divestment, is general and not specific to neoconservative parties. Since 1980 virtually all provincial governments have responded to budget crises and changing patterns of competition by reexamining their established public enterprises. The parties concerned span the ideological spectrum: New Democrats in Manitoba, Conservatives in Saskatchewan, Liberals in Ontario, and the Parti québécois in Quebec.[73] Let us look at Quebec and Saskatchewan, provinces that display very different party doctrines regarding the role of the state in economic development. The Parti québécois, as we have pointed out in previous chapters, extended a tradition set by the Liberal government in the 1960s of using Crown corporations and government investment agencies to invigorate Quebec-based industrial development. The Saskatchewan Conservative party espoused a populist, free enterprise philosophy captured by the slogan "Open for Business" and advocated privatization of public enterprises established by its social democratic predecessors. Both provinces reconsidered doctrine in the mid-1980s. The result was a retreat from privatization in Saskatchewan and a willingness to sell Crown corporations in Quebec.

Until 1985 the restructuring of the public enterprise sector in Quebec principally involved what in France was called "silent denationalizations" as government holding companies rationalized their operations. Thus the province's industrial holding company, SGF, was encouraged by a Parti québécois government under pressure of budget restrictions to reduce its costs and finance new projects with outside funding. SGF divested some assets, offered shares in some subsidiaries to the public, and negotiated joint ventures.[74] Then, however, the 1985 budget speech introduced the rationale for a much wider reconsideration of the government's role as producer and investor. The minister explained that the size of Crown corporations and the resources locked up in their assets made it imperative to reevaluate their role in economic development. Although budget considerations provoked this rethinking, he argued that the Quebec economy had matured to the point where capable private-sector actors could take on some of the functions that government had previously been obliged to assume.[75] This reorientation in PQ policy paved the way for the Liberals, upon their return to power in December 1985, to call for a "complete reexamination of the role of the state in the economy." The Quebec prime minister, Robert Bourassa, appointed a minister of privatization with a mandate to sell off all commercial corporations except for those where the public interest could justify government ownership. Invoking the international trend to privatization, notably the British experience, he hailed "a new economic era" that would see "the state as catalyst not the state as entrepreneur."[76]

Putting its policy into practice, the cabinet gave the privatization minister two years to determine the future of some thirteen companies. In the first year several commercial Crown corporations were indeed sold, most notably the regional airline, Quebecair.[77] More impressive than its sales, however, is the government's adeptness at using privatization to mobilize elite support (it concocted three advisory task forces with private-sector participation) and to improve its own balance sheet without in fact sacrificing any instruments for future intervention.[78] In the case of the mining group Soquem, profitable operations were regrouped into a new company, Cambior, which issued two-thirds of its shares to the public in 1986. The proceeds enabled Soquem (still government-owned) to pay off its long-term debts and the government, a significant shareholder in Cambior, to enjoy future dividends. In the case of SGF, the government found itself, like Ottawa, drawn into new investments despite its divestment policy. It solicited bids for SGF's stake in two major forest products companies at the same time as it was directing another SGF subsidiary to take over three money-losing companies in the shipbuilding industry, thereby protecting Quebec jobs while allowing a private enterprise to restructure its debt.[79]

In Saskatchewan the election victory of the Conservatives in 1982 ended eleven years of social democratic rule and resulted in a policy to cut back and depoliticize the public enterprise sector. A review commission was set up to reassess all government investments, and following its report the new government chose to retain but reorganize and reorient the holding company Crown Investments Corporation (CIC). Private-sector nominees replaced ministers as chairmen of each company's board (although the ministers remained as vice-chairmen). CIC, now Crown Management Board, was to take as its principal objective the maximization of revenues to the province. Each company was to be "clearly profit oriented and pay to government grants in lieu of taxes as well as set fees on borrowed funds."[80] Faced with the first provincial budget deficit in twenty years, the government in essence adopted a policy of dividend stripping—in 1982 the companies collectively lost $125 million but the holding company paid $42 million in dividends. The premier now asserted that Crown corporations, rather than being privatized, "must operate as bottom line business organizations responsible to the people of Saskatchewan for earning a profit on the investment."[81]

This turnabout was not strictly a nickel-and-dime question but reflected the Conservatives' post-election adjustment to the realities of provincial development. In conditions of recession the absence of alternative investors and continued popular support for state corporations made it unrealistic to dismantle them. As the minister of finance explained it, after expressing regrets for his government's slow progress toward more jobs and economic diversification, "it is obviously difficult with an agriculture-based economy—far from the financial, commerical and manufacturing centres—to have a private sector sufficiently well developed and diversified as to meet these objectives on its own." It was therefore necessary to discriminate between the New Democratic party's ideology, which must be rejected, and its pragmatism, which had dictated continued state ownership of the major Crown corporations.[82] Combining pragmatism and populism, the Conservatives in Saskatchewan introduced "'public participation' as opposed to 'privatization'" by selling different types of securities in major state enterprises: Saskpower savings bonds; Saskoil participatory bonds, to be extended to other state companies, with partially fixed and partially variable return; and most recently common shares linked to convertible preferred shares in Saskoil. The government expects to meet its target of $200 million in revenues and the people, it seems, "just love it."[83]

For Ottawa, then, there are both political implications in divestment and political incentives for reinvestment which preclude any wholesale privatization of all commercial corporations.[84] In prospect for the major Crown corporations, such as Petro-Canada and Air Canada, is an authorization to make partial share offerings to the public. Here we see a congruence of interests between management, which seeks to enhance its autonomy by reducing the need to come to government for approval of new financing, and government, which has its eyes riveted on the public purse. For instance, in 1984 the Conservative government decided to "cease injecting any further equity funds" in Petro-Canada. The corporation interpreted this to mean that it is "to operate in a commercial, private sector fashion, with emphasis on profitability."[85] Corporate management then lobbied for the right to finance operations by selling securities.[86] For Quebec and Saskatchewan divergent party ideologies have been modified to permit a restructuring of state investments. Their shared experience illustrates how governments across Canada are adapting state capitalism to the changing conditions of economic development and to common financial constraints.

STATE CAPITALISM RECONSIDERED

It seems evident that in Canada, as in all European countries but Britain, privatization programs serve not to dismantle the public enterprise sector but to rationalize state holdings. The state will remain a producer and investor in enterprises that compete in the marketplace, but the scope and forms of state capitalism will vary. The structural and political realities that differentiate Canada from other industrial countries preclude facile solutions and should prohibit sloganeering that favors "privatization" or "public ownership."

We do *not* argue that state enterprises have moved "beyond ideology." Rather, we argue that governments of any ideological stripe, in promoting whatever economic strategy based on whatever social values, will continue to intervene directly in production. To do so without squandering scarce resources they must recognize certain fundamentals. It is clearly inappropriate today to proceed on the neoconservative assumption that the state can or will divest itself of all commercial holdings. The catch phrase that Canada is "open for business" is grossly inadequate to grasp the complexities exposed by Canada's deteriorating position in a changing world economy. It is likewise inappropriate to resuscitate orthodox social democratic claims that regional disparities and social inequalities will be overcome if only public ownership is expanded.[87]

In Part I we argued that the Canadian experience with public enterprises cannot be divorced from the particular historical process of development. The special characteristics of the Canadian political economy are (1) Canada's dependence on trade and the country's weak manufacturing sector; (2) a pattern of truncated industrialization that renders Canada very reliant on foreign capital and technology; and (3) a federal system characterized by regional disparities and provincial governments intent on maximizing their autonomy. In the international division of labor of the 1980s we find Canada's position little changed. All advanced capitalist countries face increasing competition from newly industrialized countries; all have to face the problems of deindustrialization engendered by the global restructuring of operations on the part of large corporations. If anything, indeed, Canada's position relative to other members of the world trading system has deteriorated.

Canada's trade dependence, as measured by exports as a percentage of gross domestic product, has grown over the last twenty-five years from 20 percent in 1960 to 28 percent in 1983. Canadian trade has become increasingly concentrated as fully three-quarters of exports and imports are now with the United States (up from two-thirds a decade ago). At the same time Canada's share of world trade has fallen almost 30 percent in a decade, from 5 percent of world trade in the early 1970s to 3.6 percent in 1981.[88] The composition of Canadian exports is shifting as resource exports, so significant for the prosperity of specific provincial economies, decline in favor of manufactured end-products. But Canada's *share* of manufactured exports to other market economies also declined in the years 1970 to 1982, from 4.8 percent to 3.6 percent, while imports of manufactured end-products has remained high and the trade deficit in high-tech products has become a sensitive political issue.

Finally, if foreign ownership of Canadian industry has decreased in overall terms during the past two decades, it still remains very significant (48 percent in manufacturing; 45 percent in mining).[89]

At the same time the fragmentation of state power within Canadian federalism continues to attenuate the impact of any "national strategy." Not only do significant regional disparities persist, but provincial governments, whatever their political predisposition, are becoming increasingly attentive to any opportunity to diversify their economies so as to generate jobs and tax revenues. At the 1986 Annual First Ministers Conference, bringing together the heads of all ten Canadian provincial governments, contentious issues of unequal regional development dominated the discussions. Objecting to Ottawa's procurement policies, Premier Howard Pawley insisted that "you appear not to be aware of the relationship of Manitoba to average national wealth in Canada—we're well under average national wealth."[90] Despite the nation's partial recovery from recession after 1982, the costs of social programs and of servicing debt to cover them mean that deficits continue to handicap all provinces.[91] Although provincial governments may emphasize incentives for private-sector investment, in fact their investment in production remains central to Canadian development. The 1985 "major projects inventory" catalogued 172 investment projects in Canada worth over $100 million and identified a provincial state enterprise, a provincial government, or a mixed enterprise with significant provincial government investment as the "sponsor company" in more than 30 percent of them.[92]

Clearly the limiting conditions of Canadian development have become ever more relevant to the formulation of policy within a rapidly changing international economy. They require government in Canada, we believe, to play a directive, if highly selective, interventionist role as investor and producer in certain sectors and at certain times.[93] The "open-for-business" version of capitalism makes assumptions about market discipline in the Canadian economy which are misleading. The Canadian Chamber of Commerce's primordial criteria for evaluating government intervention—does the state "impinge on [private] property rights" or "interfere with the operation of the market system"—will not do.[94] Canada is already part of a world economy characterized by many forms of state intervention in production, by government regulations and procurement policies biased to protect national producers, and by a "free" trade that is typically an administered, intrafirm trade dominated by international oligopolists. Without a modicum of mercantilist logic to ensure Canada a share of the gains from trade and international investment, the future for national industrial development is put at risk.

As we consider the evolution of state capitalism across the industrial countries, we do not expect to see either wholesale nationalizations or full-scale privatization. Regardless of party doctrine, governments in capitalist societies must rely in part on nationally or regionally based production to provide the wherewithal (jobs and revenues) for political survival. They will not, cannot, eschew the promise of discretionary power which state investment offers. All governments likewise remain susceptible to timeless statist motives for asserting state control "in exceptional circumstances," under the legitimizing banner of national interest, defense, or security of supply. Governments on the right have made ideological-symbolic sales and married pragmatism with doctrine by turning to external sources of capital for state enterprises. Now they are legitimizing the residual role of the state as shareholder by appealing to business logic—companies will toe the bottom line, respect efficiency criteria, and so forth. State capitalism, variable in scope and in form, seems to be inherent to the mixed economy. But state capitalism within what limits and for what purposes?

We cannot conclude with Robert Heilbroner that state enterprises merely assure the conditions favorable to private capital accumulation. Heilbroner maintains that "nationalized companies play the same role as other unprofitable state activities, such as road building or education—providing the social underpinnings that business itself cannot afford to provide but must receive in order to carry out its expansive activities."[95] On the contrary, as we have sought to demonstrate, the doctrinal premise that the state cannot produce for the market in competitive and even profitable industries is false. The transnationalization of national economies made recourse to state ownership in internationally competitive industries acceptable to many governments in the 1970s. When recession increased the costs and reduced the revenues to the state sector, most governments, despite the trend to neoconservatism, have preferred to streamline rather than fully privatize their corporate holdings. Our expectations for the future of state capitalism are therefore quite different from Heilbroner's.

Across the ideological spectrum, in Europe and in Canada, state capitalism is being adapted to the exigencies of world competition, where success now seems to depend on knowledge inputs. The capacity to innovate defines leading firms as those able to adapt to rapidly changing markets and to reduce production costs by introducing new materials and new processes, which, like computer-aided design, cut across several industries. To protect the future rather than the past, most governments now recognize that rigid definitions (a "job" as opposed to a "skill," "industry" as opposed to "technology," a "national" firm as opposed to an "internationally competitive" firm) have become obsolete. Governments in Europe are facing the need to restructure their state sectors

accordingly—selling off uncompetitive companies and giving state holding companies the latitude to initiate or terminate product lines, invest
or divest, in order to survive in a changing international division of
labor. Rather than insulate their activities, state enterprise managers are
encouraged to seek out joint ventures and to co-invest, even with foreign
firms, to enhance their research and development capability and thereby
achieve flexible specialization.

At the same time the range of political tolerance for continued borrowing to cover budget deficits has narrowed. All political parties have
had to rein in their ambitions. Social democrats have come to recognize
that however laudible its original purpose, a public enterprise that loses
money has an opportunity cost. To adapt state capitalism to the exigencies of politics in a time of restraint, governments in Europe have chosen
to streamline their public enterprise sectors by extending the principles
of competitiveness and profitability. No longer simply a performance
goal for selected commercial enterprises, as in the 1970s, profitability
has become a criterion governing investment or divestment decisions for
the entire sector. To fund those state-owned enterprises deemed vital to
socioeconomic development, governments on the left are willing to go to
the stock market for financing, even when to do so reduces the formal
share of state control over the enterprise. To capture new markets,
acquire new technological capability, or tap new sources of capital governments have given priority to the more flexible forms of state capitalism—mixed enterprises, joint ventures, and activity undertaken
through holding companies and their subsidiaries. Overall, then, we
find not a pattern of denationalization or privatization but a restructuring of the entire public enterprise sector. Everywhere the state remains
in business, and everywhere the state seeks to be more businesslike.

Acronyms of Canadian Companies and Agencies

AEC	Alberta Energy Corporation
AGT	Alberta Government Telephones
ATI	Alberta Telecommunications International
BNS	Bank of Nova Scotia
CCC	Canadian Commercial Corporation
CCF	Cooperative Commonwealth Federation
CDC	Canada Development Corporation
CDIC	Canada Development Investment Corporation
CIC	Crown Investments Corporation
CN	Canadian National Railways
CRTC	Canadian Radio-television and Telecommunications Commission
CTC	Canadian Transport Commission
DREE	Department of Regional Economic Expansion
EDC	Export Development Corporation
FBDB	Federal Business Development Bank
IDEA	Innovation Development for Employment Advancement
NDP	New Democratic Party
NEB	National Energy Board
NEP	National Energy Program
NHB	National Harbours Board
NSRL	Nova Scotia Resources Limited
OEC	Ontario Energy Corporation
OEV	Ontario Energy Ventures
PCS	Potash Corporation of Saskatchewan
PIP	Petroleum Incentives Program

PQ	Parti québecois
RTI	Ridley Terminals Inc.
SCOMINEX	Scotian Mineral Exploration
SGF	Société générale de financement
SMDC	Saskatchewan Mining Development Corporation
SNA	Société nationale de l'amiante
UTDC	Urban Transportation Development Corporation

Notes

ABBREVIATIONS
AR   Annual Report
FP   Financial Post (Toronto)
GM   Globe and Mail (Toronto)

Introduction

1. Michael H. Wilson, minister of finance, Government of Canada, "Securing Economic Renewal, The Budget Speech," May 23, 1985, p. 11.
2. Maurice Dobb, *Studies in the Development of Capitalism* (New York: International, 1963), p. 23.
3. See Andrew Shonfield, *Modern Capitalism: The Changing Balance of Public and Private Power* (Oxford: Oxford University Press, 1974).
4. "The State in the Market," *Economist,* December 30, 1978, p. 37.
5. Douglas F. Lamont, *Foreign State Enterprises: A Threat to American Business* (New York: Basic, 1979), p. 53, and R. Joseph Monsen and Kenneth D. Walters, *Nationalized Companies: A Threat to American Business* (New York: McGraw-Hill, 1983). Canadian figures are from the *FP 500,* Summer 1986.
6. This observation supports Skocpol's thesis that the modern state is an organization that may compete for resources to strengthen its autonomy in competition both with other states and at times with the interests of dominant classes in society. See Theda Skocpol, *States and Social Revolution* (Cambridge: Cambridge University Press, 1979).
7. Hershel Hardin, *A Nation Unaware: The Canadian Economic Culture* (Vancouver: J. J. Douglas, 1974), pp. 54–140.
8. Aidan R. Vining and Robert Botterell, "An Overview of the Origins, Growth, Size and Functions of Provincial Crown Corporations," p. 320, and also John W. Langford and Kenneth J. Huffman, "The Uncharted Universe of Federal Public Corporations," p. 274, both in J. Robert S. Prichard, ed., *Crown Corporations in Canada* (Toronto: Butterworths, 1983).
9. "The Business of the Crown," *FP 300,* Summer 1976, p. 32.

10. Stuart Holland, "Europe's New Public Enterprises," in Raymond Vernon, ed., *Big Business and the State* (Cambridge: Harvard University Press, 1974), p. 41.

11. Thomas E. Kierans, "Privatization If Necessary But Not Necessarily Privatization," *Choices* (Institute for Research on Public Policy, Montreal), November 1984. His figures are exaggerated—see Chapter 3 below.

12. Office of the Minister of State (Privatization), "Speaking Notes for the Honourable Barbara McDougall to the Canadian Chamber of Commerce," Vancouver, September 16, 1986, p. 5.

13. "The State in the Market," *Economist*, December 30, 1978, p. 38.

14. Privy Council Office, *Crown Corporations: Direction, Control, Accountability* (Ottawa: Supply & Services, 1977), p. 25. See also Robert W. Sexty, "The Profit Role in Crown Corporations," *Canadian Business Review* 5 (Summer 1978), pp. 9–13.

15. Paul E. Martin, president and chief executive officer, The CSL Group Inc., "Random Remarks on Crown Corporations," address to the Canadian Highway Transport Lawyers' Association Annual Convention, Montreal, December 2, 1983, p. 13.

16. Thomas E. Kierans, "Strengthening the Market at the Expense of the State," *Choices*, April 1985; Jacques Parizeau (former minister of finance, Government of Quebec), "Public Enterprises: The Quebec Experience," Institute for Research on Public Policy *Newsletter* 7 (March–April 1985).

CHAPTER 1. *State Capitalism in the Industrial Countries*

1. "The 500 Largest Industrial Corporations outside the United States," *Fortune*, August 13, 1979. In 1985, eighteen of the top hundred were state-owned enterprises from the industrialized countries: "The Fortune International 500," ibid., August 4, 1986.

2. Arie Y. Lewin, "Public Enterprise, Purposes and Performance: A Survey of Western European Experience," in W. T. Stanbury and Fred Thompson, eds., *Managing Public Enterprises* (New York: Praeger, 1982), p. 52.

3. The important exception is the United States, where the federal government has rarely turned to state-owned enterprises outside wartime. The approximately thirty-five "government corporations," as they are termed in the Government Control Act, concentrate in financing (Export-Import Bank, Federal Deposit Insurance Corporation), but commercial enterprises have been created in transportation and telecommunications with a view to achieving profits (Comsat, Amtrak, Conrail). Overall, local and state authorities play the most active economic role. For a comprehensive study see Annmarie Hauck Walsh, *The Public's Business: The Politics and Practices of Government Corporations* (Cambridge: MIT Press, 1978); for an inventory of federal government corporations and policy issues surrounding them, see *Report on Government Corporations* (Washington, D.C.: National Academy of Public Administration, 1981).

4. We concur with Jorge Niosi that much analytical confusion has been created by the use of the same concept, state capitalism, to designate a phase of capitalist development (as in the orthodox Marxist theory), a mode of production (used alternately to describe Third World political economies and to castigate the Soviet Union), and a sector of activity. See Niosi, *Canadian Capitalism* (Toronto: James Lorimer, 1981).

5. We exclude the less industrialized European periphery of Turkey, Greece, Portugal, and Ireland. Fully comparable data are not available for Sweden, Denmark, and Norway.

6. Armand Bizaguet, "L'importance des entreprises publiques dans l'économie française et européenne après les nationalisations de 1982," *Revue économique* 34 (May 1983), p. 463. Figures are for 1979, EEC member-states only.

Explanation for these national differences lies in the history of state-society relationships and ruling coalitions within each country. For a framework intended to guide comparative analysis of economic policy see Peter J. Katzenstein, "Conclusion: Domestic Structures and

Strategies of Foreign Economic Policy," in Katzenstein, ed., *Between Power and Plenty: Foreign Economic Policies of Advanced Industrial States* (Madison: University of Wisconsin Press, 1978). For an impressive statistical comparison of the size, economic impact, and performance of public enterprises in seventy-seven countries, see R. P. Short's contribution to *Public Enterprise in Mixed Economies* (Washington, D.C.: IMF, 1984), pp. 110–81.

7. Niosi, *Canadian Capitalism*, p. 85, Table 4.3. Chapter 3 below describes in full the public enterprise sector in Canada.

8. Centre européen de l'entreprise publique (CEEP), *L'entreprise publique dans la communauté économique européenne* (Brussels, 1981).

9. Ibid. Italian figures are for 1978, all others for 1979. Unfortunately, despite the best efforts of CEEP to publish comparative statistics, the divergent national definitions of "sector" would make another table of country-by-country statistics misleading.

10. Ibid. for Italian statistics; French figures are from Ministère de la recherche et de l'industrie, *Une politique industrielle pour la France* (Paris: La Documentation française, 1981), p. 207.

11. *Une politique industrielle*, pp. 109 and 213. "Manufacturing" excludes the energy sector; "large" firms employ more than 2,000 persons.

12. "L'économie espagnole," *Notes et études documentaires* nos. 4643-44 (November 20, 1981). Figures are for 1977.

13. CEEP, *L'entreprise publique*, p. 44. Figures are for 1979.

14. Bizaguet, "L'importance," p. 461, draws on CEEP statistics and takes an arithmetical average of the three measures for the EEC member-states.

15. Claus Offe, "The Theory of the Capitalist State and the Problem of Policy Formation," in Leon N. Lindberg et al., eds., *Stress and Contradiction in Modern Capitalism* (Lexington, Mass.: D. C. Heath, 1975), p. 12.

16. The French Communist party devoted two volumes to elaborating why "state monopoly capitalism" is the appropriate label for the mode of production in advanced industrial economies. See Paul Boccara et al., *Traité d'économie politique: le capitalisme monopoliste d'état* (Paris: Ed. sociales, 1971). An overview and critique of this orthodox Marxist concept is offered by Bob Jessop, *The Capitalist State: Marxist Theories and Methods* (Oxford: Martin Robertson, 1982), pp. 32–77.

17. Ernest Mandel, *Marxist Economic Theory* (London: Merlin, 1968), pp. 511, 501–2.

18. Ibid., pp. 502–3.

19. James O'Connor, *The Fiscal Crisis of the State* (New York: St. Martin's, 1973), pp. 180 and 183.

20. Mandel, *Marxist Economic Theory*, p. 533.

21. The linkage between private property and individualism remains central to the liberal paradigm of the state-economy-society relationship.

22. Neoclassical economists offer other rationales for public ownership, for example, in the case of a natural monopoly. For a review see William G. Shepherd, "Public Enterprises: Purposes and Performance," in Stanbury and Thompson, *Managing Public Enterprises*, pp. 13–50.

23. Martyn Sloman reviews the British Labour party's shifting commitment to public ownership in *Socialising Public Ownership* (London: Macmillan, 1978). For France see the *Programme du parti socialiste et programme commun de la gauche* (Paris: Flammarion, 1972); for Canada, *Jobs: An Industrial Strategy* (Ottawa: New Democratic Party, 1978).

24. *Fortune 500*, August 11, 1980.

25. Stuart Holland has written two provocative analyses of the evolution of state enterprises in Europe: "State Entrepreneurship and State Intervention," in Holland, ed., *The State as Entrepreneur* (London: Weidenfeld & Nicolson, 1972), pp. 5–44, and "Europe's New Public Enterprises," in Raymond Vernon, ed., *Big Business and the State* (Cambridge: Harvard University Press, 1974), pp. 25–42.

26. John B. Sheahan, "Experience with Public Enterprise in France and Italy," in William G. Shepherd, ed., *Public Enterprise* (Lexington, Mass.: D. C. Heath, 1976), pp. 123–

84. Most students of public enterprise in France downplay the Blum government's "timid" nationalizations. See for example Christian Stoffaës and Jacques Victorri, *Natonalisations* (Paris: Flammarion, 1977).

27. This principle has been retained by subsequent French constitutions.

28. Holland, "Europe's New Public Enterprises," p. 25.

29. Ibid., p. 41.

30. Holland, "State Entrepreneurship," p. 6.

31. Holland, "Europe's New Public Enterprises," p. 31.

32. Ibid., p. 34; Nicolas Jéquier, "Computers," in Vernon, *Big Business*, pp. 195–254; Stephen Young, *Intervention in the Mixed Economy: The Evolution of British Industrial Policy, 1964–72* (London: Croom Helm, 1974), pp. 24 and 201.

33. Richard N. Cooper, *The Politics of Interdependence* (New York: McGraw-Hill, 1968).

34. U.S. Congress, Senate, Subcommittee on Multinational Corporations, *Multinational Corporations in Brazil and Mexico* (Washington, D.C., 1975), p. 5; Michael Barratt Brown, *The Economics of Imperialism* (London: Penguin, 1974), p. 220; Lawrence Franko, *The European Multinationals* (Stamford, Conn.: Greylock, 1976).

35. See Robin Murray, "The Internationalisation of Capital and the Nation State," in Hugo Radice, ed., *International Firms and Modern Imperialism* (London: Penguin, 1975), p. 131.

36. Competing explanations of the crisis are given by A. Gamble and P. Walton, *Capitalism in Crisis* (London: Macmillan, 1976), and André Gunder Frank, *Crisis: In the World Economy* (New York: Holmes & Meier, 1980).

37. Centre d'études prospectives et d'informations internationales, *Economie mondiale: La montée des tensions* (Paris: Economica, 1983), pp. 21–73. On the growing knowledge intensity of production and its consequences for competition see Lynn Krieger Mytelka, "Knowledge-Intensive Production and the Changing Internationalization Strategies of Multinational Firms," in James Caporaso, ed., *International Political Economy Yearbook* (Boulder, Colo.: Lynne Reinner, 1986).

38. UNIDO, *Industry in a Changing World* (New York, 1983), pp. 152–53, Tables VI.2 and VI.4.

39. Charles-Albert Michalet, "Crise mondiale ou crise internationale?" in Michalet et al., *Nationalisations et internationalisation* (Paris: Maspero, 1983), pp. 44 and 48–49, Tables 13, 14, 18, and 19.

40. Ibid., and UNIDO, *Industry in a Changing World*, p. 191, Table VII.3.

41. Folker Fröbel, Jürgen Heinrichs, and Otto Kreye, *The New International Division of Labour* (Cambridge: Cambridge University Press, 1980); Gerald K. Helleiner, *Intra-Firm Trade and the Developing Countries* (London: Macmillan, 1981); Louis Turner and Neil McMullen, *The Newly Industrializing Countries: Trade and Adjustment* (London: Allen & Unwin, 1982).

42. UNIDO, *Industry in a Changing World*, p. 10. The debate over "deindustrialization" started with a narrow concern about the fall of employment in manufacturing; moved to a broader concern with the decline in a country's share of world manufactured exports and has since turned to the issue of import penetration and the search for strategies to redeploy national resources in order to recapture competitiveness. An excellent collection of essays on the first two phases of the debate is Frank Blackaby, ed., *De-Industrialization* (London: Heinemann, 1979); the third is imaginatively dealt with in Michael J. Piore and Charles F. Sabel, *The Second Industrial Divide* (New York: Basic, 1984).

43. Christian Stoffaës, *La grande menace industrielle* (Paris: Calmann Lévy, 1978), and, for the conceptualization of the world economy, Charles-Albert Michalet, "Pour une nouvelle approche de la spécialisation internationale" in Michalet et al., *L'intégration de l'économie française dans l'économie mondiale* (Paris: Economica, 1984).

44. Douglas F. Lamont, *Foreign State Enterprise* (New York: Basic, 1979), Table 2.1. For a complete listing of state-owned multinational enterprises and an analysis of their corporate strategy based on interview data, see J.-P. Anastassopoulos et al., *Les multinationales publiques* (Geneva: IRM, 1985).

45. By 1979 petroleum led all other sectors represented in the *Fortune* 500 for increased sales while just five companies, four of them state-owned, accounted for 32 percent of total profits earned by all 500. *Fortune*, August 11, 1980, p. 88. See O. Noreng, "State-Owned Oil Companies," in Raymond Vernon and Yair Aharoni, eds., *State-Owned Enterprises in Western Europe* (London: Croom Helm, 1981), and Richard J. Samuels, *The Business of the Japanese State: Energy Markets in Comparative and Historical Perspective* (Ithaca: Cornell University Press, 1987), for further examples.

46. Pierre Cahuzac and Marc Giget, "L'industrie aérospatiale," *Revue d'économie politique* 5–6 (1982), p. 666; M. S. Hochmuth, "Aerospace," in Vernon, *Big Business*, pp. 145–69.

47. For the official rationale by the Secretary of State for Industry see U. K., Commons, *Debates*, 5th ser., vol. 901, (1975–76), cols. 1450–52.

48. CEEP, *L'entreprise publique*, p. 65; Aérospatiale, *AR*, 1981, p. 20; Cours des Comptes, *Rapport au président de la république sur l'activité, la gestion et les résultats des entreprises publiques* (Paris: Journaux officiels, 1982), pp. 101–7; CEEP, *L'impact économique*, p. 112.

49. Jean-Pierre Anastassopoulos, *La stratégie des entreprises publiques* (Paris: Dalloz, 1980), pp. 29–32.

50. The huge Bécancour smelter, a joint venture with the Quebec government's holding company, SGF (25 percent), and the U.S. firm Alumax Inc. (25 percent), was officially opened in 1986. At that time Péchiney—itself nationalized—claimed it would shut down aluminum plants in France in favor of its Canadian and Australian ventures unless the state enterprise Electricité de France reduced electricity rates to an internationally competitive level. *Financial Times*, September 12, 1986, p. 23.

51. All information on the coal industry in France is from Cours des Comptes, *Rapport*, 1982 and 1979 eds.

52. CEEP, *L'impact économique*, pp. 110–11.

53. Gruppo IRI, *Yearbook* (Rome: Edindustria, 1981), p. 40; Renato Mazzolini, *Government Controlled Enterprises: International Strategic and Policy Decisions* (New York: Wiley, 1979), pp. 67 and 94.

54. Lucien Rapp, *Les filiales des entreprises publiques* (Paris: Librairie générale de droit et de jurisprudence, 1983), p. 19.

55. Ibid., p. 39; H. Gresh, "Les entreprises publiques et la création de filiales," *Économie et statistique* 65 (May 1975), pp. 29–43. One reason for the reduced number of parent companies in France was decolonization—Algerian gas and Guinean mines were no longer "French" state enterprises.

56. Rapp, *Les filiales*, p. 469.

57. Ibid., pp. 300–303; Cour des comptes, *Rapport*, 1979 and 1982 eds.

58. CEEP, *L'entreprise publique*, p. 44. CEEP, *L'impact*, p. 82.

59. Frank Carmichael, "Germany [report on state investment]," *Europe*, September–October 1982, pp. 16–19; CEEP, *Impact*, p. 84. Another public share issue in 1984 reduced the government's holding to 25 percent.

60. An overall philosophy of state holding companies was articulated by Pasquale Sarceno, *Il sistema delle imprese a partecipazione statale nell'esperienza italiana* (Milan: Giuffrè, 1975).

61. According to the Minister of State for Industry in U.K., Commons, *Debates*, 5th ser., Vol. 880, (November 4, 1974), col. 667, commenting on the White Paper that set out the proposal for the NEB enacted in the Industry Act 1975. For a full discussion see Young, *Intervention*, pp. 39–120.

62. Keyser and Windle, *Public Enterprise*, pp. 67–68.

63. Per Sköld, "Statsföretag—10 Years Progress," Statsföretag *AR*, 1979, p. 2. Rankings from *Fortune 500*, August 11, 1980. E. Nowotny, "Nationalized Industries as an Instrument of Stabilization Policy: The Case of Austria," *Annals of Public and Co-operative Economy* 53 (January–March 1982), pp. 41–57.

64. Law of August 4, 1978, cited in CEEP, *L'entreprise publique*, pp. 11–12. For more detailed analyses see Brian Hindly, ed., *State Investment Companies in Western Europe* (London: Macmillan, 1983).

65. Ian Gough, *The Political Economy of the Welfare State* (London: Macmillan, 1979). James O'Connor first identified the "fiscal crisis of the state" in his study of government expenditures in the United States (see footnote 19).

66. In this struggle over budgets we see the state, like Theda Skocpol, as an organization that may compete for resources to strengthen its relative autonomy in competition both with other states and to a limited extent with the prevailing interests of dominant classes in society. See her *States and Social Revolutions* (Cambridge: Cambridge University Press, 1979), pp. 28–32.

67. Both Charles-Albert Michalet and Colin Leys regard this application of business logic to state enterprises as detrimental to social democratic movements. Governments thereby are able to rationalize their unwillingness to use public enterprise for social purposes and at the same time they dilute labor opposition to some layoffs and plant closures because such actions by a state-owned enterprise are more readily accepted as being in the "public" interest. Michalet, "France," in Vernon, *Big Business,* p. 118; Leys, *Politics in Britain* (Toronto: University of Toronto Press, 1983), pp. 259–79.

68. Groupe de travail du Comité interministeriel des entreprises publiques, *Rapport sur les entreprises publiques* (April 1967).

69. CEEP, *L'impact économique,* p. 136; CEEP, *L'entreprise publique,* p. 62.

70. National Economic Development Office, *A Study of U.K. Nationalized Industries: Their Role in the Economy and Control in the Future* (London: HMSO, November 1976), p. 89.

71. Ibid.; Richard Pryke, *The Nationalized Industries: Policies and Performance since 1968* (London: Martin Robertson, 1981), pp. 257–61. An excellent analysis of the debate over the public sector in Britain is found in David Heald, *Public Expenditure: Its Defence and Reform* (Oxford: Martin Robertson, 1983).

72. CEEP, *L'entreprise publique,* pp. 11–12.

73. Ibid., pp. 121–27. Nonetheless political interference is intrinsic to Italy's experience with public enterprises. Romano Prodi, prior to being named chairman of IRI, argued that Italian public enterprises were increasingly political creatures and that this was particularly inappropriate now that they had expanded into competitive and profitable industries. See Prodi, "Italy," in Vernon, *Big Business,* pp. 45–63.

74. Lars Tornblom, "The Swedish State Company Limited, Statsföretag AB: Its Role in the Swedish Economy," *Annals of Public and Co-operative Economy* 48 (October–December 1977), p. 453.

75. R. Joseph Monsen and Kenneth Walters present a picture of disaster in *Nationalized Companies* (New York: McGraw-Hill, 1983), pp. 80–101. Their conclusions regarding "unfair competition" are challenged by Yair Aharoni, "The State-Owned Enterprise as a Competitor in International Markets," *Columbia Journal of World Business* 15 (Spring 1980), pp. 14–22.

76. We can agree with B. J. Fine and K. O'Donnell that, for the state-owned enterprise, profitability is "a criterion for policy." Unlike the private firm where profitability serves as a control mechanism, the state-owned enterprise may continue to survive without achieving profits. See "The Nationalised Industries," in David Currie and Ron Smith, eds., *Socialist Economic Review* (London: Merlin, 1981), p. 267.

CHAPTER 2. *The Political Economy of State Intervention in Canada*

1. Hugh G. J. Aitken, "Defensive Expansionism: The State and Economic Growth in Canada," in W. T. Easterbrook and M. H. Watkins, eds., *Approaches to Canadian Economic History* (Toronto: McClelland & Stewart, 1967), p. 184.

2. See W. A. Mackintosh, *The Economic Background of Dominion-Provincial Relations* (Toronto: McClelland & Stewart, 1969), chap. 2.

3. Harold A. Innis, "Transportation as a Factor in Canadian Economic History," in

Mary Q. Innis, ed., *Essays in Canadian Economic History* (Toronto: University of Toronto Press, 1956), pp. 62–77.

4. Harold A. Innis, *The Problems of Staple Production in Canada* (Toronto: Ryerson, 1933), pp. 80–81.

5. James A. Corry, *The Growth of Government Activities since Confederation* (Ottawa: King's Printer, 1939), p. 3.

6. Alexander Gerschenkron, *Economic Backwardness in Historical Perspective* (Cambridge: Harvard University Press, 1962), chap. 1.

7. Hugh G. J. Aitken, "Defensive Expansionism," and Aitken, "Government and Business in Canada: An Interpretation," *Business History Review* 38 (September 1964), p. 8.

8. Alexander Brady, "The State and Economic Life in Canada," in K. J. Rea and J. T. McLeod, eds., *Business and Government in Canada*, 2d ed. (Toronto: Methuen, 1976), pp. 28, 40.

9. Hershel Hardin, *A Nation Unaware: The Canadian Economic Culture* (Vancouver: J. J. Douglas, 1974), pp. 59–63. Hardin's analysis is reminiscent of Louis Hartz, *The Founding of New Societies* (Toronto: Harcourt, Brace & World, 1964), and Gad Horowitz, "Conservatism, Liberalism and Socialism in Canada: An Interpretation," *Canadian Journal of Political Science* 32 (May 1976), pp. 14–171.

10. Hardin, *Nation Unaware*, pp. 54, 80–84.

11. See Peter J. Katzenstein, *Small States in World Markets: Industrial Policy in Europe* (Ithaca: Cornell University Press, 1985), pp. 81–86, for a discussion of the trade dependence, trade concentration, and industrial specialization of the small, open economies which create special vulnerabilities to change in the world economy. A more detailed profile of the Canadian economy is provided below.

12. Cf. Glen Williams, *Not for Export: Toward a Political Economy of Canada's Arrested Industrialization* (Toronto: McClelland & Stewart, 1983), pp. 15–16.

13. Ibid., p. 13. This industrialization strategy was adopted by many Latin American countries. See Albert O. Hirshman, "The Political Economy of Import Substituting Industrialization in Latin American," in Hirshman, *A Bias for Hope* (New Haven: Yale University Press, 1971).

14. For example, the following statement in the *Canadian Manufacturer*, August 15, 1890, and quoted in Williams, *Not for Export*, p. 20: "Before we worry ourselves about foreign trade in our manufacturing let us first fully occupy our home market. Let us make all such articles as we can manufacture to advantage. . . . When we have done this it will then be time to consider the question of exporting our surplus manufactures, but not till then."

15. In other words, to get protection for their patents in Canada, American patentees had to guarantee that they or their agents would manufacture the product in question within the specified time period. Williams, *Not for Export*, p. 23. See also Stephen Scheinberg, "Invitation to Empire: Tariffs and American Economic Expansion in Canada," in G. Porter and R. Cuff, eds., *Enterprise and National Development* (Toronto: A. M. Hakkert, 1973), p. 85.

16. Williams, *Not for Export*, pp. 30, 33.

17. Mira Wilkins, *The Emergence of Multinational Enterprise: American Business Abroad from the Colonial Era to 1914* (Cambridge: Harvard University Press, 1970), pp. 141–42.

18. H. V. Nelles, *The Politics of Development: Forests, Mines and Hydro-Electric Power in Ontario, 1849–1941* (Toronto: Macmillan, 1974), p. 348.

19. Tom Naylor, "The Canadian State, the Accumulation of Capital and the Great War," *Journal of Canadian Studies* 16 (Fall–Winter 1981), pp. 44–46, and Donald Creighton, *Canada's First Century* (Toronto: Macmillan, 1970), pp. 136–38.

20. Creighton, *Canada's First Century*, pp. 139–40, and Marsha Gordon, *Government in Business* (Montreal: C. D. Howe Institute, 1981), pp. 54–56. The Drayton-Acworth Royal Commission, appointed in 1916 to recommend a solution to the railway problem, recommended that the state take over the railways.

21. Naylor, "Canadian State," pp. 35–36.

22. Williams, *Not for Export*, pp. 63–65.

23. Naylor, "Canadian State," p. 45.

24. Tom Traves, *The State and Enterprise: Canadian Manufacturers and the Federal Government, 1917–1931* (Toronto: University of Toronto Press, 1979), p. 5.

25. Naylor, "Canadian State," pp. 47–49.

26. Williams, *Not for Export*, chap. 5.

27. For details of Howe's role in Canadian politics see Robert Bothwell and William Kilbourn, *C. D. Howe: A Biography* (Toronto: McClelland & Stewart, 1979).

28. Hardin, *A Nation Unaware*, p. 256.

29. Bothwell and Kilbourn, *Howe*, pp. 100–102.

30. Ibid., pp. 106–9, and Gordon, *Government in Business*, pp. 66–67 and 78. Trans-Canada Airlines became a separate entity under the name Air Canada in 1964. In 1967 a new Air Canada Act was passed which, among other changes, made the corporation responsible to the Minister of Transport and severed its connection with CN.

31. For a summary of the role of the Judicial Committee of the Privy Council in interpreting the British North America Act see Donald Smiley, *Canada in Question: Federalism in the Eighties*, 3d ed. (Toronto: McGraw-Hill Ryerson, 1980), pp. 31–37, and Garth Stevenson, *Unfulfilled Union* (Toronto: Macmillan, 1979), passim.

32. Christopher Armstrong and H. V. Nelles, "Private Property in Peril: Ontario Businessmen and the Federal System, 1898–1911," in Porter and Cuff, *Enterprise and National Development*, pp. 20–38, and Stevenson, *Unfulfilled Union*, pp. 79–93.

33. Sanford Borins, "World War Two Crown Corporations: Their Wartime Role and Peacetime Privatization," *Canadian Public Administration* 25 (Fall 1982), p. 384.

34. Ibid., pp. 390–402. At the provincial level (Saskatchewan) where a populist/socialist party gained power in 1944, a program of public ownership was central to economic strategy. See Chapter 5.

35. Donald Smiley, "Canada and the Quest for a National Policy," *Canadian Journal of Political Science* 8 (March 1975), p. 47. He quotes Galbraith at p. 48.

36. Donald Smiley, "The Federal Dimension of Canadian Economic Nationalism," *Dalhousie Law Journal* (October 1974), p. 553, and Smiley, *Canada in Question*, pp. 206–7.

37. Smiley, "Canada and the Quest," p. 49.

38. Garth Stevenson, "Continental Integration and Canadian Unity," in Andrew Axline et al., *Continental Community: Independence and Integration in North America* (Toronto: McClelland & Stewart, 1974), pp. 194–220.

39. Hugh G. J. Aitken, *American Capital and Canadian Resources* (Cambridge: Harvard University Press, 1961), p. 50.

40. *Foreign Direct Investment in Canada* (Ottawa: Supply & Services, 1972), p. 19.

41. Ibid., pp. 171–74. For a discussion of the ramifications of the growing bilateral relationship see Maureen Appel Molot and Glen Williams, "The Political Economy of Continentalism," in M. S. Whittington and G. Williams, eds., *Canadian Politics in the 1980s*, 2d ed. (Toronto: Methuen, 1984), pp. 81–104.

42. *Foreign Direct Investment*, p. 183.

43. Science Council of Canada Background Study no. 22, 1971, cited in Williams, *Not for Export*, p. 111, and *Foreign Direct Investment*, chap. 8.

44. H. G. J. Aitken, "The Changing Structure of the Canadian Economy with Particular Reference to the Influence of the United States," in Aitken et al., *The American Economic Impact on Canada* (Durham: Duke University Press, 1959), p. 11.

45. *Foreign Direct Investment*, p. 173.

46. Michael Barratt Brown, *The Economics of Imperialism* (London: Penguin, 1974), p. 220.

47. A capsule history is provided by Don Gracey, "Public Enterprise in Canada," in André Gélinas, ed., *Public Enterprise and the Public Interest* (Toronto: Institute of Public Administration of Canada, 1978), pp. 25–47.

48. Canada, Department of External Affairs, *A Review of Canadian Trade Policy* (Ottawa: Minister of Supply & Services, 1983), p. 3.

49. Williams, *Not for Export*, p. 8, Table 1.

50. *Foreign Direct Investment*, p. 8.

51. *On the Mend* (Ottawa: Supply & Services Canada, 1983), p. 23.

52. See discussion of the Quebec case below in Chapter 6.

53. Estimates from Aidan R. Vining and Robert Botterell, "An Overview of the Origins, Growth, Size and Functions of Provincial Crown Corporations," p. 320, and John W. Langford and Kenneth J. Huffman, "The Uncharted Universe of Federal Public Corporations," p. 274, both in J. Robert S. Prichard, ed., *Crown Corporations in Canada* (Toronto: Butterworths, 1983).

54. See Allan Tupper, "Pacific Western Airlines," in Tupper and G. Bruce Doern, eds., *Public Corporations and Public Policy in Canada* (Montreal: Institute for Research on Public Policy, 1981), pp. 285–318. (Alberta sold the airline to private capital in 1983). Marsha Chandler relates party ideology to different types of public enterprises in "State Enterprise and Partisanship in Provincial Politics," *Canadian Journal of Political Science* 15 (December 1982), pp. 711–40.

55. Export Development Corporation, *AR*, 1975, pp. 21–22.

56. *GM*, December 5, 1983, p. B13.

57. Jorge Niosi, *Canadian Capitalism: A Study of Power in the Canadian Business Establishment* (Toronto: James Lorimer, 1981). An excellent critique on the state of the literature in Canada prior to 1980 is Allan Tupper, "The State in Business," *Canadian Public Administration* 22 (Spring 1979), pp. 124–50.

58. Harry Johnson, ed., *The New Mercantilism* (Oxford: Oxford University Press, 1974), pp. ix–x.

CHAPTER 3. *Contemporary State Capitalism in Canada*

1. *FP 500*, Summer 1986. The editors point out (p. 66) that three other state enterprises qualified—Eldorado Nuclear, Alberta Government Telephones, and Potash Corp. of Saskatchewan—but late data submission prevented their being listed.

2. The impact of privatization programs on the state enterprise sector is analyzed in Chapter 8. For now we note that as of year-end 1986, three of the corporations listed in Table 3 had been privatized, and two others offered shares or participation bonds to the public (with the government retaining majority control).

3. "Policy Statement," June 28, 1982, p. 1.

4. Ibid. Counting Crown corporations is a never-ending shell game. Here we rely on Government of Canada, President of the Treasury Board, *Annual Report to Parliament on Crown Corporations and Other Corporate Interests of Canada, 1983–84* (Ottawa: Minister of Supply & Services Canada, 1985), pp. 6–7, and then subtract those corporations which are inactive or have since been dissolved.

5. Aiden R. Vining and Robert Botterell, "An Overview of the Origins, Growth, Size and Functions of Provincial Crown Corporations," in J. R. S. Prichard, ed., *Crown Corporations in Canada* (Toronto: Butterworths, 1983), pp. 303–67.

6. Ibid., p. 326, Table 4. Figures are from 1977. Only Nova Scotia and Prince Edward Island had less significant shares, while in Newfoundland Crown corporations' assets exceeded the provincial GDP.

7. The dilemmas encountered in defining a Crown corporation are well analyzed by John Langford, "The Identification and Classification of Federal Public Corporations: A Preface to Regime Building," *Canadian Public Administration* 23 (Spring 1980), pp. 76–104.

8. Canada, Parliament, House of Commons, Bill C-24, "An Act to Amend the Financial Administration Act in Relation to Crown Corporations and To Amend Other Acts in Consequence Thereof" (June 28, 1984), 2d sess., 32d Parliament.

9. Ibid., s. 2.1(1) and 95; information on provincial regulations throughout this chapter is from Jeanne Kirk Laux and Maureen Appel Molot, *Report on the Control and Accountability of Government Owned Corporations in Selected Provinces of Canada*, Report prepared for the President of the Treasury Board, Government of Canada, February 1984.

10. See M. J. Trebilcock and J. R. S. Prichard, "Crown Corporations: The Calculus of Instrument Choice," in Prichard, *Crown Corporations*, pp. 15–26.

11. André Gélinas, "Les entreprises publiques: Causes, modes d'établissement, types et régimes généraux de contrôle," in Roland Parenteau, ed., *Les sociétés d'état: Autonomie ou intégration* (Montreal: HEC, 1980), pp. 36ff.

12. Canada, Statistics Canada, *Federal Government Enterprise Finance*, cat. no. 61–203 (Ottawa: Statistics Canada, 1968), p. 18.

13. This definition of competition may appear broad, but note that the federal government's new competition law (1986) quite rightly recognizes that competition now takes place on a global scale. The law allows mergers by companies in sectors with high import penetration where the old combines (or monopolies) legislation would have disallowed them.

14. As noted in Chapter 1, profit mandate should not be confused with profitability. The special difficulties in assessing the profitability of a state-owned enterprise are discussed by Arie Y. Lewin, "Public Enterprise: Purposes and Performance," in W. T. Stanbury and Fred Thompson, eds., *Managing Public Enterprises* (New York: Praeger, 1982), pp. 66–70.

15. The proliferation of mixed enterprises without apparent coordination provoked the Lambert Commission in 1979 to observe that "they constitute a mixed bag" without even "the ground rules of a management and accountability relationship." Royal Commission on Financial Management and Accountability, *Final Report* (Ottawa: Minister of Supply & Services Canada, 1979), p. 355. Federal legislation now requires disclosure of indirect investments by stipulating that Crown corporations' plans and capital budgets "shall encompass all the business and activities, including investments of the corporation and its wholly-owned subsidiaries." Moreover, no Crown corporation or subsidiary may incorporate a new company in which it will hold any portion of the equity, nor can it buy shares in an established corporation without cabinet approval. Ministers and public servants are forbidden to make share purchases unless their department has received parliamentary sanction within an approved program. Canada, "Financial Administration Act" (above, note 8), s. 129(1) and 131(2). See also s. 100 and 101 regarding new incorporations.

16. Treasury Board of Canada, Secretariat, "Crown Corporations and Other Canadian Government Corporate Interests" (Ottawa: Minister of Supply & Services, 1983), p. 2. This list is based on information provided by the corporations in response to a questionnaire.

17. Canada Development Corporation, *AR*, 1981, pp. 53–54. The government excluded CDC holdings from its list in deference to the corporation's desire to be seen as independent (see Chapter 4), while the bank's equity placements were considered to be for security purposes only (see Chapter 6).

18. E. Craig Elford and W. T. Stanbury, "Mixed Enterprises in Canada," in vol. 2 of the research studies prepared for the Royal Commission on the Economic Union and Development Prospects for Canada, *Industry in Transition* (Toronto: University of Toronto Press, 1986), p. 280.

19. Ibid., pp. 284–85, Table 6.10.

20. Ibid., p. 288.

21. Herbert Morrison, *Socialisation and Transport* (London: Constable, 1933), p. 149.

22. *Parliaments, Governments and Public Enterprises* (London: Commonwealth Secretariat, 1981), p. 16; Gélinas, "Entreprises publiques," pp. 44–47; V. Seymour Wilson, "Beyond the Ministerial Departments: The Behemoth of Public Enterprise," in Wilson, *Canadian Public Policy and Administration* (Toronto: McGraw-Hill Ryerson, 1982), pp. 366–68.

23. Canada, Privy Council Office, *Crown Corporations: Direction, Control, Accountability* (Ottawa: Supply & Services, 1977), p. 7. New Democratic governments do not fully espouse the arms-length assumption. In Saskatchewan, for example, the government ap-

pointed ministers to the boards to ensure that the corporation's activities reflected its policies.

24. Ira Sharkansky offers a polemical survey of the ways in which the modern state hives off activities in *Whither the State? Politics and Public Enterprises in Three Countries* (Chatham, N.J.: Chatham House, 1979).

25. A critique of the public enterprise from this perspective is T. M. Ohashi and T. P. Roth, eds., *Privatization, Theory and Practice* (Vancouver: Fraser Institute, 1980), pp. 151–79.

26. According to André Gélinas's summary of reports by experts from eight countries in "Public Enterprise and Public Interest: Independence and Accountability—Summary of Discussions," *Public Enterprise and the Public Interest* (Toronto: Institute of Public Administration of Canada, 1978), p. 1; and *Parliaments, Governments*, which distilled these trends from some one hundred studies on European, Canadian, and U.S. public administration and public enterprises.

27. The notable exceptions are Italy, which has a Ministry of State Investments; Austria and Sweden, which use the state holding company format; and Spain, which has introduced general legislation governing state enterprises.

28. Raymond Vernon underscores the many factors shaping relations between state enterprises and government which make it unlikely that long-term commitments in such contractual arrangements will prove meaningful. See Vernon, "Linking Managers with Ministers: Dilemmas of the State-owned Enterprise," *Journal of Policy Analysis and Management* 4, 1 (1984), pp. 39–55.

29. The Ontario Government's *Manual of Administration* identifies 275 agencies of which 82 are active corporations submitting annual financial statements. Of these, fourteen are placed on a special Schedule II reserved for commercial corporations intended to be self-financing and whose boards of directors may make investments without returning to the government for authorization.

30. Canada, "Financial Administration Act" (above, note 8), s. 129.

31. These documents, approved by cabinet and tabled in the legislature, can stipulate that "the Minister may contract with the Corporation for the performance of individual projects"—Memorandum of Understanding between the Minister of Transportation and Communications and the Urban Transportation Development Corporation, June 12, 1979, art. III.1.28ff.

32. Canada, "Financial Administration Act" (above, note 8), s. 99.

33. It remains a subject of debate whether public servants effectively represent the public interest: their attendance at board meetings is usually erratic, and they are not always well briefed on corporate activities. For an assessment of the quality of Crown corporation boards see Tom Mitchell, ed., *The Role of the Board of Directors in Crown Corporation Accountability* (Ottawa: Conference Board of Canada, 1985). To date only the province of Manitoba has an explicit, if embryonic, policy of appointing representatives of the workforce to the boards, although this is an occasional practice in other jurisdictions, especially when Social Democratic parties are in power.

34. See Harvey B. Feigenbaum's review article "Public Enterprise in Comparative Perspective," *Comparative Politics* 15 (October 1982), p. 117, and the literature scan by Howard Thomas, "Strategic Management and State-Owned Enterprises: A European Perspective," in Anant R. Negandhi et al., *Multinational Corporations and State-Owned Enterprises* (London: JAI Press, 1986), p. 119.

35. Gélinas, "Public Enterprise," p. 19.

36. *Parliaments, Governments*, p. 27. For a cogent essay on these paradoxes, leading to a policy-making typology, see J. P. Nioche, "Gérer l'ambiguïté," in J. P. Anastassopoulos and Nioche, *Entreprises publiques, entreprises comparées* (Paris: FNEGE, 1982), pp. 11–18.

37. Privy Council Office, *Crown Corporations*, p. 25. Robert W. Sexty, "The Profit Role in Crown Corporations," *Canadian Business Review* 5 (Summer 1978), pp. 9–13, first traced the origins of this trend to commercialization.

38. For example, kickbacks to agents representing Atomic Energy of Canada, invest-

ment by Polysar in South Africa, and creation of an unauthorized subsidiary by Air Canada.

39. *Report of the Auditor General of Canada to the House of Commons, Financial Year Ending 31 March 1976* (Ottawa, 1976), pp. 53–65.

40. Marsha Gordon, *Government in Business* (Montreal: C. D. Howe Institute, 1981), p. 49.

41. See Richard Bird, *Financing Canadian Government* (Toronto: Canadian Tax Foundation, 1979), p. 45.

42. On the experiments see Douglas Hartle, *The Expenditure Budget Process in the Government of Canada* (Toronto: Tax Foundation, 1978), and Richard D. French, *How Canada Decides: Planning and Industrial Policymaking, 1968–1984* (Toronto: James Lorimer, 1984).

43. Royal Commission on Financial Management and Accountability, *Final Report* (Ottawa: Supply & Services, 1979).

44. Canada, "Financial Administration Act" (above, note 8), s. 2.1(6).

45. "Policy Statement" (above, note 3), p. 1.

46. Privy Council Office, *Crown Corporations*, p. 42. The Consolidated Revenue Fund is the account in which government funds are kept.

47. Canada, Laws, Statutes, etc., *Air Canada Act*, s. 7(2). For an assessment of both the CN and the Air Canada restructuring, see E. G. Davis and P. B. Mokkelbost, "The Recapitalization of Crown Corporations," *Canadian Public Policy* 9 (June 1983), pp. 181–88. It is unlikely that lenders assess the debt : equity ratio of a Crown corporation in the same manner as they do for a private enterprise. Both Crown corporation managers and government officials are nonetheless fond of validating their performance by reference to private-sector norms.

48. Crown Investments Review Commission, *Report to the Government of Saskatchewan* (December 1982), p. 43.

49. British Columbia Railway, *AR*, 1982, p. 1. B.C. Rail, mainly a natural resource–carrying railway, was asked by government to develop the Tumbler Ridge branch to expedite coal exports to Japan. The government purchased shares for $45 million in 1982 to help meet the costs of the line. British Columbia Railway, *AR*, 1982; British Columbia, Legislative Assembly, Committee on Crown Corporations, "Fifth Annual Review of Operations" (April 1, 1982–March 31, 1983), pp. 8–13. By 1985 BC Rail had become Canada's twenty-first-ranking company in terms of profit margin. *FP 500*, Summer 1986, p. 105.

50. "Memorandum of Understanding" (above, note 31).

51. Citations are from the annual reports of, respectively, Petro-Canada, *AR*, 1983, p. 3; Northern Transportation Company, *AR*, 1982, p. 1 (this company was privatized in 1985); and Atomic Energy of Canada, *AR*, 1983–84, pp. 1 and 5.

52. For background on the cases examined below see Gordon, *Government in Business*, pp. 19–45. We do not include Canada's largest hydroelectrical company, Ontario Hydro, because it is if anything overanalyzed elsewhere. The trend is similar, however, since Ontario Hydro was reorganized in 1974 from a commission to a corporation with an independent board of directors. Paul McKay gives a highly critical account of its corporate strategy in *Electric Empire: The Inside Story of Ontario Hydro* (Toronto: Between the Lines, 1983).

53. *FP 500*, Summer 1986, pp. 66 and 112.

54. Hydro-Québec, *Plan de développement d'Hydro-Québec, 1984–1986* (Montreal, December 1983), pp. 30, 40, and 46. Details on export contracts are provided in Philippe Faucher and Johanne Bergeron, *Hydro-Québec: La société de l'heure de pointe* (Montreal: Presses de l'Université de Montréal, 1986), pp. 108–10. The authors are persuaded that the export market is residual—that is, to absorb surplus capacity.

55. Hydro-Québec, *AR*, 1985.

56. Hydro-Québec, *Plan*, p. 50.

57. Interview with company president Guy Coulombe, "Corporate Style," *FP 500*, Summer 1985, p. 19. A full-scale analysis of Hydro-Québec's strategy, emphasizing its "commercialization" after 1983, is presented by Faucher and Bergeron, *Hydro-Québec*.

58. B.C. Hydro, *AR*, 1982–83, p. 1.
59. Ibid., p. 4.
60. Ibid., pp. 1 and 5.
61. *GM*, February 13, 1986, p. B9. The declining value of the Canadian dollar pushed up the share of B.C. Hydro's expenditures going to service its debt to 40 percent (more than half of it owed to U.S. creditors). For details on the export contracts see *Canadian Energy News* 3, no. 19 (1984), p. 149, and ibid., no. 20, p. 158.
62. The Canadian companies include Lavalin and the SNC Group. *GM*, March 6, 1987, p. B17.
63. Alberta General Telephones, *AR*, 1982, p. 4.
64. Ibid., p. 14.
65. Ibid., p. 4.

CHAPTER 4. *Business as Usual: Public Enterprises and Public Policy*

1. Canadian National Railways, *AR*, 1977, p. 21.
2. *Report of the Auditor General of Canada to the House of Commons* (Ottawa: Supply & Services Canada, 1982), p. 11.
3. Maurice Strong, "Government-Private Sector Relations in Canada—The Federal Government as Investor in Business," James Gillies Alumni Lecture, York University, Toronto, March 23, 1983, pp. 14–15.
4. Robert W. Sexty, "The Profit Role in Crown Corporations," *Canadian Business Review* 5 (Summer 1978), p. 12.
5. W. T. Easterbrook and Hugh G. J. Aitken, *Canadian Economic History* (Toronto: Macmillan, 1956), p. 443. The mythical image of railroad building in Canada is well captured by Pierre Berton, *The National Dream: The Great Railway, 1870–1881* (Toronto: McClelland & Stewart, 1970).
6. The mandate is quoted in John Gratwick, "Canadian National: Diversification and Public Responsibilities in Canada's Largest Crown Corporation," in W. T. Stanbury and Fred Thompson, eds., *Managing Public Enterprises* (New York: Praeger, 1982), p. 237. CN's problems are elaborated by Garth Stevenson, "Canadian National Railways," in Allan Tupper and G. Bruce Doern, eds., *Public Corporations and Public Policy in Canada* (Montreal: IRPP, 1981), pp. 319–51.
7. Stuart Holland, "Europe's New Public Enterprises," in Raymond Vernon, ed., *Big Business and the State* (Cambridge: Harvard University Press, 1974), p. 25. See Chapter 1 for the full typology.
8. Stevenson, "Canadian National Railways," p. 341.
9. Gratwick, "Canadian National"; Canada, Laws, Statutes, etc. *National Transportation Act*, R.S.C. 1970, c. N-17, s. 3(c), specifies that a company "so far as practicable, receives compensation for the resources, facilities and services that it is required to provide as an imposed public duty."
10. The corporate reorganization is described in CN's 1977 *AR*.
11. Supplementary Estimates are increments to approved levels of spending for government departments or corporations. The practice of introducing new programs in the guise of financial adjustments has brought strong objections in Parliament. VIA Rail was declared a Crown corporation by Order in Council P.C. 1978–954 on April 1, 1978.
12. Canada, Laws, Statutes, etc., *Canadian National Railways Capital Revision Act*, S.C. 1977–78, c. 34, s. 6, 7, 9 and 10. CN must first make payments on interest of securities held by the public; on indebtedness to the Crown; and of income taxes. The government may direct CN to make a higher dividend payment.
13. For example, with its AA2 rating from Moody's Investors Service, CN successfully issued $100 million of Eurobonds in 1985.
14. David Perry, "Keeping the Country on the Move," *FP 500*, June 1982, pp. 55–56. The rankings are found in ibid., Summer 1986.

15. Dividend figures are given in the corporation's annual reports.

16. Transport Canada—Marine, "Elements of an International Shipping Policy for Canada," prepared by H. J. Darling, August 16, 1974, p. vi.; and personal interview, Transport Canada, Policy and Planning, Marine—Deputy Administrator, Ottawa, April 1983.

17. Transport Canada—Marine, "Elements," p. iv.

18. Ibid., p. 12; GM, May 9, 1983, p. B13. On the politics of international shipping see Lawrence Juda, "World Shipping, UNCTAD, and the New International Economic Order," International Organization 35 (Fall 1981), pp. 493–516.

19. GM, May 29, 1981, p. B4.

20. Shareholders' Agreement, sec. 2.1 and 4.4—Exhibit CN-1 in File W110.15.11, Canadian Transport Commission, Water Transport Committee.

21. Canadian Transport Commission, Water Transport Committee, Case No. W-1/75, vol. 4, pp. 439–41; pp. 395ff. for the Union position; vol. 1 for Canadian Pacific's position.

22. GM, May 29, 1981, p. 84.

23. The Canadian National Railways Act, sec. 31, specifies that "with the approval of the Governor-in-Council [cabinet]," CN can invest in "any business that in the opinion of the Board of Directors may be carried on in the interests of the National Company."

24. See the series of articles by Lyndon Watkins in GM, September 21, 1982, p. B11; October 30, 1982, p. B16; November 5, 1982, p. B11; and November 23, 1982, p. B9.

25. CN, AR 1981, p. 44. GM, April 24, 1982, p. B1, and January 14, 1983, p. B1.

26. GM, July 18, 1983, p. B16. For reports of the cabinet's assessment see FP, July 2, 1983, p. 4. The Royal Bank was sole owner of Cast, the largest North Atlantic container operator, until 1985 when it sold a majority interest; GM, December 20, 1985, p. B1.

27. Sandford F. Borins, "World War II Crown Corporations," in J. Robert S. Prichard, ed., Crown Corporations in Canada (Toronto: Butterworth, 1983).

28. F. C. Philips, "A History of Aerospace Research and Development in Canadair Limited," Canadian Aeronautics and Space Journal 25 (Second Quarter 1979), pp. 112–21.

29. The Avro Arrow project has immense symbolic importance in the debate over technological sovereignty in Canada. It involved Canadian government–funded design and manufacture of a supersonic all-weather fighter intended for the Canadian forces by A. V. Roe Canada (controlled by British Hawker Siddeley). It was to have been powered by a revolutionary new jet engine, the Iroquois, designed, produced, and flight-tested in a six-year development program by Orenda Engines—a subsidiary of A. V. Roe. Government cancellation of both the engine and the aircraft in February 1959 resulted in a drop in employment at Orenda from 5,000 to 1,000 as the company became simply a repair and overhaul center and A. V. Roe moved out of aviation entirely. A massive emigration of brain-power followed. See James Dow, The Arrow (Toronto: Lorimer, 1979).

30. Canada, Minister of State, "A Report by Senator Jack Austin on Canadair Ltd. to the Standing Committee on Public Accounts and to the Standing Committee on Finance, Trade and Economic Affairs," June 7, 1983, p. 14–15.

31. Ibid., p. 15.

32. Evidence for the board's role comes from testimony before the House of Commons Public Accounts Committee during hearings held from June to November 1983. The summary report concludes, "your Committee feels that Canadair's Board of Directors failed to exercise its responsibilities." Canada, Parliament, House of Commons, Standing Committee on Public Accounts, Minutes of Proceedings and Evidence 93 (November 27, 1983), p. 6.

33. Canadair imported its engines from Avco Lycoming and General Electric in the United States; in Canada engines are manufactured by a subsidiary of United Technologies—Pratt and Whitney of Canada.

34. GM, June 8, 1983, p. 1.

35. CBC, The Fifth Estate, April 13, 1983.

36. FP editorial, June 18, 1983, p. 4; GM, June 8, 1983, p. 3.

37. See Keith Hayward, *Government and British Civil Aerospace* (Manchester: Manchester University Press 1983), intro., pp. 1–12.

38. Modification of the Lear jet design to give a more comfortable, wide-bodied plane reduced the Challenger's range and fuel efficiency. Certification was delayed, and sales orders dropped in consequence. Attempts to develop a stretch version of the Challenger in 1980 were aborted the following year after expenditures of some $9 million, as the requisite wing modifications and engine upgrading would have made the plane uncompetitive.

39. Canada, Minister of State, "Report," p. 30.

40. Supplementary Estimates (E) 1981–82, Industry and Commerce, Item 6e, March 1982.

41. Canada, Minister of State, "Report," p. 47.

42. CDIC, "Background Notes on 1982 Canadair Ltd. Financial Statements" (Ottawa, 1983); and Canadair Ltd., *AR* 1983, pp. 1 and 17.

43. Both Canadair and De Havilland were sold in 1986; see Chapter 8 for a detailed account of the privatization program. In the case of Canadair, the government has been left holding over one billion dollars in debts by the nature of the company's restructuring in 1983. Canadair's enormous "negative net worth" obviously jeopardized its commercial future, and to resolve this problem the holding company, CDIC, created a new subsidiary, calling it Canadair, while the former company changed its name to Canadair Financial Corporation Inc. The new Canadair acquired all the assets of the old, leaving government-owned Canadair Financial Corporation with $1.1 billion in debt and accrued interest. See CDIC, "Financial Statements for the Period Ending March 31, 1984."

44. Canada, Parliament, House of Commons, *Debates*, February 23, 1971, p. 3667.

45. All quotations on the CDC's purposes and powers are from Canada, Laws, Statutes, etc., *Canada Development Corporation Act*, S.C. 1970–71, c. 42.

46. The federal government held 100 percent of the shares until 1975. Public share offerings reduced government ownership to 46.6 percent in 1981. As part of its privatization policy, the Conservative government announced its intention to divest completely in 1984, but at year end 1986 the government still held 13.6 percent of CDC's voting stock.

47. These examples are drawn from Canada Development Corporation, *AR*, 1977–1981.

48. CDC, *AR*, 1980, p. 3.

49. Canada, Parliament, House of Commons, Standing Committee on Public Accounts, *Minutes of Proceedings and Evidence* 39 (July 5, 1977), pp. 3–18; the auditor general is quoted on p. 4.

50. "CDC at the End of Ten Years," remarks delivered by H. Anthony Hampson, president and chief executive officer, to the Toronto Society of Financial Analysts, December 10, 1981, pp. 11–12.

51. *GM*, May 29, 1980, p. B1.

52. Strong was elected a director. His recollection of events is given in Peter Foster, "Ottawa's Man: The Interventionist Politics of Maurice Strong," *Saturday Night*, August 1983, pp. 17–23.

53. Letter from Senator Jack Austin to H. A. Hampson, president and chief executive officer, Canada Development Corporation, May 27, 1982, reprinted in CDC, *AR*, 1982, pp. 49–50. See Chapter 6 for an assessment of the CDIC.

54. Philippe Faucher, "La stratégie de l'entreprise d'état," in Faucher and Johanne Bergeron, *Hydro-Québec* (Montreal: Presses de l'Université de Montréal, 1986), pp. 19–34. See also Harvey Feigenbaum, *The Politics of Public Enterprise: Oil and the French State* (Princeton: Princeton University Press, 1985), who vigorously argues that "the profit-maximizing orientation of French public enterprise, combined with managerial autonomy, leads to behavior that is inconsistent with the purported goals of French petroleum policy" (p. 147).

55. Taieb Hafsi, *Enterprise publique et politique industrielle* (Paris: McGraw-Hill, 1984), and Hafsi, "The Strategic Decision-Making Process in State-Owned Enterprises" (diss., Harvard Business School, 1981).

56. In addition to funding, legal organization, market structure, internationalization, and diversification, Aharoni emphasizes the number and complexity of corporate goals, company size, national interest, technical nature of information required, and the quality of management personnel. Yair Aharoni, "Managerial Discretion," in Aharoni and Raymond Vernon, eds., *State Owned Enterprises in the Western Economies* (New York: St. Martin's, 1980), pp. 189–91.

CHAPTER 5. *The State in Business: Beyond Profits*

1. This concept has recently come under criticism as being imprecise and leading to undue emphasis on jurisdictional confict. R. A. Young, Philippe Faucher, and André Blais, "The Concept of Province-Building: A Critique," *Canadian Journal of Political Science* 17 (December 1984), pp. 783–818. For the concept of nation building see Karl Deutsch, *Nationalism and Social Communication: An Inquiry into the Foundation of Nationality* (New York: Wiley, 1953).

2. See for example S. D. Berkowitz, "Forms of State Economy and the Development of Western Canada," *Canadian Journal of Sociology* 4 (Fall 1979), pp. 287–312. Marsha Chandler accepts the importance of province building but also argues that there is a relationship between party ideology and the expanding provincial state sector; not only are parties of the left (which she identifies as the New Democratic party, which has governed the provinces of Manitoba, Saskatchewan, and British Columbia at various times since 1944, and the Parti québécois, in power in Quebec from 1976 to 1985) more likely to use state enterprises as public tools, but they also see them more clearly as agents of economic and social control. Chandler, "The Politics of Public Enterprise," in J. Robert S. Prichard, ed., *Crown Corporations in Canada: The Calculus of Instrument Choice* (Toronto: Butterworths, 1983), pp. 185–218.

3. Albert Breton, "The Economics of Nationalism," *Journal of Political Economy* 72 (August 1964), pp. 376–86.

4. Pierre Fournier, *The Quebec Establishment*, 2d rev. ed. (Montreal: Black Rose, 1978), chaps. 10 and 11, and Fournier, *Les sociétés d'état et les objectifs économiques du Québec: Une évaluation préliminaire* (Quebec: Office de planification et de développement du Québec, 1979).

5. Jorge Niosi, *Canadian Capitalism: A Study of Power in the Canadian Business Establishment* (Toronto: Lorimer, 1981), pp. 94–96. Unlike Fournier, however, Niosi sees the outcome of the emergence of a francophone bourgeoisie as a necessary integration of this new group with existant capital rather than the consolidation of a provincial economy that could enhance the viability of the separatist option. Ibid., p. 150.

6. John Richards and Larry Pratt, *Prairie Capitalism: Power and Influence in the New West* (Toronto: McClelland & Stewart, 1979).

7. Berkowitz, "Forms of State Economy."

8. See G. O. Vagt, "Asbestos," and G. S. Barry, "Potash," in Energy, Mines and Resources, *Canadian Minerals Yearbook, 1985* (Ottawa: Supply & Services Canada, 1986), p. 9.9, Table 4, and p. 48.14 respectively.

9. Calculated from Barry, "Potash," p. 48.10, Table 2. The percentage of Saskatchewan potash exported to the United States has declined since the government takeover, and that sold offshore has increased.

10. Statistics Canada, *International Investment Catalogue* 67–202 (Ottawa, 1984).

11. See Richards and Pratt, *Prairie Capitalism*, pp. 137–38.

12. B. W. Boyd, "Potash," in Energy, Mines and Resources, *Canadian Minerals Yearbook 1976* (Ottawa: Supply & Services Canada, 1977), p. 38.4, Table 2.

13. Energy, Mines and Resources, *Asbestos*, MR 155 (Ottawa, 1976), pp. 7 and 19.

14. Section 109 of The Constitution Act, 1867, gives the provinces jurisdiction over natural resources. Section 92A, added in 1982, makes explicit the provinces' ability to

make laws relating to the development, management, and conservation of nonrenewable natural resources. The Constitution Act, 1982.

15. Michael J. Prince and G. Bruce Doern, *The Origins of Public Enterprise in the Canadian Mineral Sector: Three Provincial Case Studies*, Working Paper no. 33 (Kingston: Centre for Resource Studies, 1985), p. 109, list 21 federal and 52 provincial government enterprises as participating in the mining and petroleum sectors.

16. See *Central Canada Potash Co. Ltd. v. Saskatchewan* (1978), 23 N.R., which questioned the constitutionality of the Potash Conservation Regulations designed to regulate production levels in the face of reduced demand; and *Amax Potash Ltd. v. Saskatchewan* (1977), 2 S.C.R., which tested provisions of the reserve tax legislation. For details on the first case see Richards and Pratt, *Prairie Capitalism*, pp. 294–301.

17. Allan Blakeney, quoted in *Leader-Post* (Regina), June 20, 1972, p. 1.

18. Parti québécois, *Dossier-Programme, 4: Les richesses naturelles* (Montreal: National Electoral Committee, 1973), pp. 3 and 16.

19. The Cooperative Commonwealth Federation became the New Democratic party in 1961.

20. A government holding company for Crown corporations, the Government Finance Office, was established in 1947. In 1978 the GFO became the Crown Investments Corporation with responsibilities for long-term planning and capital requirements for all state enterprises. Under the Conservative government the CIC became the Crown Management Board in 1983, but its responsibilities remain much the same.

21. For a discussion of the Quiet Revolution and expanding role of the government in Quebec see Kenneth McRoberts and Dale Postgate, *Quebec: Social Crisis and Political Change*, rev. ed. (Toronto: McClelland & Stewart 1980), chap. 6. Quebec state ventures, including those in the mining sector as well as financial institutions, are discussed in Chapters 6 and 7 below.

22. Pierre Fournier, "The National Asbestos Corporation of Quebec," in Allan Tupper and G. Bruce Doern, eds., *Public Corporations and Public Policy in Canada* (Montreal: Institute for Research on Public Policy, 1981), p. 356, and Mary Beth Montcalm, "Class in Ethnic Nationalism: Quebec Nationalism in Comparative Perspective" (diss., Carleton University, 1983), p. 211. An annual listing of Quebec state enterprises and their financial statements is found in Gouvernement du Québec, Ministère des finances, *Entreprises du gouvernement du Québec 198–, états financiers.*

23. *FP 500*, Summer 1985, pp. 84 and 90.

24. For details of the government-industry conflict see Maureen Molot and Jeanne Laux, "The Politics of Nationalization," *Canadian Journal of Political Science* 12 (June 1979), pp. 235–37.

25. Allan Blakeney quoted in *Ottawa Citizen*, November 14, 1975, p. 5.

26. Raymond Mikesell, "International Collusive Action in World Markets for Nonfuel Minerals: Market Structure and Methods of Market Control," Special Report no. 4 (Washington, D.C.: Department of State, September 1974), pp. 4–5; Mikesell, *New Patterns of World Mineral Development* (Washington, D.C.: British North American Committee, 1979), pp. 40–45. For a discussion of the problem of nationalization in the copper industry and the "loss of insulation" as a result of state intervention that put new state enterprises at risk, see Michael Shafer, "Capturing the Mineral Multinationals: Advantages or Disadvantages?" *International Organization* 37 (Winter 1983), pp. 93–119.

27. See W. E. Koepke, *Structure, Behaviour and Performance of the World Potash Industry*, Mineral Bulletin MR 139 (Ottawa: Department of Energy, Mines & Resources, 1973), p. 52.

28. Although there is now some potash production in the province of New Brunswick, these sites had not been developed when the Saskatchewan takeover occurred (and, in fact, were brought on stream by companies unhappy with the production atmosphere in Saskatchewan).

29. Pragmatism provoked criticism from the left. See the critique by the Waffle faction

(a splinter left group within the NDP), "Potash Nationalism: Socialism or Smoother Capitalism?" *Next Year Country*, June–July 1977, pp. 14–19.

30. The Potash Corporation of American has constructed a mine in New Brunswick and is now producing potash. International Minerals and Chemical Corporation has explored potash deposits in Manitoba but has not moved beyond exploration. Although potash deposits outside Saskatchewan are not nearly as extensive as those inside the province, their availability and the corporate preparedness to explore them illustrates the interprovincial competition for investment dollars in Canada and the ability of corporations to play off one province against another.

31. Government Finance Office Saskatchewan, *Public Enterprise in Saskatchewan* (Regina, April 1977), p. 30.

32. *GM*, March 19, 1979, p. B2.

33. *GM*, December 4, 1980, p. B11, and interview, official of United Steel Workers of America (Canada), November 1980.

34. Interview, Saskatoon, June 1982.

35. For example, PCS buys from a company in Regina conveyer belts for carrying mined potash. It was at the suggestion of the Saskatchewan Department of Industry and Commerce that the company began to manufacture the conveyer belts. Previously the belts had been imported from the United States. *FP*, October 3, 1981, p. S5.

36. PCS, *AR*, 1982, p. 16.

37. As a result of the fall in demand several privately owned potash producers laid off workers during 1982.

38. *GM*, June 11, 1982, p. B6.

39. PCS, *AR*, 1983, p. 6.

40. Ibid., 1985, p. 6.

41. Ibid., 1984, p. 4.

42. Ibid., 1985, p. 4, and *FP*, May 24, 1986, p. 7.

43. New Brunswick now has two operating potash mines. Manitoba recently announced a joint venture in which it will participate to build a potash mine: *FP*, May 24, 1986, p. 17.

44. *Montreal Star*, October 20, 1977, p. C12, and October 21, 1977, p. A2.

45. Normand Alexandre, *Vers une politique québécoise de l'amiante* (Quebec: Quebec Ministry of Natural Resources, 1975). For a summary of the report's major recommendations see the memorandum to cabinet from Jean-Gilles Massé, Liberal minister of natural resources at the time. The report was tabled in the Quebec legislature in late 1978. Québec, Assemblée nationale, *Documents de la session* no. 37, 1978.

46. *GM*, January 26, 1977, p. A1. Brian Tanguay, "Quebec's Asbestos Policy: A Preliminary Assessment," *Canadian Public Policy* 11 (June 1985), pp. 227–40, examines the motives that brought the PQ to participate in the asbestos industry.

47. The then premier of Quebec, Maurice Duplessis, was well known for his support of capital at the expense of labor. His government passed extremely restrictive labor legislation, and, as premier, he used the provincial police to ensure labor peace. For a description of the asbestos strike that catapulted the author into prominence in Quebec see Pierre Elliot Trudeau, *La grève de l'amiante: Une étape de la révolution industrielle du Québec* (Montréal: Cité Libre, 1956).

48. The Société nationale de l'amiante was established by Bill 70, introduced into the Quebec National Assembly on November 29, 1977, and passed on May 23, 1978.

49. *Montreal Star*, November 9, 1977, p. B1, statement by Premier Lévesque.

50. Asbestos Corporation had announced reserves of 200 million tons according to a survey. Energy, Mines and Resources, *Asbestos*, p. 7. Because Asbestos Corporation sold virtually all of its output to a refining company in Nordenham, West Germany, there was no concern about potential difficulties with the United States over nationalization of the kind that had arisen with potash. See Molot and Laux, "Politics of Nationalization."

51. *Montreal Star*, October 22, 1977, p. A8.

52. *GM*, March 17, 1981, p. B8. In December 1978 the Quebec government introduced

Bill 121 into the National Assembly. This legislation empowered the government to expropriate the assets of the Asbestos Corporation. The bill also provided for an arbitration board of three to establish a price for Asbestos Corporation shares if the parties could not agree on compensation.

53. Quoted in Roma Dauphin, "Asbestos," in Carl E. Beigie and Alfred O. Hero, Jr., eds., *Natural Resources in U.S.-Canadian Relations* (Boulder, Colo.: Westview, 1980), 2:260.

54. See Pierre Fournier, "The National Asbestos Corporation of Quebec," in Tupper and Doern, *Public Corporations and Public Policy*, p. 359.

55. SNA, *AR*, 1984–85. p. 2.

56. See *Gazette* (Montreal), April 25, 1979, p. 49, and Tupper and Doern, *Public Corporations and Public Policy*, p. 361; and on the Thetford Mines plant, *GM*, March 27, 1982, p. B4.

57. *La Presse* (Montreal), October 18, 1979.

58. SNA operates its share of Asbestos Corporation through its SNA Mines Division, which holds 51 percent voting interest in General Dynamics Canada. *FP*, February 20, 1982, p. 3.

59. Interviews, Government of Quebec, Ministère du Conseil exécutif—Développement économique; Ministère des Finances—Direction des sociétés d'état; and Ministère de l'énergie et des ressources, January 1984.

60. The U.S. Environmental Protection Agency has proposed a ban on asbestos with a final decision to be made in mid-1987. With sales already dropping, the Quebec and federal governments are helping the industry counter the E.P.A. policy. See *GM*, April 29, 1986, p. B2, and July 19, 1986, p. B18; *FP*, April 5, 1985, p. 12.

61. *FP*, April 5, 1986, p. 12.

62. *GM*, June 17, 1982, p. B10.

63. *GM*, November 11, 1984, p. B4. The SNA Asbestos Hill Mine closed its operations in January 1984 with the loss of two hundred jobs. *GM*, October 28, 1983, p. B10.

64. SNA, *AR*, 1984–1985, p. 8–9.

65. Sorès Inc. and A. D. Little Inc., *Étude des possibilités de fabrication des produits d'amiante au Québec*, Phases I and II (Montreal, 1977 and 1978).

66. *Ottawa Citizen*, September 16, 1983, p. 43.

67. SNA, *AR*, 1982–83, p. 3; 1983–84, p. 3, and 1984–85, p. 3.

68. *GM*, July 31, 1986, p. B4.

69. *GM*, December 10, 1986, p. B3.

70. See Pierre Fournier, "The Parti québécois and the Power of Business," *Our Generation* 12, 3 (1979), p. 13. Robert Armstrong also discusses SNA's health record in "Nationalizing Asbestos: Takeover in Perspective," *Canadian Forum*, August 1979.

71. *SNA, AR*, 1984–1985, p. 9.

72. *GM*, October 28, 1983, p. B10.

73. *GM*, June 14, 1984, p. B13.

74. *GM*, June 6, 1984, p. B4, and January 3, 1985, p. B9.

75. *GM*, March 1, 1986, p. B3.

76. Jacques Parizeau, "Public Enterprises: The Quebec Experience," in W. T. Stanbury and Thomas Kierans, eds., *Papers on Privatization* (Ottawa: Institute for Research on Public Policy, 1985), p. 92.

77. See *GM*, July 31, 1986, p. B4, and *Ottawa Citizen*, July 31, 1986, p. C10.

CHAPTER 6. *The State as Investor*

1. See Chapter 3 for the complete inventory of mixed enterprises; for a survey of motives for establishing them, see Anthony Boardman, Catherine Eckel, and Aiden Vin-

ing, "The Advantages and Disadvantages of Mixed Enterprises," in Anant R. Negandhi, ed., *State-Owned Enterprises* (London: JAI Press, 1986), pp. 235–37.

2. See Walter B. Meigs et al., *Accounting*, 3d Canadian ed. (Toronto: McGraw-Hill Ryerson, 1981), p. 603.

3. The risk to government of using debt financing is analyzed by Allan M. Maslove, "Loans and Loan Guarantees: Business as Usual versus the Politics of Risks," in G. Bruce Doern, ed., *How Ottawa Spends Your Tax Dollars 1983* (Ottawa: School of Public Administration, Carleton University, 1983), pp. 121–32.

4. We have not included the "joint enterprises" formed between two governments. They express a particular political logic of the 1970s when the Trudeau government sought to assert Ottawa's ability to shape economic development through the Department of Regional Economic Expansion (DREE). DREE was empowered to sign formal regional development agreements with provincial governments and could incorporate jointly owned corporations to carry out projects. (See the DREE Act, in Canada, Law, Statutes etc., 1970, c. R-4, s.8(3)(c).) Some half-dozen joint enterprises were so established—usually to undertake highly visible tasks such as expansion of the port at Quebec City and development of Mirabel International Airport.

5. A plausible further purpose in these cases is to protect society from such "dangerous" activities, but over time the real objectives appear more pecuniary than regulatory.

6. CN, *AR*, 1983, pp. 46 and 48.

7. Canada, *Public Accounts, 1980–81*, sec. 6, "Loans Investments and Advances," p. 38.

8. Allan Tupper gives an overview of assistance programs in *Public Money in the Private Sector: Industrial Assistance Policy and Canadian Federalism* (Kingston: Institute of Intergovernmental Relations, Queens University, 1982).

9. *Federal Business Development Bank Act* (1975), s. 20(2)(b).

10. According to the prospectus issued by Salomon Brothers, Wood Gundy Inc., Goldman Sachs and Company (New York and Toronto, May 5, 1981), p. 6, which also notes that FBDB made some 83 equity-related investments worth over $14 million in 1980.

11. Federal Business Development Bank, "FBDB Equity Financing," October 1981.

12. FBDB, *AR*, 1984, p. 4, and *GM*, July 5, 1986, p. 32.

13. Petro-Canada, *AR*, 1982, p. 22.

14. The actual history of this mixed enterprise turned out to be a dreary series of disagreements concerning overdue payments and cost overruns on the government side. The company never managed to hire native peoples for more than an average of 24 percent of its work force rather than the 60 percent agreed upon. In October 1986 the government sold its interest for $6 million to the majority shareholder, MRI.

15. See Bruce Doern and James A. R. Brothers, "Telesat Canada," in Allan Tupper and Doern, eds., *Public Corporations and Public Policy in Canada* (Montreal: Institute for Research on Public Policy, 1981), pp. 221–50. Other considerations certainly entered into the decision—for example, rivalry with provincial governments to stake out federal control in an area of some constitutional ambiguity. For a careful analysis of the decision-making process see Stephen Brooks, "Direct Investment by the State: Mixed Enterprise in Canada" (diss., Carleton University, 1985).

16. Canada, Laws, Statutes, etc., 1968–69, c. 51, Telesat Canada Act.

17. In 1977 the cabinet did not accept the CRTC's ruling that Telesat membership in the TransCanada Telephone System would reduce competition; in 1981 cabinet rejected the CRTC's requirement that Telesat liberalize its marketing and leasing policies.

18. Brooks, "Direct Investment," argues that the example of government sponsorship provided by Comsat in the United States also influenced thinking in Ottawa toward a mixed enterprise format.

19. Government of Canada, Ministry of State for Economic Development, *News Release*, December 4, 1981, pp. 2 and 4. For press accounts of this case see *GM*, August 16, 1980, p. B16; *FP*, February 21, 1981, p. 4; *GM*, October 31, 1981, p. B1.

20. The ad hoc nature of government investment, and the fact that information avail-

able to Parliament is "fragmented and incomplete," continues to perturb the Auditor General. See paras 5.87 and 5.89 in *Report of the Auditor General of Canada to the House of Commons, Fiscal Year Ended 31 March 1985* (Ottawa: Minister of Supply & Services, 1985), which devoted a chapter to "Mixed and Joint Enterprises."

21. CDIC, *AR*, 1983, p. 2.

22. For an assessment of this economic strategy in the context of the world economic crisis, see François Houle, "Economic Strategy and the Restructuring of the Fordist Wage-Labour Relationship in Canada," *Studies in Political Economy* 11 (Summer 1983), pp. 127–47.

23. Larry Pratt, "Energy: Roots of National Policy," *Studies in Political Economy* 7 (Winter 1982), p. 37.

24. G. Bruce Doern and Glen Toner, *The Politics of Energy: The Development and Implementation of the NEP* (Toronto: Methuen, 1985), pp. 430–39. Megaprojects included the tar sands project Alsands and the heavy oil upgrader project at Cold Lake.

25. Repatriation involved ending the British Parliament's formal right to approve constitutional amendments. See Michael B. Stein, "Canadian Constitutional Reform, 1927–1982," *Publius* 14 (Winter 1984), pp. 121–39.

26. James Laxer, *Rethinking the Economy* (Toronto: New Canada, 1984), p. 68. See p. 69, Table 5, for figures on the decline of real GNP, industrial production, and employment.

27. In 1981 the government had to write off its $125 million equity investment in Consolidated Computer Inc. following intense bureaucratic infighting and embarrassing exposures in the press. See Sandford Borins with Lee Brown, *Investments in Failure: Five Government Corporations That Cost the Canadian Taxpayer Billions* (Toronto: Metheun, 1986).

28. The CDC's *AR*, 1982, reprinted the letter from Senator Jack Austin to H. A. Hampson, president and chief executive officer, CDC, dated May 27, 1982, on pp. 49–50.

29. Strong's extraordinary career combines successful entrepreneurship in private business (e.g., president of Power Corporation in the 1960s), key assignments with international organizations (e.g., coordinator of world relief to Ethiopia in 1985), and political brokerage within the Liberal party. See Peter Foster, "Ottawa's Man: The Interventionist Politics of Maurice Strong," *Saturday Night,* August 1983, pp. 17–23, and Alexander Ross, "Strong Medicine," *Canadian Business,* April 1983, pp. 38–41 and 107–12.

30. Maurice F. Strong, "Government-Private Sector Relations in Canada—The Federal Government as Investor in Business," James Gillies Alumni Lecture, York University, Toronto, March 23, 1983, p. 6.

31. Canada, Privy Council Office, PC 1982–2843 (September 15, 1982). The CDIC was also declared to be a Crown corporation.

32. Ibid., PC 1982–3579 (November 23, 1982). Emergency advances up to this amount are authorized by the Financial Administration Act but seldom used.

33. These maneuvers were uncovered and documented by journalist Michael Valpy—see *GM,* May 20, 1983, p. 6, and February 10, 1983, p. 6.

34. Canada, Parliament, House of Commons, "An Act Respecting the Canada Development Corporation, Canada Development Investment Corporation and Certain Other Corporations," Bill C-25, 2d sess., 32d Parliament, 1983–84, s. 11(1).

35. Comparing types of holding companies, Stephen Brooks quite properly locates the CDIC with those which undertake "the competitive rehabilitation of firms experiencing financing difficulties." Brooks, "The State as Entrepreneur: From CDC to CDIC," *Canadian Public Administration* 26 (Winter 1983), p. 541.

36. Canada, Minister of State, "Statement by Senator Jack Austin," Press Conference, Canada Development Investment Corporation (March 20, 1984), p. 6, and oral remarks supplementing the prepared text.

37. In the late 1970s and early 1980s a series of takeovers took place, favored by the banks' excess liquidity and revisions to the Income Tax Act which allowed deductions for costs of shares purchased. The debt : equity ratios of many companies rose to a point where the companies became vulnerable to small changes in the interest rates.

38. Detailed case studies of the fourteen major bailouts—including Massey-Ferguson, Dome Petroleum, and Chrysler Canada—are in Michael Trebilcock et al., *The Political Economy of Business Bailouts*, vol. 1 (Toronto: Ontario Economic Council, 1985). An analytical framework showing when and why the Canadian government chooses to bailout is provided in ibid., 2: 345–69.

39. Canada, Laws, Statutes, etc., 1980–83, c. 172, "Atlantic Fisheries Restructuring Act," s. 3 and 4(1)(a).

40. Canada, Task Force on Atlantic Fisheries, *Navigating Troubled Waters: A New Policy for the Atlantic Fisheries* (Ottawa: Minister of Supply & Services, 1982).

41. Ibid., p. 35.

42. Ibid., p. 40.

43. Ibid., and *GM*, November 4, 1983, p. 10.

44. Quoted in "The Fishery Fight," editorial, *GM*, August 30, 1983, p. 7.

45. "Agreement between the Government of Canada and the Government of Newfoundland and Labrador Concerning the Restructuring of the Newfoundland Fishery" (September 26, 1983), art. 2(e). The agreement stipulates that "plant closure, plant mergers, mechanization or trawler transfers resulting in a significant permanent change in employment in excess of 100 people, or one-half the workforce . . . associated with any single plant location would be subject to the approval of both governments." Where one government opposes closure, it will be obligated to compensate the company for the loss of income (to be determined by outside accountants).

46. Ibid., arts. 2(d) and 4. Ottawa held 62 percent of the shares, Newfoundland 25 percent, and the BNS 12 percent for four years before reprivatization in 1987.

47. Canada, Fisheries and Oceans, "Federal Provincial Agreement to Cooperate in Restructuring Two Major Nova Scotia Deep-Sea Fishing Companies," *News Release* (September 30, 1983), pp. 2 and 5.

48. Quoted in *GM*, January 18, 1984, p. B5.

49. *GM*, March 24, 1984, p. 3. The tenor of Nova Scotia's opposition to federal government involvement in the industry is well captured in the *Chronicle Herald* (Halifax), January–March 1984. If Ottawa and the Bank of Nova Scotia are formally separate registered owners, the main beneficial owner of NatSea is NS Holdco—a 50-50 partnership between these two shareholders which holds their 34 percent voting stock and, according to the shareholder's agreement, must approve any major changes to the company's structure or financing. Although it has no voting stock, the provincial government does name one director to the board of NatSea.

50. In 1983 Ottawa announced that it would bail out the Quebec fisheries cooperative, Pêcheurs unis du Québec, already dependent on credit guaranteed by the federal government. Ottawa paid the shareholders $15.2 million and transformed the cooperative into a Crown corporation. Why, asked an editorial in Montreal's *Devoir*, $15.2 million when the market value of the shares was not quite a third of that amount? Because it coincided exactly with the debts owed the two secured creditors, the Banque nationale and the Caisse populaire. See Canada, Fisheries and Oceans, "Government of Canada to Fund Restructuring of Pecheurs Unis du Québec," *News Release* (October 16, 1983), and *Le devoir*, February 7, 1984, p. 6. The cooperative was reprivatized in 1986 for $5 million.

51. *FP*, January 1, 1983, p. 4.

52. The structure of capital markets in Canada, the concentration of financial resources among the chartered banks, and the overreliance of many corporations on debt financing gave the commercial banks exceptional influence in the 1980s. See John Calvert, *Government, Limited—The Corporate Takeover of the Public Sector in Canada* (Ottawa: Canadian Centre for Policy Alternatives, 1984). For a broader, comparative analysis of the way in which financial systems shape the ability of governments to influence industrial development see John Zysman, *Governments, Markets, and Growth* (Ithaca: Cornell University Press, 1983).

53. Government of Alberta, *Proposals for an Industrial and Science Strategy for Albertans, 1985–1990* (Edmonton, July 1984), p. 41.

54. Alberta, Legislative Assembly, "The Alberta Heritage Savings Trust Fund Act," Bill-35 (1976).

55. For historical background and an analysis of the role of this provincial government in the economy see John Richards and Larry Pratt, *Prairie Capitalism: Power and Influence in the New West* (Toronto: McClelland & Stewart, 1979).

56. A. F. Collins (deputy provincial treasurer), "The Alberta Heritage Savings Trust Fund: An Overview of the Issues," *Canadian Public Policy*, supplement VI (February 1980), p. 159.

57. Alberta Heritage Savings Trust Fund, *AR*, 1980–81, p. 7. For a critical review of Alberta's development strategy and the role played by the fund see Melville L. McMillan and Kenneth H. Norrie, "Province-Building and Rentier Societies: Alternative Approaches to the Deployment of Natural Resource Rents," in T. M. Ohashi and T. P. Roth, eds., *Privatization in Theory and Practice* (Vancouver: Fraser Institute, 1980), pp. 183–86.

58. Alberta, Legislative Assembly, AHSTF Act. For an interpretation of the actual exercise of powers during the first years of the fund's operations see L. R. Pratt and A. Tupper, "The Politics of Accountability: Executive Discretion and Democratic Control," *Canadian Public Policy*, supplement VI (February 1980), pp. 254–64.

59. This is the title of Peter Foster's best-selling *The Blue-Eyed Sheiks: The Canadian Oil Establishment* (Toronto: Totem, 1979).

60. AHSTF, *AR*, 1980–81, p. 8.

61. AHSTF, *AR*, 1980–81, p. 2; for the issues of contention see Doern and Toner, *Politics of Energy*, pp. 266–75, "Alberta's Response."

62. Collins, "Alberta Heritage," p. 162.

63. Gilles Gherson, "The Living Want a Piece of Alberta Heritage Fund," *Financial Post 500*, June 1981, p. 48.

64. AHSTF, *AR*, 1980–81, p. 7.

65. AEC, *AR*, 1981, p. 4. The Alberta Energy Corporation became a public company in 1975 when the government and the general public each subscribed $75 million shares. AEC is involved in conventional oil and gas production but also in coal, forest products, and petrochemicals. In 1985 the government reduced its ownership share to 37 percent by having AEC buy back shares for cancellation, thus generating $125 million for general government revenues. AEC, *AR*, 1985.

66. Personal interviews, Government of Alberta, Treasury Department, June 1982; *GM*, September 1, 1983, p. B3; and June 16, 1982, p. B6.

67. See McMillan and Norrie, "Province Building."

68. James Pesando, "An Economic Analysis of Government Investment Corporations, with Attention to the Caisse de dépôt et placement du Québec and the Alberta Heritage Fund," Economic Council of Canada Discussion Paper 277 (Ottawa 1986).

69. The newly elected Conservative government premier, Don Getty, committed himself, despite continuing budget deficits, not to touch the fund's principal and to make economic diversification the top policy priority. *GM*, May 7, 1986, p. A4.

70. *FP 500*, Summer 1985. Since 1983 the Caisse has also made foreign investments.

71. Jorge Niosi, *Canadian Capitalism* (Toronto: Lorimer, 1981), pp. 108–9; Fernand Martin, "La SGF et ses filiales: Une étude de cas," paper prepared for the Economic Council of Canada (October 18, 1984), pp. 25–26.

72. Douglas Fullerton, "La Caisse de dépôt—un regard en arrière," in Claude E. Forget, ed., *La Caisse de dépôt et placement du Québec* (Montreal: C. D. Howe Research Institute, 1984), p. 27, our trans.

73. Ibid., pp. 2–30, explains the thinking behind these choices.

74. See Niosi, *Canadian Capitalism*, pp. 108–9; Martin, "SGF," pp. 25–35.

75. Caisse, *AR*, 1985, p. 21. The SGF was revamped as a 100 percent government-owned holding company in 1972 and directed by government in the 1980s to concentrate investments in five sectors identified as strategic for industrial development. SGF, *AR*,

1984, p. 4; Jean-Claude Lebel, "Les sociétés d'état au Québec: Un outil indispensable," *Canadian Public Administration* 27 (Summer 1984), p. 256.

76. Quebec, National Assembly, 1st sess., 1965, "An Act Respecting the Caisse de Dépôt et placement du Québec," s. 32(a).

77. Pierre Fournier, *Les sociétés d'état et les objectifs économiques du Québec* (Québec: Office de planification et de développement du Québec, 1978), p. 29, our trans.

78. Ibid., chap. 2.1 on the Caisse.

79. Stephen Brooks and A. Brian Tanguay, "Québec's Caisse de Dépôt et Placement: Tool of Nationalism?" *Canadian Public Administration* 28 (Spring 1985), p. 119.

80. Caisse de dépôt et placement du Québec, *AR*, 1981, p. 15. At the same time, to increase the profitability of its real estate portfolio, the Caisse established two wholly owned subsidiaries—one to manage these investments and the other to administer the properties acquired.

81. Jacques Parizeau, "Public Enterprises: The Quebec Experience," Institute for Research on Public Policy *Newsletter* 7 (March–April 1985).

82. A listing of all the Caisse's investments in corporate securities worth over $5 million or representing more than 10 percent of voting rights is provided as an insert to its *AR*, 1985.

83. *GM*, April 11, 1981, p. 1; *Toronto Daily Star*, November 3, 1981, p. 1. The logical conclusion was reached in 1985 when Gaz-Metro, still majority-controlled by the two state agencies, bought out Inter-Cité, thus eliminating the Winnipeg company that held 40 percent of this second gas distributor. *GM*, May 8, 1985, p. B20.

84. *GM*, August 20, 1981, p. B1. The Caisse still holds a 15 percent interest in Domtar. The SGF maintains a 28 percent share through its majority-owned holding company, Dofor. Although privatization was announced, no serious offers were received. See Dofor Inc., "Quarterly Report at September 30, 1986" (Montreal, 1986), and *GM*, February 19, 1987, p. B5.

85. *GM*, January 21, 1982, p. B5; November 11, 1982; and June 13, 1984, p. B1.

86. March Côté and Léon Courville, "La perception de la Caisse de dépôt et placement du Québec par les chefs d'entreprise," in Forget, *La Caisse de dépôt*, pp. 74–91. This distinction between board membership and executive committee membership suggests the impotence of many corporate boards today. In all instances the hostility of the English-speaking executives toward the Caisse was even more pronounced than that of their French-speaking counterparts.

87. David Olive, "Caisse Unpopulaire," *Canadian Business*, May 1982, pp. 94–101.

88. Canada, Parliament, Senate, Bill S-31, "An Act to Limit Shareholding in Certain Corporations," 1st sess., 32d Parliament, November 2, 1982, s. 3 and s. 6.

89. Allan Tupper, "Bill S-31 and the Federalism of State Capitalism," Discussion Paper no. 18 (Kingston: Institute of Intergovernmental Relations, n.d.), p. 19.

90. Ibid., pp. 24–25; Roy Romanow (cabinet member, Government of Saskatchewan), "Bill to Limit Provincial Ownership Full of Flaws," comment in *FP*, January 1, 1983, p. 6, and supporting letter from British Columbia cabinet minister R. Mair, "Forced March of Centralization," *FP*, January 15, 1983, p. 8.

91. Caisse, *AR*, 1985, p. 5.

CHAPTER 7. *Collaborating with Private Capital: Joint Ventures*

1. See Frank Swedlove, "The Joint-Venture Alternative for Investing in Canada," *Foreign Investment Review* 2 (Winter 1977–78), p. 16, and Allen R. Janger, *Organization of International Joint Ventures*, Report no. 787 (New York: Conference Board, 1980), pp. 4–5.

2. See Frank Swedlove, "Business-Government Joint Ventures in Canada," *Foreign Investment Review* 3 (Spring 1978), pp. 13–16. Joint venturing is an established practice in many countries. See for example Lloyd Musolf, *Mixed Enterprise: A Developmental Perspective* (Lexington, Mass.: Lexington, 1972).

3. Swedlove, "Business-Government," p. 13.

4. Nova Scotia Resources Ltd., *WHO? WHY? HOW?* a brochure published by NSRL (n.p., n.d.).

5. For a list of these subsidiaries see Government of Canada, President of the Treasury Board, *Annual Report to Parliament on Crown Corporations and Other Corporate Interests of Canada, 1983–84* (Ottawa: Minister of Supply & Services, June 1985), p. 344.

6. Quoted in *GM,* November 18, 1980, p. B2.

7. The constitution stipulates that "each province is given exclusive power to make laws in relation to exploration, development, conservation, and management of non-renewable natural resources" and that they may "levy both direct and indirect taxes with respect to non-renewable resources." The Constitution Act, 1982, sec. 92A.

8. See Ted Greenwood, "Uranium," in Carl Beigie and Alfred Hero, Jr., eds., *Natural Resources in U.S.-Canadian Relations* (Boulder, Colo.: Westview, 1980), 2:345, 354. Uranium is the one exception to the constitutional provision cited in note 7 above. Prior to 1970 there were no restrictions on foreign investment in the uranium industry. Concern about foreign ownership developed in 1970 when a Canadian-owned uranium company wished to sell its assets to an American company. The federal government disallowed the sale and announced general controls on the level of foreign ownership.

9. For a detailed discussion of the National Energy Program see G. Bruce Doern and Glen Toner, *The Politics of Energy* (Toronto: Methuen, 1985).

10. For a discussion of NDP philosophy see Chapter 5. Other Saskatchewan Crown corporations also engage in joint ventures; for example, Saskoil has oil and gas joint ventures with Canadian and foreign-owned oil companies.

11. See G. Bruce Doern, *Government Intervention in the Nuclear Industry* (Montreal: Institute for Research on Public Policy, 1980), pp. 19–24.

12. *GM,* November 5, 1979, p. B6.

13. SMDC, *AR,* 1985, p. 5, and 1984, p. 4.

14. *Financial Times* (Toronto), April 8, 1985, p. 25.

15. SMDC, *AR,* 1983, p. 3.

16. Ibid., 1985, p. 21.

17. SMDC, *AR,* 1983, p. 9. SMDC originally acquired a share in the Key Lake project in 1974 when the site was in the early phases of exploration and raised its interest in the venture to 50 percent in 1979 when Inexco Oil Company of Houston sold its one-third interest.

18. Amok is controlled by three French companies: Cogema, a subsidiary of the French Atomic Energy Commission, which has a 38 percent interest; CFM-Mokta, which is in turn a subsidiary of Imetal, a French mining company with overseas interests, 37 percent; and PUK, a large aluminum producer (nationalized by the French government in 1982), with a 25 percent interest.

19. Interviews, SMDC, Saskatoon, April 1983. Cluff Lake produced its first uranium in 1980. Expansion of initial capacity at the Cluff Lake site began almost as soon as the first uranium was produced, with Phase II of the mine commencing the extraction and milling of ore in 1984. SMDC, *AR,* 1984, p. 10.

20. SMDC, *AR,* 1983, p. 17, and 1984, p. 4.

21. Interviews with company officials, Saskatoon, April 1983.

22. Calculated from SMDC annual reports, 1981 to 1985 inclusive. SMDC markets its share—50 percent—of the uranium from the Key Lake mine. Amok sells all of the uranium from the Cluff Lake mine and distributes the profits.

23. For example, Cogema of France has a long-term contract to purchase uranium produced by the Cluff Lake mine. SMDC, *AR,* 1983, p. 7.

24. Ibid., 1985, p. 5.

25. The last time the number had been so low was the 1976–77 exploration year. SMDC, *AR,* 1982, p. 3, and 1983, p. 17.

26. SMDC began to explore for base metals outside Saskatchewan in the 1976–77 explo-

ration year. SMDC's extraprovincial activities were carried on by a wholly owned subsidiary, SMD Mining Co., now inactive.

27. Interview, Saskatoon, April 1983.

28. SMDC, *AR*, 1985, p. 3.

29. Among the many Quebec state enterprises that engage in joint ventures are Rexfor, Société générale de financement, and Sidbec. The last joined with British Steel Corporation and Quebec Cartier Mining Co. of Montreal, a unit of United States Steel, in Sidbec-Normines Inc., a mining and pelletized ore operation. Sidbec entered the joint venture because it wanted a secure supply of pelletized ore. The venture was not a success, and the plant was sold for a nominal sum to Quebec Cartier Mining. *GM*, May 17, 1985, p. B4.

30. Interviews, Quebec City, August 23, 1982.

31. An Act Respecting the Société québécoise d'exploration minière, Revised Statutes of Quebec 1977, c. S-19 as amended, sec. 3.

32. Calculated from Soquem annual reports, 1981–1985.

33. See Pierre Fournier, *The Quebec Establishment*, 2d rev. ed. (Montreal: Black Rose, 1976), p. 188.

34. Patrick Caragata, *National Resources and International Bargaining Power: Canada's Mineral Policy Options* (Kingston: Centre for Resource Studies, 1984), p. 78. Soquem and Teck Corporation each had a 50 percent interest in the Niobec mine.

35. Soquem, *AR*, 1983/84, p. 19; *GM* September 11, 1985, p. B6, April 20, 1986, p. B6, and February 27, 1987, p. B4.

36. Soquem, *AR*, 1984/1985, pp. 4–5, and *GM*, July 22, 1985, p. B4.

37. Soquem, *AR*, 1983/1984, p. 5. Share sales later reduced Soquem's interest in this company from 43 to 31 percent. *GM*, August 25, 1985, p. B6.

38. *GM*, April 30, 1986, p. B6. Soquem's interest in Cambior could be reduced to 21 percent by 1990 if all the warrants available with the sale of shares are exercised. Interview, Soquem, October 27, 1986. A more complete discussion of Quebec's privatization program is given in Chapter 8.

39. Fournier, *Quebec Establishment*, pp. 191, 192.

40. An Act Respecting the Société québécoise d'initiatives pétrolières, Revised Statutes of Quebec 1977, c. S-22 as amended, secs. 3 and 17.

41. Quoted in *GM*, September 22, 1983, p. B13.

42. Done through a GNC Québec Ltd. joint venture established in 1982 in which Soquip has a 25 percent share, Gaz Métropolitain 25 percent, and CNG Fuel Systems 50 percent. See Soquip, *AR*, 1984/1985, pp. 17, 18.

43. Ibid., 1980/1981, p. 4. See also An Act Respecting the Société québécoise d'initiatives pétrolières, sec. 3.

44. Soquip, *AR*, 1981/1982, p. 1, and 1985/1986, inside cover.

45. Ibid., 1985/1986, p. 2. Gaz Métropolitain, which is 20 percent owned by Soquip, acquired all of the common shares of Gaz Inter-Cité as well as two other companies in the spring of 1985. See Chapter 6 for further details.

46. Soquip subsequently sold 50 percent of the assets to Westmin Resources of Calgary. Soquip, *AR*, 1984/1985, p. 8.

47. Ibid., 1984/1985, p. 11, and 1985/1986, p. 8. The Quebec minister for privatization has indicated that Soquip Alberta will be put up for sale, saying "it's not up to the Quebec Government to pump money into Alberta" (quoted in *GM*, February 23, 1987, p. B4).

48. Ibid., 1985/1986, p. 4.

49. *FP*, June 30, 1984, p. 23.

50. Soquip, *AR*, 1983/1984, p. 15, and 1984/1985, pp. 12–13.

51. Ibid., 1985/1986, p. 23. Exploration Soquip also undertook a major exploration program in Hudson Bay which associated it with state and private-sector corporations including Onexco Oil & Gas and Trillium Exploration, subsidiaries of the provincial government enterprise Ontario Energy Corporation.

52. Ibid., pp. 12, 28, 29. Soquem owns 50 percent of the consortium. Its other partners are Alberta Natural Gas and the SNC Group.

53. NSRL, *AR*, 1984, p. 1, emphasis added, and 1982–83, p. 2.
54. Ibid., 1985–86, p. 4.
55. Ibid., 1982–1983, p. 5. In 1983–84 PIP payments totaled 65 percent of funds expended on exploration. Ibid., 1984, p. 3.
56. Ibid., 1985–86, p. 3.
57. Ibid., 1984, p. 6.
58. Ibid., 1985–86, p. 10.
59. Ibid., 1982–1983, p. 11, and 1984, p. 9. With the submission of its report the consortium fulfilled its mandate, and since none of the participants was prepared to commit further resources to the project, the consortium was disbanded.
60. OEC, *AR*, 1984, p. 2.
61. The Ontario government paid $650 million for a 25 percent share of Suncor by paying $325 million in cash and borrowing another $325 million at 14 percent from Suncor. *GM*, November 25, 1981, p. 6; *FP*, November 6, 1982, p. 6, and February 23, 1985, p. 5.
62. Ironically perhaps, in view of the furor over the purchase, OEC was not Suncor's first choice as a vehicle for Canadianization. Toronto *Financial Times*, October 19, 1981, pp. 18 and 41. The Ontario government never exercised its option to purchase another 26 percent of Suncor, nor could it find any private-sector investors interested in buying its interest. *GM*, March 20, 1985, p. 26.
63. OEC, *AR*, 1985, p. 3.
64. Peter Lamb, notes for Panel Discussion at the National Energy Program Seminar, Toronto, January 17, 1983, pp. 3–5.
65. See table on p. 6 of OEC, *AR*, 1985. Trillium participated in six of the fourteen significant hydrocarbon discoveries made by the petroleum industry in Canada's frontier regions in 1984.
66. Panarctic Oil, a consortium of companies, was established in the late 1960s to undertake high-risk oil and gas exploration in the Arctic. The federal government purchased a 45 percent controlling interest in Panarctic shortly after its establishment, an interest that was transferred in 1976 to Petro-Canada.
67. OEC, *AR*, 1985, p. 2.
68. Ibid., p. 20, and 1984, pp. 5–8; *GM*, March 20, 1985, p. B12.
69. Manitoba also got into the act. In 1982 the province set up the Manitoba Oil and Gas Corporation in order to explore, develop, transport, or sell petroleum and natural gas and empowered it to "participate with others either directly or in partnership or through subsidiaries or through operating companies established to carry on joint operations for the participants." The Manitoba Oil and Gas Corporation Act, Sec. 4(b).
70. OEC, *AR*, 1984, p. 2, and 1985, pp. 9–13.
71. Ibid., 1984, p. 2, and 1985, p. 11.
72. IDEA Corporation, *AR*, 1983, p. 6. See also *GM*, December 31, 1983, p. 42. Efforts to combine the innovative capability of private-sector, university, and government research centers have become increasingly common in North America in the 1980s. The Saskatchewan government, for example, has joined forces with the University of Saskatchewan and private investors in SED Systems Inc., which now has a government holding of 23 percent of share capital, to promote new communications technology. SED Systems entered into a joint venture with White Radio in Ontario to enhance marketing of its satellite television receivers. *FP*, February 18, 1984, p. 11.
73. IDEA also sought to promote technology transfer. The corporation acted as a technology broker by arranging licenses for new products and processes; it also developed public policies and education programs that contribute to public understanding and debate on issues related to technological innovation. IDEA Corporation, *AR*, 1984, p. 1.
74. Ibid., 1983, p. 6.
75. Ibid., pp. 7–8, 17, for lists and descriptions of the specific funds.
76. Ibid., 1984, p. 2.
77. *GM*, May 14, 1986, p. A6, and *FP*, April 5, 1986, p. 5.

78. For a list of these capital sources see IDEA Corporation, *AR*, 1984.

79. *FP*, April 5, 1986, p. 5.

80. Ministry of Industry, Trade and Technology, Ontario, *News Release*, February 19, 1986. The government, still concerned about promoting industrial innovation in Ontario, replaced IDEA with an older modality, a high-technology fund to be administered by a tripartite council of representatives from business, universities, and government. *Toronto Star*, April 19, 1986, p. A1.

81. Interviews, Edmonton, November 1983, and *FP*, October 3, 1983, pp. 18–19.

82. *Financial Times* (Toronto), February 17, 1986, p. 10.

83. Memorandum of Understanding between the Minister of Transportation and Communications and the Urban Transportation Development Corporation, June 12, 1979, art. 4.

84. UTDC was established in 1973 as the Ontario Transportation Development Corporation under the Ontario Business Corporations Act. UTDC received letters patent in October 1974 under the federal Canada Corporations Act. For background and a critical assessment see Christopher J. Maule, *The Urban Transportation Development Corporation: A Case Study of Government Enterprise*, Discussion Paper no. 281 (Ottawa: Economic Council of Canada, 1985), pp. 21–22.

85. Quoted in Marsha Gordon, *Government in Business* (Montreal: C. D. Howe Institute, 1981), p. 185.

86. Among UTDC's other objectives were to coordinate research activities in the industrial, commercial, and academic sectors; and to ensure that Ontario municipalities did not face a monopoly in equipment supply. Maule, *Urban Transportation Development Corporation*, pp. 4–5.

87. *GM*, April 1, 1985, p. B12.

88. UTDC, *AR*, 1985, p. 4, and 1984, pp. 9, 15; *GM*, April 1, 1985, p. B12.

89. UTDC, *AR*, 1984, pp. 9, 20.

90. Ibid., and *GM*, March 11, 1985, p. B10.

91. UTDC, *AR*, 1985, pp. 20, 22.

92. *GM*, February 8, 1986, p. B2, and Maule, *Urban Transportation Development Corporation*, pp. 35–41. While in opposition the Liberal party was highly critical of UTDC's operations and its accounting practices.

93. Quoted in *FP*, August 2, 1986, p. 3.

94. *GM*, July 15, 1986, p. A4.

95. *GM*, October 31, 1980, p. B6.

96. Petro-Canada, *AR*, 1984, p. 34.

97. *GM*, November 29, 1982, p. B5.

98. Quoted in *FP*, January 7, 1984, p. 5.

99. Petro-Canada, *AR*, 1984, p. 34. The directive came as Privy Council Order PC1984–4187. The new government explained that its decision to abandon Canertech was intended to leave "more room for the private sector to exploit market opportunities." Canada, Department of Finance, *A New Direction for Canada: An Agenda for Economic Renewal* (Ottawa, November 8, 1984), p. 65.

CHAPTER 8. *Looking Ahead: State Capitalism in Question*

1. For a survey of trends see "Privatisation—Everybody's Doing It, Differently," *The Economist*, December 21, 1985, pp. 71–86. National policy debates are analyzed in the special issue "Privatization of Public Enterprise, a European Debate," *Annals of Public and Co-operative Economy* 57 (April–June 1986).

2. United Kingdom, Commons, Debates, 5th ser., vol. 967 (1979–1980), cols. 48–49 (May 15, 1979): Spanish instruction as quoted in *FP*, November 17, 1984, p. B14.

3. Disagreement over the limits to nationalization subsequently contributed to the

break-up of the Union de la gauche in September 1977. The Communists wanted to specify that some 700 *subsidiaries* of the conglomerates to be nationalized would also be taken over, but the Socialists refused. Point 21 of the Socialist program for the 1981 elections nonetheless reaffirmed a commitment to nationalization. The thinking behind this platform is detailed in the proceedings of the party conference on industrial policy and nationalizations: *Socialisme et industrie* (Paris: Club socialiste du livre, 1980).

4. The tortuous process of getting the nationalization legislation passed, including challenges before the Constitutional Court, is chronicled in André G. Delion and Michel Durupty, *Les nationalisations 1982* (Paris: Economica, 1982), pp. 75–116. The law is no. 82-115, published in the *Journal officiel*, February 13, 1982.

5. Three major banks were in fact *re*nationalized. The Banque nationale de Paris, Crédit Lyonnais, and Société générale had been nationalized in the 1940s and then authorized by a 1973 law to issue up to 25 percent of their shares to their employees. The five conglomerates were Compagnie générale d'électricité, Pechiney-Ugine-Kuhlmann, Rhône Poulenc, St. Gobain, and Thomson-Brandt.

6. Protocols signed October 8 and 12, 1981, respectively. The previous government had already negotiated a minority shareholding in Dassault and a double-weighted vote at the Board of Directors on specified questions. In 1981 company president Marcel Dassault made the government a personal gift of the shares required to bring the state's holding to 51 percent.

7. CII-Honeywell Bull in the computer industry, where government enhanced its 47 percent interest to 80 percent; Roussel-Uclaf, the chemical and pharmaceutical company controlled by the German group Hoechst, where it took a minority interest sufficient to confer veto power; and the Compagnie générale de constructions téléphoniques, owned by U.S. ITT, which after bitter bargaining became a wholly owned state enterprise.

8. The Finance Law of November 18, 1981, converted the government's loans to equity.

9. Comparing nationalized industry after 1982 to the manufacturing and energy sectors, some statistical sources show its shares as high as 25 percent of employment, 56 percent of investment, 30 percent of value added, and 32 percent of export value. See "Nationalisations industrielles et bancaires," *Cahiers français* no. 214 (January–February 1984), p. 22. State ownership figures are from Delion and Durupty, *Nationalisations*, p. 191.

10. Christian Stoffaës, *Politique industrielle* (Paris: Les cours de droit, 1984), p. 585; "Nationalisations industrielles," p. 7, and "Annex 5" on St Gobain, p. 1.

11. This is not to deny that ideology was the driving force behind the nationalization policy. The Socialists were indeed committed to the premise that a shift in the balance of power from private to public sector was required to protect the public interest. Concentration within French industry, they argued, placed undue power in the hands of a narrow economic elite motivated by short-term financial gain. At one level the simple legal transfer of property to the state resolved this problem. French Socialists rejected "statism," however, insisting that public ownership was merely a prerequisite for progressive industrial and social policy.

12. These objectives were voiced by the prime minister before the Assembly September 16, October 14, and November 21, 1981; by the president in his press conference September 24, 1981. It was assumed that industrial democracy would reinforce the first policy priority—competitiveness—since workers with a voice in decision making would be more likely to support the government's modernization and restructuring plans.

13. Letter from Pierre Dreyfus in "Nationalisations industrielles," p. 12. Mitterrand's thinking is said to have been influenced by his key adviser, Alain Boublil, whose 1977 book, *Le socialisme industriel*, argued for a modern strategy of nationalization wherein state-owned firms would be technology leaders, independently managed, and capable of recapturing competitive success for a French company that would otherwise be restructured by multinational firms in the interests of international capital.

14. As for the socialists' second objective, the Law of Democratization was passed July

26, 1983. It introduced a tripartite decision-making structure to the Boards of Directors in all state-owned or -controlled firms with more than 1,000 employees: six representatives each from government, workers, and "competent" individuals chosen by the government from outside the firm. (Smaller companies were to have two workers' representatives on the board following the passage of a second democratization law on February 13, 1984.) During 1984 new boards were elected on this basis for over six hundred state-controlled companies. A far cry from the self-management schemes promoted by some socialists, these measures permitted only formal worker participation—both because candidates had to be approved either by the established unions or by workers' committees in place since the 1940s and because, however construed, Boards of Directors exercise very limited power in France.

15. The "contrats de plan," cosigned by the president of a state enterprise and the minister of industry, were announced in the 1982 nationalization law. These documents are just a variation on the program contracts used by the previous government. They clarify corporate intentions and government preferences in reaching mutual agreement on the areas for state financing. For their history and an optimistic view of their efficacy see Haut Conseil du Secteur Public, *Rapport, 1984* (Paris: La documentation française, 1984), vol. 1, pt. 2, chap. 3.

16. *Le matin*, August 31, 1982, and "Contrats de Plan, signature chez Rhône Poulenc et Usinor," *Le nouvel journal*, February 18, 1983.

17. For detailed descriptions of restructuring by sector see Stoffaës, *Politique industrielle*, chaps. 5 and 6.

18. On this crucial turning point in the Socialist government's economic strategy see Peter Hall, "Socialism in One Country: Mitterrand and the Struggle to Define a New Economic Strategy for France," in P. Cerny and M. Schain, eds. *Socialism, the State and Public Policy in France* (London: Pinter, 1984), and Vincent Wright, "Socialism and the Interdependent Economy: Industrial Policy-Making under the Mitterrand Presidency," *Government and Opposition* 19 (Summer 1984), pp. 287–303. An acerbic interpretation from within the French intellectual left is Alain Lipietz, *L'audace ou l'enlissement: Sur les politiques économiques de la gauche* (Paris: Le découverte, 1984).

19. "Le fardeau du secteur public," *Expansion*, April 22–May 5, 1983, p. 59.

20. Haut Conseil, *Rapport, 1984* 1:36, 2:252.

21. "Le fardeau du secteur public," p. 55.

22. Fabius is quoted in "Nationalisations industrielles," p. 71. The renewed emphasis on managerial autonomy commenced with President Mitterrand's chastisement of Chevènement at the February 1983 cabinet meeting after many state enterprise executives had complained of excess *dirigisme*. See *Le monde*, February 3–9, 1983, p. 1. The government did not even maintain a "global level." A new sectoral plan for steel was implemented in spring 1984 which closed plants and put more than 25,000 steelworkers out of work. The political costs were enormous. Massive demonstrations denounced the betrayal of socialist ideology, and by summer the Communists had withdrawn from the coalition government to move into political opposition.

23. "Nationalisations industrielles," p. 37. The Haut Conseil's 1984 *Rapport* gives a detailed breakdown of the multinational operations of nationalized industries (vol. 1, Annexe 1, p. 307).

24. Examples from Haut Conseil, *Rapport, 1984*, 2:83 and 93–97. This freedom should not be exaggerated. When a private or public company's decision had high political visibility, ministers intervened and, in the public sector, they prevailed. Thus Thomson was obliged to reverse its January 1983 decision to sign a market-sharing agreement with an American group after intense lobbying by groups opposed to the consequent closure of a plant in France. See ibid., 2:63.

25. Haut Conseil, *Rapport, 1984*, 1:258–59; *Les échos*, June 18, 1985, p. 1.

26. Interview by the minister of industry, Edith Cresson, in the popular daily *Liberation* as interpreted in *L'Express*, May 3, 1985, pp. 26–28.

27. The French stock as opposed to bond market is traditionally marginal in financing investment, and the share of the population holding shares is likewise tiny compared to most industrial countries. For analysis of impediments to privatization see François de Witt, "Dénationalisation, les dix pièges," *Expansion*, April 18–May 1, 1986, pp. 93–101. The Privatization Law of August 6, 1986, was put through after President Mitterrand refused to sign executive decrees authorizing sales. See "Privatisations: Querelle sur la liste," *L'Express*, April 18, 1986, pp. 28–29.

28. By early 1987 the government had successfully floated the shares in St Gobain—an issue fourteen times oversubscribed—and in the state banking group Paribas. It had also divested 11 percent of its holding in the mixed enterprise Elf Aquitaine and invited bidders to purchase the telephone equipment maker CGCT. Statist considerations prompted restrictions—the privatization legislation stipulated a 20 percent ceiling on foreign ownership and gave government the right to take a special share (an "action spécifique d'état," like the British golden share) for five years in any defense or strategic industry. For example the oil company Elf was designated strategic for reasons of national energy independence. The government could thus approve or reject any shareholder's seeking more than 10 percent of the company's stock. *Le monde*, September 17, 1986, p. 45.

29. Her Majesty's Treasury, "Privatization in the United Kingdom, Background Briefing," no. 18/1 (London, n.d.) p. 1.

30. Amersham was formerly a profit center within the Atomic Energy Authority. A detailed status report on privatization legislation as at April 1982 is an appendix to D. A. Heald and D. R. Steel, "Privatizing Public Enterprise: An Analysis of the Government's Case," *Political Quarterly* 53 (1982), pp. 346–49.

31. Were all targeted companies to be sold, the state enterprise share of Britain's GDP would be 6.5 percent rather than 10 percent in 1979, when the Thatcher government was formed. *The Economist*, December 21, 1985, p. 85. British Gas Corp.'s shares, worth some £16 billion, went on sale in November 1986; the share issue for British Airways took place in February 1987 after two postponements; legislation to transform the water authorities into private limited companies has not been introduced at the time of writing.

32. Indispensable are Frank Blackaby, ed., *De-Industrialisation* (London: Heinemann, 1979); Colin Leys, "Thatcherism and British Manufacturing: A Question of Hegemony," *New Left Review* 151 (May–June 1985), pp. 5–25; Stephen Wilks, "Introduction: Industrial Policy and Industrial Decline," in Wilks, *Industrial Policy and the Motor Industry* (Manchester: Manchester University Press, 1984); and Peter A. Hall, "The State and Economic Decline," in Bernard Elbaum and William Lazonick, eds., *The Decline of the British Economy* (Oxford: Oxford University Press, 1986), pp. 226–302.

33. United Kingdom, Commons, *Debates*, 5th ser. vol. 967, 1979–1980, cols. 710–711 (May 21, 1979).

34. See *Manchester Guardian Weekly*, October 2, 1983, p. 3. The debate over the real impact of privatization on public-sector borrowing rates (the PSBR) is never-ending. For an attempt at measurement see R. Buckland and E. W. Davis, "Privatization Techniques and the PSBR," *Fiscal Studies* 5 (August 1984), pp. 44–53; for a skeptical political analysis see David Heald, "Will the Privatization of Public Enterprises Solve the Problem of Control?" *Public Administration* 63 (Spring 1985), pp. 11–12.

35. HM Treasury, "Why Privatize?" speech by John Moore, financial secretary and minister responsible for co-ordinating the privatization program, November 1, 1983, p. 1. The business press remained skeptical, however, as the *Economist* expressed concern that "raising money has become more important than promoting competition," December 21, 1985, p. 86. The theoretical underpinning for the government's initial program was provided by economists Michael Beesley and Stephen Littlechild, "Privatization: Principles, Problems and Priorities," *Lloyd's Bank Review* 149 (July 1983), pp. 1–20.

36. See David Heald, "Privatization: Analysing Its Appeal and Limitations," *Fiscal Studies* 5 (February 1984), pp. 36–46. A provocative example of militant Conservative support for privatization, showing twenty-two ways Thatcher used to carry out the program, is

Madson Pirie, "The British Experience," in S. Butler, ed., *The Privatization Option* (London: Heritage, 1985), pp. 53–68. A critical assessment of the actual relationship between change of ownership and competition policy is J. A. Kay and Z. A. Silberston, "The New Industrial Policy: Privatization and Competition," *Midland Bank Review*, Spring 1984, pp. 8–16.

37. Heald and Steel, "Privatizing Public Enterprise," p. 334.

38. HM Treasury, "A People's Capital Market," speech by John Moore, financial secretary, December 5, 1984. From the outset of privatization in 1981, a portion of shares was normally reserved for employees who were offered special incentives (in the case of Amersham International, some shares were given away).

39. Ibid. In many instances, as might be expected, a concentration followed the initial share offering as small shareholders sold to make a short-term gain and institutional investors accumulated shares. One year after privatization, for example, the number of shareholders in British Aerospace had diminished from 158,000 to 28,000, those in Amersham International from 65,000 to 10,000. F. E. Dangeard, "Nationalisations et dénationalisations en Grande Bretagne," *Notes et études documentaires*, 4739–4740 (November 14, 1983), p. 43.

40. For contending explanations of Thatcher's political success see Stuart Hall and M. Jacques, eds., *The Politics of Thatcherism* (London: Macmillan, 1983); its critique by Bob Jessop et al., "Authoritarian Populism: Two Nations and Thatcherism," *New Left Review* 147 (September–October 1984), pp. 32–60; and the rejoinder by Hall, "Authoritarian Populism: A Reply to Jessop et al.," *New Left Review* 151 (May–June 1985), pp. 104–23.

41. By year end 1986 Rolls-Royce, the state-owned aircraft engine maker, had returned to profitability and was sold during 1987, and some of British Shipbuilders' warship yards had been divested. On British Steel see *GM*, July 9, 1986, p. B11.

42. *The Guardian*, November 28, 1982, p. 3. Britoil was, however, fully privatized in 1985.

43. British Leyland had been nationalized in the early 1970s to salvage jobs and export earnings. Tory objections were not to privatization as such but to foreign takeover that threatened job losses (and hence parliamentary seats) in the Midlands and a possible shift away from U.K. component suppliers. After negotiations with GM broke down in March 1986, the state-owned firm was reorganized and renamed the Rover Group. Its subsidiary RRONA opened a U.S. headquarters to help sell Range Rovers in North America. Rover's van operations and Leyland Trucks were later merged in a new group partly owned by Rover but controlled by the Dutch vehicle manufacturer Daf, itself partly state-owned. See the *Economist*, February 8, 1986, pp. 53–54; and March 29, 1986, p. 45; *Manchester Guardian Weekly*, March 30, 1986, p. 3; and *Financial Times* (London), November 4, 1986, p. 7, and February 20, 1987, p. 1.

44. After the official bidding, however, RTZ managed to accumulate a 29.9 percent interest by buying shares on the market. *Financial Times* (London) July 3, 1984, p. 1.

45. HM Treasury, "Privatization Achievements," speech by John Moore, financial secretary, July 18, 1984, p. 18.

46. British Aerospace, *Prospectus* (April 3, 1985), pp. 8, 19. Some special shares had specified dates of expiry. For details see Heald, "Will the Privatization," pp. 18–19.

47. *FP*, November 17, 1984, p. B14; *GM*, November 12, 1984, p. 184; *New York Times*, January 6, 1986.

48. IRI quoted in *GM*, February 25, 1985, p. IB4. Riccardo Parboni attributes these losses to the jump in interest rates, doubling from 1975 to 1980. State-owned enterprises were highly leveraged due to the government's preference for debt rather than equity financing. He also argues that some privatization was undertaken to assist *private* enterprises restructuring to meet international competition, as when ENI took over losing plants in the chemicals industry from private firms and then rationalized them. See Parboni, "La privatizzazione dell'economia italiana," *Stato e Mercato* no. 12 (December 1984), pp. 385–430.

49. The president of ENI, the energy holding company, was quoted as saying he "hopes

to raise about $1 billion (U.S.) from the injection of private capital into several of its companies and from asset disposals over the next three years," *GM*, June 18, 1984, p. IB3.

50. Quoted in *GM*, April 16; 1984, p. IB5. See *The Economist*, January 5, 1985, p. 59, or *GM*, June 10, 1985, p. 10, where numerous additional examples are given.

51. In socialist Sweden, too, the government opted to eliminate subsidies to state enterprises and sell out interests worth several hundred million dollars in order "to improve the efficiency and competitiveness of the Group." Statsföretag, *AR*, 1982, p. 2.

52. Objections within the party, which had centered around Edward Heath, broadened by summer 1985 to include many Conservative MPs when cuts in social spending hit hospitals and schools. Business elites also turned away from Thatcherism. The Confederation of British Industires was notably unenthusiastic about privatization in its consultation document "Change to Succeed" published in March 1985: "There will continue to be a number of industries in state ownership for the foreseeable future. In some cases privatisation, or at least an influx of private capital, may well be appropriate. If and when an industry is privatised, [the decision] . . . should be determined by the need to encourage greater efficiency and competition, rather than by the drive to maximise the proceeds to the Treasury" (p. 59).

53. Bonn's privatization program began with a May 1983 cabinet decision to reduce the government's ownership share in VEBA (while retaining veto power). Then in January 1985 a government catalogue listing potential privatization candidates was published. See J.-M. Messier and André Barbé, "La République fédérale allemande," in Barbé et al., *Dénationalisations* (Paris: Economica, 1986), pp. 47–68. On Lufthansa see *FP*, April 16, 1985, p. 14 and *GM*, August 6, 1985, p. B14.

54. *Financial Times* (London), November 15, 1984, p. 2. Since this evaluation, Finance Minister Gerhard Stoltenberg has twice proclaimed his intent to further reduce government equity holdings (when introducing the 1985 and 1986 budgets). Selling off Bonn's stake in VW and VEBA, he noted, could raise 4.5 billion marks. The VEBA group, however, made record profits in 1985, and the prospect of elections in January 1987 no doubt dampened other ministers' interest in making such a controversial move official policy. *GM*, June 28, 1986, p. B6, and July 3, 1986, p. B9.

Dutch experience is somewhat similar. Finance Minister Onno Ruding's statement on the 1987 budget foresaw revenues from sales of state holdings. Although the government did reduce its shareholding in KLM by 23 percent, privatization in Holland has mainly taken the form of contracting out services (for example printing) to cut the number of civil service employees. Concern about budgetary spending produces contrary effects—postal services, until now provided by a Dutch government ministry, will be assumed by a new state-owned enterprise incorporated under private companies law. *Financial Times* (London), September 12, 1986, p. 2, and *Dagblad*, September 17, 1986, p. 3.

55. Canada, Department of Finance, *The Budget Speech* (Ottawa, May 23, 1985), p. 10.

56. Michael H. Wilson, minister of finance, *Economic and Fiscal Statement*, delivered in the House of Commons (November 8, 1984), pp. 1–2.

57. Quoted in the *Toronto Star*, October 31, 1985, p. 1.

58. President of the Treasury Board, *Annual Report to Parliament on Crown Corporations and Other Corporate Interests of Canada, 1983–1984* (Ottawa: Minister of Supply & Services Canada, 1985), p. iv. His views are consistent with the recommendations made by the Conservative party's pre-election task force on privatization and basically replicate the policy statements made by the short-lived 1979 Conservative government.

59. The Nielsen Task Force on Program Review was the most ambitious of these initiatives. See Canada, Department of Finance, *Budget Papers* (May 23, 1985), pp. 25–34.

60. The government holding company Canada Development Investment Corporation (see Chapter 6) had publicly identified Eldorado for divestment in 1983 and proposed the sale of Teleglobe following a telecommunications policy review. Indeed, NTCL, the first Crown corporation actually sold by the Conservatives, had been put up for sale by the

Liberals in March 1984 and the valuation process begun. CDIC, *AR*, 1983; *GM*, March 3, 1984, p. B1; Department of Transport, *Press Release*, December 21, 1984.

61. This is not to say that Canada's Conservative government lacked zest in introducing market-driven policies. But privatization of Crown corporations was not linked dynamically to these broader policies.

62. Canada, Department of Finance, *A New Direction for Canada: An Agenda for Economic Renewal* (November 8, 1984), p. 63.

63. Personal interviews, Task Force Secretariat, Ottawa, August 1985. The only exceptions were the Bank of Canada and the Royal Canadian Mint. *Toronto Star*, September 17, 1986, p. C6. Appointed in June 1986, the minister chairs a new Cabinet Committee on Privatization, Regulatory Affairs and Operations, comprised of eleven ministers. To support the minister, a staff with the usual hierarchy from deputy minister down was put in place.

64. The assets transferred to the public by the B.C. government were valued at $151 million (in 1978 Canadian dollars). See T. M. Ohashi, "Privatization in Practice: The Story of the British Columbia Resources Investment Corporation," in Ohashi and T. P. Roth, *Privatization: Theory and Practice* (Vancouver: Fraser Institute, 1980), pp. 3–107.

65. A relatively small share of assets has been privatized because the four credit institutions (e.g., the Export Development Corporation) represent half of the total. The government has also sold some subsidiaries of Crown corporations, for example CN's trucking operations, CN Route, and some investments in mixed enterprises, for example, its 18 percent interest in the Nanisivik lead-zinc mine (see Chapter 6). Divestments of the further holdings of large Crown corporations have been part of the normal course of business for decades, and thus we do not attribute them to the Convervatives' privatization program.

66. The government offered 23 million shares for sale to be paid in two installments. It thus intended to retain just over 10 percent of the voting shares to respect convenants on debt instruments which stipulated continued government participation (then set by CDC's governing legislation at a minimum of 10 percent). After the second installment in 1986, 95 percent of the offering was fully subscribed. *GM*, September 27, 1986, p. B3.

67. Canada, Parliament, House of Commons, *Minutes of Proceedings and Evidence of the Legislative Committee*, 2 (October 1, 1985) and 6 (October 15, 1985), in particular the testimony of Anthony Hampson, president of the CDC, and Sinclair Stevens, minister of industry. For the exact provisions restricting ownership see Canada, Parliament, House of Commons, "An Act Respecting the Reorganization of the Canada Development Corporation" (enacted December 20, 1985), 1st sess. 33d Parliament, secs. 5 and 10.

68. Analysts' skepticism about privatization is expressed in the *Financial Times* (Toronto) editorial title, "The Seedy Saga of CDC's Sell-Off," September 21, 1986, p. 1. Divestment of corporate assets by way of bidding also put the government in some awkward situations. In the case of both De Havilland Aircraft and Canadian Arsenals, government was accused of prevarication or bias by the companies that lost the bidding competition. Regarding De Havilland, see testimony by Ian McDougall, chief executive officer, Rimgate Holdings, in Canada, Parliament, House of Commons, *Minutes of Proceedings and Evidence*, Standing Committee on Regional Development, 35 (January 28, 1986), pp. 20–23; for Arsenals, *FP*, December 14, 1985, p. 4.

69. Teleglobe averaged a 40 percent return on equity in the 1980s. The government skimmed profits prior to the sale, declaring a $108 million dividend in 1986 when reported net earnings were just $43 million. *FP*, January 18, 1986, p. 5. Headline from *GM*, September 25, 1985, p. B16. See Government of Canada, "Government Calls Bids for Teleglobe Canada," *News Release*, DRIE 75/85 (August 1, 1985), for the guidelines.

70. *GM*, September 14, 1986, p. A3. Teleglobe's February 1987 sale to a small Canadian company, Memotec Data, itself the creature of two venture capital companies set up to invest funds for a conglomerate of large private and state enterprises, surprised the business press. (Only days before the decision, the *Financial Post* explained in great detail why another bidder would win the competition. See *FP*, February 9, 1987, p. 3.) Critics sug-

gested that cash rather than telecommunications policy had motivated the choice of bidder, because the sale proceeds permitted the minister of finance to reach his announced deficit target in the 1987 budget speech. See *Le Devoir* (Montreal), February 12, 1987, p. 1; *GM*, March 2, 1987, p. B5.

71. The interests at stake and the convoluted dealings involved are recounted in Peter Foster, *The Masterbuilders; How the Reichmanns Reached for an Empire* (Toronto: Key Porter, 1986), pp. 123–129. It was the Reichmann brothers' company, Olympia and York Developments, which bought out Gulf Canada.

72. The minister is quoted in the *Calgary Herald*, August 13, 1985, p. B8, the MP in *FP*, August 24, 1985, p. 4, and *Ottawa Citizen*, August 17, 1985, p. B1. At the same time Ottawa was backed into approving another $130 million for state-controlled Fisheries Products International (see Chapter 6). As long as market conditions precluded privatization, the intractable problems of regional disparities in Canada and the terms of the 1983 intergovernmental agreement obliged the federal government to support the company's five-year business plan with this further investment. FPI has since turned an operating profit after an upswing in the U.S. seafood market, and the government filed a prospectus to offer shares to the public in February 1987. See *FP*, October 12, 1985, p. 12, and *GM*, February 19, 1987, p. B5.

73. Since assuming office in May 1985 the Liberal government of Ontario has folded one Crown corporation (IDEA) into a government department, sold a second (UTDC), and is dismantling a third (OEC). See Chapter 7 for details.

74. For example, SGF's subsidiary, Dofor Inc., itself a holding company for several investments in forestry products companies, issued shares with a fixed dividend and voting rights on the Montreal Stock Exchange in June 1985. Other examples are given in SGF, *AR*, 1984, p. 4, and *Rapport Trimestriel* (June 30, 1985).

75. Government of Quebec, Budget 1985–1986, *Discours sur le Budget*, pp. 26–28.

76. Government of Quebec, Ministère des Finances, Ministre délégué à la privatisation, *Privatisation de sociétés d'état, orientations et perspectives*, February 1986, pp. 11–13, 32, and 50. *GM*, December 13, 1985, p. 1.

77. The government also agreed to divest its 35 percent holding in Nordair, one member of the consortium of private companies which purchased the airline. *FP*, August 9, 1986, p. 2. Other sales include three small subsidiaries of the National Asbestos Corp. (each under fifty employees) and a sugar refinery that was sold to its competitor to be shut down. See *GM*, July 31, 1986, p. B4, and March 11, 1986, p. B4.

78. The task forces dealt with privatization of services, reorganization of government, and divestment of corporate holdings. The last report, submitted in June 1986, called for the immediate sale of ten industrial Crown corporations, preferably by way of public share issues with Quebecers retaining control. Sales should increase competition, not just financial gains to the government. Monopolies such as Hydro-Québec should have their statutes revised to allow for competition, but not necessarily be privatized. Report of the Committee on the Privatization of Crown Corporations, *From the Quiet Revolution to the Year 2000* (Quebec, June 1986).

79. On Soquem see *GM*, December 18, 1986, p. B1, and discussion in Chapter 7. On SGF see *GM*, October 15, 1986, p. B1 and Chapter 6. *Le Devoir* (Montreal), October 9, 1986, p. 13, details the takeovers by Marine Industrie (65 percent controlled by SGF, 35 percent by the French state enterprise Alsthom Atlantique) of the holdings of Vancouver-based Versatile Corporation.

80. Crown Investments Review Commission (The Wolff Commission), *Report to the Government of Saskatchewan* (December 1982), pp. 43, 45. See also "State Enterprise and the Tories," *Maclean's*, March 8, 1982, p. 39.

81. Quoted in Potash Corporation of Saskatchewan, *News Release*, January 21, 1983. See also *FP*, May 21, 1983, p. 6.

82. Robert Andrew, minister of finance, Government of Saskatchewan, "Public Participation in Crown Corporations: A Saskatchewan Perspective," Institute for Research on

Public Policy *Newsletter*, March–April 1985. The Conservatives actually created two new Crown corporations in 1986; one was the Agriculture and Commercial Equity Corporation to invest in new agribusiness ventures. *FP*, April 5, 1986, p. 10.

83. Premier Grant Devine, quoted in *FP*, August 31, 1985, p. 50. France had introduced this participatory bond ("titre participatif") formula in 1983. In the Saskoil case, shares were sold in units so that the purchase of one common share required the purchase of two convertible preferred shares. See *FP*, November 23, 1985, p. 27, and the advertised public offering in the *Ottawa Citizen*, December 19, 1983, p. D11.

84. By institutionalizing privatization in a new Ministry of State (see note 63 above), the government enshrined it as official policy and also routinized procedures, thereby reducing the need and the incentive for dramatic action. Indeed, official statements began to emphasize the importance of caution, even when addressed to business audiences. For example, "we are progressing with our privatization initiatives in a careful, considered and businesslike fashion, there are many complex issues at stake and there are many interests to consider. Just as the government's power to own should not be used indiscriminately, our decisions to sell must be subject to complete and careful consideration." Office of the Minister of State (Privatization), Speaking Notes for the Honourable Barbara McDougall to the Canadian Chamber of Commerce, Vancouver, September 16, 1986, p. 7.

85. Canada, *New Direction*, p. 65; Petro-Canada, AR, 1984, p. 2.

86. *GM*, September 21, 1985, p. B1, reported that "a special internal committee of Petrocan's 15-member board of directors, as well as two securities firms hired by Petrocan, are deciding the mechanics of how a share issue will be done." Since then, although the minister of finance told a receptive Alberta audience that he saw no reason not to privatize Petro-Canada, no official proposals have been made. See *Sunday Star* (Toronto), March 8, 1987, p. 1. Air Canada's chairman, Claude Taylor, anxious to secure capital for fleet renewal, constantly speaks out in favor of privatization, arguing that "there are no longer any public policy reasons justifying Air Canada being retained as a Crown corporation." Quoted in *GM*, January 13, 1987, p. B1.

87. John Calvert, in *Government Limited: The Corporate Takeover of the Public Sector in Canada* (Ottawa: Canadian Center for Policy Alternatives, 1984), expresses this faith. Calvert, however, recognizes that in practice the "failure of public enterprises to operate as models of open, democratic, publicly accountable organizations," requires rectification (p. 146).

88. Trade dependence figures from Canada, Department of External Affairs, *Competitiveness and Security* (Ottawa: Minister of Supply & Services, 1985), p. 5, fig. 1. Share of world trade from Canada, Department of External Affairs, *A Review of Canadian Trade Policy* (Ottawa: Minister of Supply & Services, 1983), p. 16, Table 1.

89. Share of exports from *Competitiveness and Security*, p. 19. The federal minister for science and technology warned that Canada would become "a banana republic" unless the $12.5 billion in high-tech products could be reversed. *Toronto Star*, October 4, 1986, p. B1. On foreign ownership see Statistics Canada, *International Investment Catalogue*, 67–202 (Ottawa: Minister of Supply & Services, 1984).

90. Quoted in *GM*, November 21, 1986, p. A1.

91. Social welfare costs, a function of high unemployment, accounted for 90 percent of the total 1985 provincial deficits according to the Canadian Bond Rating Service as reported in *GM*, July 23, 1985, p. B16.

92. Office of Industrial and Regional Benefits, Department of Regional Industrial Expansion, *Major Project Inventory* (Ottawa: Minister of Supply & Services, 1985).

93. For other perspectives on the state and industrial development in Canada see, in addition to earlier references, Michael Jenkin, *The Challenge of Diversity: Industrial Policy in the Canadian Federation*, Science Council of Canada Background Study no. 50 (Ottawa: Supply & Services Canada, 1983); André Blais, Research Coordinator, *Industrial Policy* (Toronto: University of Toronto Press, 1986); and James Laxer, *Rethinking the Economy* (Toronto: New Canada, 1984), pp. 123–24.

94. Canadian Chamber of Commerce (Ottawa), "Submission on the Commercialization of Crown Corporations: Report of the Canadian Chamber's Task Force on Crown Corporations to the Hon. Robert De Cotret, President of the Treasury Board" (May 1985), p. 8.

95. Robert Heilbroner, "The Coming Invasion," *New York Review of Books*, December 8, 1983, p. 25.

Index

"An Act to Limit Shareholding in Certain Corporations" (Bill S-31), 149–150
Aerospatiale, 18, 25–26
AGIP, 125
AGIP Canada, 157
Aharoni, Yair, 98
Air Canada, 48, 49, 62, 66, 70, 74, 125, 193, 198
Aircraft industry, 88–90. *See also* Canadair
Aitken, Hugh, G. J., 37, 40
Alberta:
  Crown corporations: administration, 71; commercialization, 77–78
  mixed enterprises, investment in, 126–127. *See also* Alberta Heritage Savings Trust Fund
  state ownership defined in, 64
  venture capitalism, 169–170
Alberta Energy Corporation (AEC), 143
Alberta Government Telephones (AGT), 50, 62, 77–78
Alberta Heritage Savings Trust Fund, 140–146
  joing venture funding, 169–170
Alberta Telecommunication International (ATI), 77
Alexandre Report, 115
Alfa Romeo, 18, 29
Alta-Can Telecom, 77
American Motors, 29
Amersham International, 183, 187
Amok Mining, 156
Anastassopoulos, Jean-Pierre, 26

Asbestos Corporation, 105, 117, 118, 119, 120, 121
Asbestos industry:
  foreign investment in, 104–105
  importance to Canadian economy, 104
  nationalized companies vs. private firms, 116
  See also Société nationale de l'amiante
Atlantic Fisheries Restructuring Act of 1983, 136
Atomic Energy of Canada, 62, 75
Automobile industry, 28–29, 186–187
Austin, Jack, 133, 135
Austrian public enterprises, 12, 13, 14, 19, 32
Avro Arrow, 90

Bailouts, 7, 126, 135–139
Bandeen, Robert, 84
Bank of Nova Scotia (BNS), 137–139
B.C. Rail, 62, 74
Beck, Adam, 42
Belgian public enterprises, 13, 14, 32, 34
Bell Asbestos, 117, 120, 121
Bennett, R. B., 49
Berkowitz, S. D., 103
Blakeney, Allan, 108
Board of Grain Supervisors, 46–47
Bourassa, Robert, 196
Bow Valley Industries of Calgary, 163
Brady, Alexander, 40, 41
Brascan group, 194
Breton, Albert, 102

Potash Corporation of Saskatchewan
(PCS), 6, 57, 62, 101, 107–114, 122
Potash industry:
foreign investment in, 104, 105
government takeovers in, 108
importance to Canadian economy, 104
nationalized companies' ability to compete with private firms, 108–109, 116
See also Potash Corporation of Saskatchewan
Pratt, Larry, 102
Privatization, 2, 8, 175, 188–191, 202
See also Canadian privatization program; *under* Britain *and* France *and* European state capitalism
Province building, 101–103, 114, 140, 153
Provincial governments:
Crown corporations: commercialization of, 74, 75–78; holdings in, 57, 63–64; and political objectives, 101–103, 106–107. *See also* Potash Corporation of Saskatchewan; Société nationale de l'amiante
economic intervention (pre-1960), 41, 49–51, 53
independence from national government, 50–51
mixed enterprises, involvement in, 66, 126–127, 144–145. *See also* Alberta Heritage Savings Trust Fund; Caisse de dépôt et placement du Québec
privatization program, impact on, 195–198
resource sector, conflicts with federal government about, 105–106
utility company commercialization, 75–77
See also Joint ventures; province building; *specific provinces*
Public enterprises: *See* Crown corporations; European state capitalism; *specific countries and enterprises*
Pulp and paper industry, 148–149

Quebec:
Crown corporations: administration of, 70, 118; commercialization of, 75–76; political purpose of, 102, 106, 107. *See also* Parti québécois; Société nationale de l'amiante
joint ventures, 153, 158. *See also* Société québécoise d'exploration minière; Société québécoise d'initiatives pétrolières

mixed enterprises, investment in, 126–127, 144–145. *See also* Caisse de dépôt et placement du Québec
privatization in, 121, 160–161, 196–197
Quebecair, 197
"Quiet Revolution," 107

RailTrans Industries of Canada, 171
Renault, 11, 18, 28–29, 30, 181
Resources Aiguebelle, 160
Resource sector, 57
Crown corporations in. *See* Potash Corporation of Saskatchewan; Société nationale de l'amiante
federal-provincial conflicts about, 105–106
foreign investment in, 104–105
importance to Canadian economy, 104
nationalized companies' ability to compete with private firms, 108–109, 116
state intervention, background to, 103–107
U.S. domination of, 53–55
See also under Joint ventures
Rhône Poulenc, 181
Richards, John, 102
Ridley Terminals Inc. (RTI), 130–131
Rio Tinto Zinc (RTZ), 187
Rolls Royce, 18, 25, 32, 183
Royal Bank of Canada, 88, 138

Sable Gas Systems, 165
Sacilor, 177
St Gobain group, 177, 178, 181
Saipem, 189
Salzgitter, 11, 15, 18
Samaero, 26
Sanofi, 30
Saskatchewan:
Crown corporations: administration of, 69, 70, 71; commercialization of, 74; political purpose of, 103, 106–107, 111–112, 198. *See also* New Democratic party; Potash Corporation of Saskatchewan
economic intervention (pre-1960), 41, 50
joint ventures. *See* Saskatchewan Mining Development Corporation
privatization in, 196, 197–198
Saskatchewan Mining Development Corporation (SMDC), 155–158
Saskatchewan Oil and Gas Corporation (Saskoil), 57, 62, 198
SCOMINEX, 165

Library of Congress Cataloging-in-Publication Data
Laux, Jeanne Kirk, 1942–
    State capitalism.
    (Cornell studies in political economy)
    Bibliography: p.
    Includes index.
    1. Government business enterprises—Canada. I. Molot,
Maureen Appel, 1941–   . II. Title. III. Series.
HD4005.L38 1987   338.6′2′0971   87-47600
ISBN 0-8014-2079-2 (alk. paper)
ISBN 0-8014-9469-9 (pbk. : alk. paper)